Confucia.. _____

A Comparative Study of Self, Autonomy, and Community

The Chinese ethical tradition has often been thought to oppose Western views of the self as autonomous and possessed of individual rights with views that emphasize the centrality of relationship and community to the self. The essays in this collection discuss the validity of that contrast as it concerns Confucianism, the single most influential Chinese school of thought. Alasdair MacIntyre, the single most influential philosopher to articulate the need for dialogue across traditions, contributes a concluding essay of commentary.

This is the only consistently philosophical collection on Asia and human rights and could be used in courses on comparative ethics, political philosophy, and Asian area studies.

Kwong-loi Shun is Professor of Philosophy and East Asian Studies at the University of Toronto.

David B. Wong is Professor of Philosophy at Duke University.

Confucian Ethics

A Comparative Study of Self, Autonomy, and Community

Edited by

KWONG-LOI SHUN

University of Toronto

DAVID B. WONG

Duke University

CAMBRIDGE
UNIVERSITY PRESS

CAMBRIDGE UNIVERSITY PRESS
Cambridge, New York, Melbourne, Madrid, Cape Town,
Singapore, São Paulo, Delhi, Mexico City

Cambridge University Press
32 Avenue of the Americas, New York, NY 10013-2473, USA

www.cambridge.org
Information on this title: www.cambridge.org/9780521796576

First published 2004
Reprinted 2013

A catalog record for this publication is available from the British Library.

Library of Congress Cataloging in Publication Data

Confucian ethics : a comparative study of self, autonomy, and community / edited by
Kwong-loi Shun, David B. Wong.
  p. cm.
Includes bibliographical references and index.
ISBN 0-521-79217-7 – ISBN 0-521-79657-1 (pbk.)
1. Confucianism. 2. Confucian ethics. I. Shun, Kwong-loi, 1953– II. Wong, David B.
BL1853.c66 2004
170´.951–dc22   2004040409

ISBN 978-0-521-79217-2 Hardback
ISBN 978-0-521-79657-6 Paperback

Contents

Contributors

Chung-ying Cheng, Professor of Philosophy, University of Hawaii at Manoa

Chad Hansen, Professor of Philosophy, University of Hong Kong

Craig K. Ihara, Professor of Philosophy, California State University at Fullerton

Joel J. Kupperman, Professor of Philosophy, University of Connecticut

Alasdair MacIntyre, Professor of Philosophy, University of Notre Dame

Henry Rosemont, Jr., Professor Emeritus, St. Mary's College of Maryland, and Professorial Lecturer, School of Advanced International Studies, Johns Hopkins University

Kwong-loi Shun, Professor of Philosophy and East Asian Studies, University of Toronto

Bryan W. Van Norden, Associate Professor of Philosophy, Vassar College

David B. Wong, Professor of Philosophy, Duke University

Confucian Ethics

A Comparative Study of Self, Autonomy, and Community

Introduction

East–West comparative ethics has drawn increased attention in recent years, especially comparative discussion of Confucian ethics and Western thought. Such interest stems in part from a growing concern with the political systems of Asian countries, which are often viewed as informed by Confucian values. Critics of such systems accuse them of a form of authoritarianism that is at odds with Western democratic ideals. Defenders of such systems reject the imposition of Western political ideals. Some argue that such systems are characterized by a democracy of a distinctively Asian kind, and some even argue that Western notions of rights and democracy are inapplicable to Asian political structures. Underlying this rejection of Western political ideals is the view that values espoused by Asian ethical and political traditions, and more specifically the Confucian tradition, are radically different from and no less respectable than those of Western traditions, a view that has led to a growing interest in the "Asian values" debate.

The interest in comparative ethics also stems in part from a concern to understand Asian ethical traditions as a way to unravel philosophical presuppositions behind Western ethical traditions. Setting the different traditions alongside each other helps to put in sharper focus the presuppositions that shape the development of each, thereby preparing the ground for a comparative evaluation and possible synthesis. The Confucian tradition, with its long history, rich content, and extensive influence on Asian communities, has drawn much attention in such comparative discussions. The scope of discussion includes not just its political ideal but also the conception of the self that underlies such an ideal. As Alasdair MacIntyre observes in his reflection on these essays, Confucianism, more than any other Asian standpoint, challenges some of the key assumptions of Western morality effectively, while providing a viable alternative to them.

A final reason for the growing interest in Confucianism in particular is that an increasing number of Westerners, not only philosophers and academics, have themselves challenged key assumptions of Western morality in ways that might naturally suggest the possibility of Confucianism as a viable alternative. According to one kind of challenge, the centrality accorded to individual rights and autonomy in Western morality has resulted in a stunted understanding of responsibilities the individual has to others. The United States in particular is often presented as the preeminent case in point: the world's most affluent country and yet one of the most unequal, failing to provide basic necessities in health and education for all its members. According to another related challenge, Western morality provides ineffective grounding for duties to others because it cannot show the individual how the performance of these duties is related to achieving a specific conception of the good and worthwhile life. MacIntyre has been among the most influential critics in this regard. By contrast, one of the strengths of Confucianism is frequently thought to lie in the way it conceives a fully human life in terms of relationship to others, structured by a set of duties to them that realize the self rather than constrain it. At the same time, critics of Confucianism often flip this apparent strength into a moral failing: that it neglects individual rights and autonomy in favor of a life of relationship. Moreover, the favored set of relationships is frequently criticized as patriarchal and oppressively hierarchical, reputedly stifling the self.

The first two sections of this anthology reflect the various reasons for increased attention to Confucianism and the ensuing controversies over rights and conceptions of the self's relation to others. The first section discusses the notion of rights and other related notions such as autonomy and respect in relation to Confucian ethics, while the second discusses the Confucian conception of the self and its moral development. Perhaps the order of these sections should be reversed, as Alasdair MacIntyre suggests in the final section, if one is to begin with what is foundational in Confucian ethics. Our decision to begin with the section on rights follows the more typical path of recent interest: the possibility that Confucianism offers an alternative perspective on rights and autonomy has motivated inquiry into the foundations of this perspective in a moral psychology of the self.

In the first section, Craig Ihara, David Wong, and Henry Rosemont argue that certain insights can be extracted from the Confucian tradition that bear on our understanding of rights and a range of related ideas. Chad Hansen's essay sets out certain methodological constraints on any attempt to appeal to the Confucian tradition in evaluating such ideas. In the second section, the essays by Joel Kupperman and Chung-ying Cheng discuss the Confucian conception of the self and of moral development. Kupperman discusses the role traditional and communal values play in shaping the self at a less reflective stage of moral development, while Cheng focuses on the more reflective role the self plays in the process of self-cultivation. On the other hand, Bryan Van Norden discusses the Confucian emphasis on the role of shame in self-cultivation, while Kwong-loi Shun provides a methodological discussion of the recent interest in the applicability of Western notions to Confucian thought.

Craig Ihara's essay argues that the absence of a conception of individual rights from Confucian thought does not render the Confucian tradition problematic, as the range of ideas associated with the notion of rights and to which we attach significance are still instantiated in Confucian thought. Such ideas include those of wrongdoing and of one's having a legitimate claim against others that should be protected, as well as the ideas of respect and equality. What is distinctive of Confucian thought is that it regards the legitimate claims one has against others as generated by social norms that bind a community together, and human beings as equally deserving of respect in virtue of their capability of membership in community. Indeed, according to Ihara, the idea of individual rights is itself a construct that serves a role only under certain specific circumstances, such as in a dysfunctional society in which one has to be protected against those who refuse to fulfill their responsibilities.

In contrast to Ihara's essay, David Wong's employs a notion of rights more broadly construed and distinguishes between two kinds of grounding for rights. Rights can be defended on autonomy grounds and viewed as constraints on the extent to which individual interest may be sacrificed for the public good, or on communal grounds and viewed as something necessary for promoting the common good. According to Wong, Confucian thought contains the germs of viable arguments for rights of certain kinds, such as the right to speak, on communal grounds. Starting with the observation that even some Confucian texts regard an official's duty to speak up as promoting the common good, Wong argues that there can be communal grounds for the right to speak because instituting and protecting such rights helps to resolve disagreements about the common good, thereby enabling the peaceful transformation of communities. Indeed, there is a mutual interdependence between rights and community: just as community-centered traditions should take into account the point that instituting and protecting certain rights help to promote the common good, right-centered traditions should acknowledge that we need viable communities to nurture effective moral agency and to make effective use of the democratic machinery.

Henry Rosemont's essay argues that while Confucian thought does not have a conception of individual rights grounded in a view of human beings as free autonomous individuals, it does have room for a conception of rights that is grounded in a view of the self as relational rather than autonomous, a view that emphasizes social interactions and regards human excellences as something realized in such interactions. Furthermore, according to Rosemont, there are certain values central to Western intellectual traditions that the majority of liberals also endorse, on the basis of which one can show the superiority of classical Confucian thought to modern Western liberalism. Indeed, according to Rosemont, Asian countries like Malaysia and Singapore have accomplished more and in a shorter time than the United States in promoting such values, such as by doing more in nourishing those qualities of character that enable citizens to be self-governing and by sustaining those institutions necessary for self-government to be effective.

While these three chapters are all sympathetic to the Confucian tradition and argue that something of value can be extracted from it, Chad Hansen's paper raises questions about the normative relevance of a study of comparative ethics and, more specifically, of an appeal to Confucian ethics. The mere fact that certain ideas can be extracted from Confucian thought cannot by itself give normative significance to such ideas; indeed, grounding normative claims on an appeal to tradition itself goes against an aspect of Confucian thought that seeks to establish Confucian values on grounds independent of tradition. On the other hand, if the normative significance of the relevant ideas is independent of their being espoused in Confucian thought, it remains unclear what significance there is to an appeal to the Confucian tradition. In the end, Hansen suggests that the ideas that can be extracted from the Confucian tradition must stand on their own merits and bear normative relevance to one's own moral philosophizing to the extent that they present a sufficiently different but credible alternative to the ideas in one's home tradition.

In their chapters, Ihara, Wong, and Rosemont consider how the distinctive Confucian conception of the self emphasizes membership in community rather than individual autonomy and how this conception bears on a discussion of the notion of rights in relation to Confucian ethics. Recent interest in the Confucian conception of the self also stems from the revival of interest in virtue-centered theories as a major theoretical alternative to consequentialist and deontological theories. Since character development is a major focus of the Confucian tradition, a study of the Confucian conception of the self and of self-cultivation also contributes to this recent development by providing an example of how an emphasis on character may shape the development of an ethical tradition.

In the second section, Kupperman's essay discusses how traditional and communal values play a role in the development of the self at a less reflective stage, through the influences of parents, of role models conveyed through stories, and of ritual and music. Such influences play not just a causal but also a constitutive role in that the styles of behavior and feeling of one's parents and of the past are made part of oneself through such influences. Such influences do not undermine the creativity of the self, as creativity itself is possible only against the background of traditional and communal values that one has acquired.

Chung-ying Cheng's essay focuses on the creativity and freedom of the self in shaping its own development. It begins with a distinction between two aspects of the self – the active self, which is engaged in actual activities, and the transcendent self, which is capable of reflecting on and reshaping the active self. It considers how interplay between these two aspects of the self makes possible the process of reshaping oneself on the basis of one's own self-reflection and discusses the sense in which the self is capable of free choice in this process.

Bryan Van Norden's essay takes up the role of shame in self-cultivation, a theme consistently highlighted in different branches of Confucian thought. It discusses the way Confucian thought emphasizes the significance of shame in moral development, criticizes various attempts to characterize Chinese culture as a shame-based rather than guilt-based culture, and argues that shame is indispensable to moral development as it is presupposed in one's having some ideal conception of one's own character. Furthermore, it argues that the Confucian emphasis on shame can be separated from the larger cosmological framework within which it is embedded, and that an understanding of the role of shame shows how moral development can be given a naturalistic basis.

Kwong-loi Shun's essay, the last of this section, considers a claim often found in comparative discussions of Confucian ethics, to the effect that certain Western notions are inapplicable to Confucian thought. It discusses the claim in connection with the notions of rights and autonomy, the idea of a mind–body distinction, and the relation between the self and the social order. In the process of the discussion, it makes the methodological proposal that the substantive issues involved can be better addressed by focusing less on the applicability of such notions or distinctions and more on the extent to which the range of phenomena associated with such notions are instantiated in Confucian thought.

Questions about the applicability of key Western notions to Chinese traditions arise frequently throughout the essays in this volume. One lesson to draw from the varying results of these discussions is that such notions are highly elastic, especially when put into the service of comparison across traditions. Those intent on emphasizing differences (such as "this tradition makes individual rights central while that tradition lacks any comparable notion" or "this tradition conceives the self as autonomous while that tradition has no comparable notion of autonomy") tend to employ more specific, thick conceptions of the relevant notions. Those intent on emphasizing similarities tend to employ broader, thinner conceptions capable of spanning certain differences in more specific content. More productive comparative discussions might take place with the recognition that both differences and similarities have normative relevance.

The anthology concludes with an essay by Alasdair MacIntyre that reflects on the preceding essays. A number of the essays in this volume attest to MacIntyre's influence in arguing first that moral notions must be understood in the context of the traditions giving them substantive meaning and second that one can identify the theoretical and moral resources of one's own tradition for defense against rival traditions only when one formulates the best case against that tradition from rival traditions. MacIntyre begins his discussion of the Confucian tradition with its foundations in moral psychology. He observes that Confucians take human nature to be developed most fully when it is guided and self-guided into the practice of the virtues, understood in distinctly Confucian terms, and into social relationships governed by distinctively Confucian norms. He observes that Confucianism implies not only a rejection of Western deontology and utilitarianism, but also a rejection of most Western versions of an ethics of virtue.

MacIntyre raises as a problem for Confucians the tension, and frequently stark contradiction, between the assumption in Mencius and

Xunzi that all people have the potential for goodness and the traditional hierarchical structures of Confucian society that have practically denied this potential for the great numbers who have sustained that society. In asking how Confucians might envision a social, political, and economic form that was not oppressive and exploitative, MacIntyre suggests that a notion of rights might have fruitful application, though the content and justification of rights will again be distinctively Confucian. MacIntyre concludes with a twist, however. At a time when individuals everywhere must live within a modern state and deal with the powerful impact of multinational corporations, Confucians might find it necessary to develop not only a distinctive notion of rights that is compatible with a Confucian vision of harmonious community, but also a Western notion of rights as protections against unwanted interventions into their affairs by governmental and other corporate bureaucracies. In MacIntyre's view, modern states cannot be governed by shared inquiry into the nature of the common good. Confucians within such states may therefore be forced to live double lives with a different conception of rights in each life.

It is appropriate that the volume should end on such a note of moral complexity. Comparative ethics has drawn increased attention partly because powerful forces draw all of us closer in a common condition, but our traditions continue to shape responses to that common condition that are at once profoundly similar and profoundly different.

I

RIGHTS AND COMMUNITY

Are Individual Rights Necessary?

A *Confucian Perspective*

Craig K. Ihara

I. WHERE INDIVIDUAL RIGHTS ARE OUT OF PLACE

I would like to begin by considering some familiar contexts in which talk
of rights, especially those one person might claim against another, seems
quite out of place.

1. On sports teams, say basketball, people have assigned roles appropriate to their various talents. A point guard is, among other things, in
charge of running the offense, doing most of the ball handling, setting
up plays, and getting the ball to people in scoring position. A center, usually the tallest player on the team, is responsible for dominating the area
under the basket, rebounding, blocking shots, and scoring from inside.
Suppose that on a specific occasion, the point guard fails to pass the ball
to the center who is wide open under the opposing team's basket. What
might one say? That the point guard made a mistake, did something
wrong or incorrect, did not do what she was supposed to, failed to do
her job, messed up, or fouled up. If, for whatever reason, she regularly
misses such opportunities, she can be regarded as a poor or bad point
guard and is likely to lose her position. Other members of the team can
legitimately complain about her incompetence, lack of court sense, or
selfishness, although in the name of team spirit they should not be too
quick to criticize.

What we have in basketball or any similar game is a practice – to use
Alasdair MacIntyre's term[1] – in which participants have roles and responsibilities, criteria of good and bad performances within the context of the
game, and an array of critical responses. In such practices people have

duties in the sense of role responsibilities, but they do not, I maintain, have individual rights.

What supports this claim? First of all it is a straightforward fact that the language of rights is not used within the game of basketball, although it is used outside of the game during professional contract negotiations or in other legal or quasi-legal situations. It would at least be unusual to say when the point guard failed to pass the ball to the center that she had failed to respect the center's rights or infringed or violated the center's right to the ball.

Suppose that we were to attribute rights to the center in this situation, what more would we be saying than we have already, namely that the point guard had failed to do her job, did the wrong thing, et cetera? We would be saying that in this situation the center had something, a right to the ball, which the other players on the team did not have, and that in failing to do what she was supposed to do, the point guard injured the center by denying her what was rightfully hers. The point guard not only did the wrong thing, she wronged the center, violated her rights, and deprived her of her due. Consequently the center is not only more justified than her other teammates in being angry and indignant, but she is also justified in demanding some sort of compensation. I maintain that talking this way about basketball or any sport is odd to say the least, and, if taken seriously, changes the game in a fundamental way. It reconceptualizes the activity in a way that makes basic the individual, and not the team.

Now it is certainly true that players get mad at each other, even if they are on the same team. In the play described, it would not be surprising if the center were even more upset with the point guard than the other players were. After all, because of the point guard's mistake, the center missed an easy opportunity to score and help the team win. But though this is understandable, it does not follow that the center's rights had been violated by the point guard. Indeed if she were to chastise the point guard for what she had done *to her*, as opposed to what she had done to injure the team's chances to win, she would be condemned for lack of team spirit.

Other rather different kinds of examples can be drawn from sports in which the use of rights language is at least unusual and unnecessary. These concern rule infractions, rather than failures to fulfill role responsibilities. As with most sports, basketball has a number of rules about what players can and cannot do in the course of a game. When players violate a rule, they are penalized, and this is not typically articulated or conceptualized in terms of rights violations. For example, traveling (sometimes called taking steps) is a rule violation resulting in turning the ball over to the opposing team. Many infractions – stepping over the line when shooting a free throw, or substitution violations – are like this; they do not directly involve an opposing player, and it would be difficult to translate or conceptualize them in terms of a violation of rights.

There are other kinds of examples of rule violations in basketball where rights-talk would not be so difficult or awkward but would still be unusual and unnecessary. Consider instances when a player is fouled by a member of the opposite team. In such cases players frequently complain to the referee in words that say in effect, "Did you see what she did (to me)?" There is nothing inappropriate in saying this insofar as the player is pointing out behavior that violates the rules. Anyone, including the fans, can do this. The key question is whether it *must* be conceptualized in terms of a violation of rights.

So for example, a defensive player who holds an opponent in order to prevent her from driving to the basket is committing a foul; we might even say that she is fouling that player, breaking the rules, doing what is not allowed, doing what she shouldn't do, or not playing fairly. But we don't normally say that she is violating the player's rights. It isn't that we couldn't conceptualize it in this way, but there would not be a point in doing so. Clearly, if the defensive player has committed an infraction, there should be a penalty. If no penalty is called, anyone, including the fans, has grounds to protest. But what they will cry is "Foul," or even "She was fouled," not "Her rights were violated." Note that even "She was fouled" need not be conceptualized as a violation of rights. "She was fouled" can be construed as comparable to "She was injured," something that can be perfectly well understood without invoking or even understanding the concept of rights. All that is necessary is the understanding that the offending player did something she should not have done according to the rules. Introducing the notion of rights here takes the focus away from the team and is unnecessary for playing the game.

2. Consider another context – dance. In a ballet people have their parts to play, they each have sequences of movements that they should perform. But even though the dancers in *Swan Lake* each have their individual roles and responsibilities, it is, I maintain, conceptually wrongheaded to think of dancers as having rights against each other within the context of the dance.

For one thing, there are no rules in ballet on which to base individual rights or duties. For another, dancers would not claim that their rights are violated when others fail to do what they should. If I forget my routine, then I can be said to dance poorly. I might even feel obliged to apologize to my dancing partner, or to the entire group. However, in making a misstep – for example, I fail to help you complete a pirouette – it would be odd to say that I infringed on your rights. I may be frustrating you, making you angry, or letting you down in the sense of disappointing you, and you may have good reason to criticize my performance or insist on a better effort on my part, but such criticism and insistence can be understood quite independently from talking about violating your rights.

Of course you might have a right to expect that I do certain things in the sense that you know what has been choreographed, but your expectations are not based on some obligation I have to you. The right here is epistemic. There is a reasonable basis for your belief, a normal expectation that I will perform in a specific way. In other words, you might be said to have a right, in the sense of a rational justification, to point out my failure to live up to my role. That justification you have in common with anyone else who sees and appreciates my mistake. But this is not a case where doing wrong constitutes a violation of your rights.

3. Consider a third context. Ceremonies and rituals are perhaps more like dance performances than competitive games, but they share some basic features with both. On the one hand, like ballet, they are practices in which people assume roles, and those roles have stipulated responsibilities. As in dance, success depends on a kind of cooperation, a joint effort in which the fulfillment of any one person's objectives largely depends on the efforts of everyone else, and even more importantly the objectives of any individual largely coincide with the common good.

On the other hand, as in competitive games, rituals and ceremonies often have rules, albeit of a different type; so, for example, a state dinner has a certain protocol. More than any other, this context of rituals and ceremonies, along with its role responsibilities and rules of behavior, resembles the Confucian vision of an ideal society.

Now I claim that in these and other contexts talk of individual rights is at least unusual and unnecessary. Later I will also claim that these practices resemble the Confucian social ideal in some fundamental ways. They are all intended to describe contexts in which there need not be any individual rights in the sense of special moral claims to something or other that one person has and that can be infringed by others. Although it has taken some time to get to the issue, I hope that keeping those examples in mind, and elaborating on some of the differences between them, will provide a contrast that will facilitate our discussion from this point on.

II. THE DEBATE OVER THE IMPORTANCE
OF INDIVIDUAL RIGHTS

In recent years, important specialists in Confucian philosophy, such as Tu Wei-Ming, Henry Rosemont, Roger T. Ames, and Chad Hansen,[2] have all claimed that there is no concept of rights in traditional Confucian thought.[3] Although this claim is itself controversial,[4] and the debate concerning it far from over, I would wager that a majority of Confucian philosophers would concur. I would also speculate that philosophers specializing in other non-Western ways of thought are likely to hold comparable positions about their respective moral traditions.

At the same time important figures in Anglo-American moral philosophy, including Ronald Dworkin, Joel Feinberg, Alan Gewirth, Judith Jarvis Thomson, A. I. Meldon, and J. L. Mackie, have forcefully argued in various ways for the fundamental importance of rights, not just for Western ethical theory, but for any philosophically acceptable morality.[5] To quote Alan Gewirth, "recognition and protection of human rights is a necessary condition of the moral legitimacy of societies."[6]

It seems that if the Confucian specialists are correct and there are no rights in Confucianism, we have a dilemma: either Confucian ethics is morally deficient in a fundamental way or Western advocates of rights have somehow gone wrong. It is this dilemma that I will begin to explore in this chapter by examining the arguments presented by Joel Feinberg in his well-known and influential article, "The Nature and Value of Rights."[7] I will use Feinberg to illustrate how Anglo-American rights advocates overstate their case, and how, even without the concept of individual rights, Confucian ethics is not vulnerable in the way Feinberg's argument suggests.[8]

III. FEINBERG'S "NOWHERESVILLE" AND ITS IMPLICATIONS

In his article, "The Nature and Value of Rights," Joel Feinberg asks us to imagine a world, "Nowheresville," in which people have no rights in the sense that they cannot make moral claims against each other, but where:

1. People are as virtuous as we can imagine, consistent with what we know of human nature.

2. People have imperfect duties (e.g., charity), which are not to any other specific person or persons.

3. People have a weak sense of dessert, that is, they can see that some rewards and punishments are fitting, as when the best contestant wins the prize, but in which people cannot demand what is fitting any more than a servant has grounds to insist on extra pay for especially fine work.

4. In order to have institutions such as property, promises and contracts, bargains and deals, appointments and loans, and marriages and partnerships, Nowheresville has a "sovereign right-monopoly" in which all such practices entail rights, but only those of the sovereign.[9]

According to Feinberg, even though Nowheresville is as morally good a place as we can imagine without rights, there is something missing. Feinberg states:

The most conspicuous difference . . . between the Nowheresvillians and ourselves has something to do with the activity of claiming.[10]

This leads us to the following questions: What does Feinberg mean by "the activity of claiming"? Is it true that without rights we cannot make claims? And if so, why is that important? It seems that those of us who wish to defend Confucian ethics must argue either that claiming is possible in Confucianism even without rights, or that being devoid of claiming is not a fatal flaw in a moral system. I will argue that being able to make individual claims against others is not an essential feature of all philosophically acceptable moral systems, Confucianism in particular.

In order to clarify his position, Feinberg proceeds to distinguish between "claiming that" and "making claims" in the following way:

It is an important fact about rights (or claims), then, that they can be claimed only by those who have them. Anyone can claim, of course, that this umbrella is yours, but only you or your representative can actually claim the umbrella. . . . One important difference then between making legal *claim to* and *claiming that* is that the former is a legal performance with direct legal consequences whereas the latter is often a mere piece of descriptive commentary with no legal force. Legally speaking, making claim to can itself make things happen.[11]

Feinberg implicitly extends his claim about legal claiming to moral claiming, such that making moral claims apparently is a moral performance with direct moral consequences and can itself make things happen, while claiming that something is or is not the case is morally often a mere piece of descriptive commentary with no moral force.[12]

Feinberg goes on to argue in roughly the following fashion: a society without rights is one in which making claims is impossible. Without the ability to make individual claims, there can be no sense of what is mine, hence (1a) no harm is grounds for complaint, and (1b) every benefit granted to another is supererogatory (not morally required); (2) we lack a sense of human dignity, self-respect, and equality. Since these implications are morally and philosophically unpalatable, we have good reason to reject any society or morality that does not have a concept of individual rights. As Feinberg says:

these are facts about the possession of rights that argue well their supreme moral importance. More than anything else I am going to say, these facts explain what is wrong with Nowheresville.[13]

If the Confucian scholars cited above are correct, it could just as easily be concluded that this lack of individual rights is what is wrong about Confucianism or other non-rights-based traditions.

IV. A REPLY TO FEINBERG

Now let us consider Feinberg's objections in more detail. First of all he says:

Nowheresvillians, even when they are discriminated against invidiously, or left without the things they need, or otherwise badly treated, do not think to leap to their feet and make righteous demands against one another.[14]

The example implicitly presents us with a false dilemma: either we have claim rights or we must passively accept all forms of ill-treatment without objection. But a conception of rights is not necessary to recognize or to register complaints against others. Take, for example, the violation of a taboo in some traditional culture. Anyone in that society can and probably would protest taboo violations. That protest would not be grounded on the claim that it violated the rights of the other inhabitants individually, or even collectively. It is far more likely to be condemned on the grounds that it was a violation of some supernatural sanction. In such a case, protesting villagers are not only *claiming that* something is being done and *that* it is a violation of a taboo, they are also *making a claim* that "can make things happen." This is not, of course, making a claim in Feinberg's sense, because it is not a claim made by specific persons whose rights have been infringed. But such villagers can recognize that there has been a wrongdoing, and they can and do actively protest that behavior.

What is true of the villagers is even true in Nowheresville, where Feinberg stipulates that people will

incur genuine obligations toward one another; but the obligations . . . will not be owed directly to promisees, creditors, parents, and the like, but rather to God alone, or the members of some elite, or to a single sovereign under god.[15]

But, if this is so, imagine what would happen if someone, A, promises the sovereign not to take things from other people against their will, but in fact ends up doing so. The person who has something taken from her, B, may well recognize that the promiser had not done what she was obligated to the sovereign to do, and could very well claim that the promiser should be forced to return what was taken or be punished or both. What this shows is that even Nowheresville is not the passive place Feinberg takes it to be. Even though it is a place where there are no rights in the sense that people cannot make direct claims against others (e.g., "You have wronged me"), it is still possible to make claims that "will make things happen." Nowheresville may be a world in which there are no claim rights, but it is not a world in which violations of promises and contracts cannot be recognized or must be ignored.

These are but two examples of many in which wrongdoing and effective protests against wrongdoing can be made without individuals having rights against one another. Other examples include role-governed activities – like the examples of basketball, ballet, or ceremonies with which we began. Another example is etiquette, where specific violations of the rules of etiquette are not conceptualized as infringements of rights – eating peas with a knife does not violate the rights of the other diners – but it can still be recognized as improper and can be effectively protested.

In baseball, suppose that a second baseman tags out a base-runner after pushing her off second base. Such an action is forbidden by the rules, and the runner can protest on those grounds. If the umpire agrees, then the runner is allowed to stay on second base. Now suppose a runner maintained that "My rights have been violated." Not only is there no explicit mention of "rights" in the rule book, but it would also be a very odd and uncommon thing to say. But whether or not we think of the runner, or even the team, as having rights, my main point is that we need not conceptualize the violation in terms of rights in order to complain about the behavior. All that is essential for complaint are authoritative rules or roles. The second baseman violated the rules, she did something that a second baseman is not supposed to do, and that is a sufficient basis conceptually to protest and to seek some official remedy.

Now it might be objected that these examples of games and etiquette are frivolous, and therefore irrelevant. Morality is serious business, and when things of real importance are at issue, like human life, then the language of rights is indispensable.

To such an objection I should like to make three responses. For one, although games and etiquette may indeed be frivolous compared to morality, it is difficult to deny that there are some striking structural similarities between them. Whether these similarities are significant depends in part on one's conception of morality, but I think such comparisons can illuminate the relationships among rules, role responsibilities, and rights and lead us to think of morality from a new perspective. They have the additional advantage of being less controversial and less emotionally charged than other more serious examples.

For another, whatever their more general significance, these examples are offered specifically as responses to Feinberg's claim that in Nowheresville – which is just as frivolous an example as any game – people will not think to protest no matter how badly treated they are. Of course the frivolity of one example does not justify frivolity in another, but these examples, if they provide concrete and familiar contexts in which actions can be recognized as wrong, can be protested, can be corrected without relying on or entailing the concept of rights, and should be accorded as much weight as Feinberg's Nowheresville example.

Finally, more serious examples can be provided. However, it is difficult to present examples that are uncontroversial for at least a couple of reasons. For one, it is difficult to abstract serious examples from our own competitive and individualistic social framework. So for example, a team of scientists, hired perhaps for something like the Manhattan Project, would from a strictly scientific point of view be quite a good example of the kind of cooperative enterprise where I maintain talk of rights is unnecessary. However, it might be objected that a right to intellectual property would not be unnecessary in such a situation. The presupposition behind such an objection is that there is a larger market system within which this activity takes place and with which the scientists are only too concerned. It is also assumed that there is no other impartial mechanism by which monetary or other rewards can be distributed, such that individuals must protect themselves vis-à-vis the claim to certain rights.

Another obstacle to introducing more serious examples is that many people are inclined to conceptualize all important human relationships in terms of rights. Given this, perhaps the least contentious serious example is that of traditional families, especially Asian families. Such families have always been conceptualized as natural, organic units whose principal purpose is the continuation and promotion of the family, and they are regarded as an entity that extends both backward in time to include familial ancestors and forward to include descendants. In such families, roles and responsibilities are well defined, everyone has a job to do, and at least one of their principal goals in life is to do that job well. A mother who regularly forgets to provide her child food is a bad mother. It isn't necessary to conceptualize her behavior as violating the child's right to food. An older brother who does not care for a younger sibling as directed by his parent is doing the wrong thing, but that should not be equated with violating his sibling's rights.

Examples similar to those given previously can also show what is wrong with the second part of Feinberg's first claim (1b): that people without a conception of rights must regard all benefits they receive as gratuities or acts of supererogation.

In many societies, including China, it is thought that the ruler must perform certain ceremonies during the spring of the year to ensure a good harvest. This performance is not regarded as an act of supererogation on the part of the ruler, but as an essential part of the responsibilities of that position. Failure would bring about censure. Performance, even superlative performance deserving praise, would not be regarded as supererogatory. But in neither case are rights attributed to the people, even though they are the ones that stand to gain or lose the most.

A squeeze play in baseball is an analogous example. By laying down a good bunt, the batter enables the runner to fulfill her role and her objectives. The runner depends on and benefits from the batter's performance. But, although praise would be appropriate, gratitude on the part of the runner would not. Like the ruler, what the batter did was not supererogatory but her responsibility as a batter. It is something the batter was obligated to do, but not for the sake of the runner. This contradicts Feinberg's view that, without claim rights, benefits would have to be regarded as supererogatory.[16]

Finally, consider the following case in the context of Nowheresville. Suppose the sovereign commands all spouses to take care of each other such that husbands have an obligation to the sovereign to care for their wives, and wives have an obligation to the sovereign to care for their husbands. Now by hypothesis husbands in Nowheresville do not have claim rights against their wives, and vice versa. And yet neither would have to regard dutiful spousal behavior as exceptional or to regard it as above and beyond the call of duty, any more than a baseball player would regard with gratitude the dependable play of a teammate.

V. INDIVIDUAL RIGHTS AND A CONFUCIAN VIEW
OF HUMAN VALUE

Given the examples provided previously, perhaps Feinberg might concede that people in Nowheresville, even though they do not have individual claim rights, can protest misbehavior and can accept certain benefits without regarding them as gratuities. But he might maintain that neither the protests nor the acceptances are based on the appropriate reason, namely the moral status of the people who stand to be harmed or benefited. In other words, their responses are not grounded on the fact that they are human beings deserving respect and dignity for their own sake. This in effect brings us to Feinberg's second argument about the value of rights. To quote him at length:

Having rights, of course, makes claiming possible; but it is claiming that gives rights their special moral significance. This feature of rights is connected in a way with the customary rhetoric about what it is to be a human being. Having rights enables us to "stand up like men," to look others in the eye, and to feel in some fundamental way the equal of anyone. To think of oneself as the holder of rights is not to be unduly but properly proud, to have that minimal–self respect that is necessary to be worthy of the love and esteem of others. Indeed, respect for persons . . . may simply be respect for their rights, so that there cannot be the one without the other; and what is called "human dignity" may simply be the recognizable capacity to assert claims. To respect a person then, or to think of him as possessed of human dignity, simply is to think of him as a potential maker of claims . . . these are the facts about the possession of rights that argue well their supreme moral importance. More than anything else I am going to say, these facts explain what is wrong with Nowheresville.[17]

In this passage Feinberg actually suggests two, importantly different, positions. Early on he says, "claiming *enables* us 'to stand up like men'" [italics mine] et cetera. In other words, he says that making claims is either itself *sufficient* to "stand up like men" or at least part of a sufficient condition for doing so. This view does not necessarily entail a criticism of Confucianism or other moral systems that do not posit rights because it leaves open the possibility that there are other ways that are sufficient to recognize dignity and equality between human beings.

However, further on in the passage he strongly suggests that thinking of others as having rights, conceived as the capacity to make claims, is at least a *necessary* condition, and may even be equivalent to respect for persons, or human dignity. Although at one point Feinberg qualifies this with a "may," this position is fundamental to his defense of rights. Without it rights are not "supremely important," but potentially eliminable, and Nowheresville is not necessarily the defective society that he says it is.

But if rights are a necessary condition for equality, self-respect, respect for persons, and human dignity, then Feinberg is posing an extemely strong challenge not only to Nowheresville but to any moral philosophy, such as Confucianism, which does not recognize or place central importance on rights.[18]

Where should a response to Feinberg's second claim begin? First of all, it is important to emphasize what I have been assuming all along, that he is not simply extolling the virtues of rights understood as claims, but the notion of *individual* rights and claims. In other words, it is conceptually possible to have the concepts of rights and claims without attributing them to individuals. Instead rights might only be attributed to groups such as families, as was the case in Tokugawa Japan. And yet if this were so we would have to rethink what Feinberg says. Would he still say that people could have a sense of equality, dignity, self-respect, and the rest?

On the one hand, if he did, people would not have these things because they individually had rights, but rather because they each belonged to a group that had such rights. But then being able to make claims as individuals would not be essential to feelings of self-worth and respect for others. Given that Feinberg's examples are always examples of individuals and their rights, it is extremely unlikely that he could or would adopt this alternative.

On the other hand, suppose group rights were not sufficient for feelings of self-worth and human dignity. If so, then it would not simply be rights that are necessary but *individuals having those rights*. Indeed, I maintain that this is precisely what is presupposed in Feinberg's argument. His analysis, and much of the philosophical literature about rights, purports to be arguing for the value of rights, when it is actually arguing for the value of the rights of individuals.

Second, if Feinberg is correct, then he must hold that for every system of morality either it must have the concept of rights, or it is not possible for people within it "to have a feeling of equality, minimal–self respect, the love and esteem for others, respect for persons, or human dignity." But these claims seem either false or true only by definition.

Take Feinberg's assertion that thinking of oneself as a holder of rights is essential for "the minimal–self respect necessary to be worthy of the love and esteem of others." If "self-respect" is understood straightforwardly as a psychological concept, the obvious fact is that a person's minimal–self respect is primarily a function of the love and regard of those important to her, especially during childhood. But it is implausible to suppose that love, especially familial love, is based on "thinking of oneself as a holder of rights" or "thinking of one's child as a potential maker of claims." In addition, the regard of others depends on what is valued in the culture in question, which may or may not include having the capacity to make claims against others. So it seems quite possible that one might be valued by others and have self-respect but not have any conception of oneself as the individual bearer of rights.

Now Feinberg can maintain that people in such a society don't really respect themselves because they don't see themselves as rights-bearers. However, not only does this seem question begging, but given what he says – "minimal–self respect is necessary to be worthy of the love and esteem of others" – it also entails that no one in these societies is "worthy of the love and respect of others," a view that Feinberg would surely not want to maintain.

Consider from a Confucian perspective another claim that Feinberg makes, namely, that being able to make claims is necessary for human equality, human dignity, and respect for persons: the Confucian world is a part of a universe well-ordered by Heaven (*Tian*). Everything has what we would call an essential nature, a characteristic role to play in this universe, and when everyone and everything does its part, all goes smoothly, harmoniously, as it should. It is an orderly conception of the world, much more like Western views prior to the scientific revolution than our views today.

In the Confucian view, human beings are part of the natural order. The natural state, even for human beings, ought to be one of harmony, not discord. Life in a harmonious society is the one human beings are both best suited for and toward which they are most naturally inclined. The Confucian conception of human equality lies in the belief that all human beings are born with a capacity for moral feelings such as compassion, respect, and propriety, and for human relationships based on them.[19] The basic tenet in orthodox Confucian thought is that "All people are by nature good," where this means that everyone is born with the four feelings that are the beginnings of the four virtues (*Mencius* 2A:6). According to Confucianism, it is because of this, and not because people are rights-bearers or are potential makers of claims, that human beings have a moral status deserving respect.

Herbert Fingarette has another related way of describing human equality and value in Confucianism.[20] In his book, *Confucius: The Secular as Sacred*, Fingarette likens the Confucian conception of human life to a sacred ceremony. Human beings are like "holy vessels" because they have a role in that ceremony.[21] It is important to see, as Fingarette takes pains to point out, that human beings have an intrinsic value, not because they are individual rights-bearers, but because they are constitutive parts of an intrinsically valuable whole. Human beings have value, not because they are individuals, but because they are interrelated.

To use another image of Confucianism, one very close to Fingarette's notion of a sacred ceremony, life is like a sacred dance in which we all have parts to play, and in which it is only through the successful performance of the dance that we can individually and collectively attain fulfillment. Human beings deserve respect because they are participants in the sacred dance of life as beings who have roles, such as those of child or parent, and capacities to relate to one another in characteristically human ways. In this picture people deserve respect and have dignity in two distinguishable ways: (1) externally, from the point of view of an observer, because they are integral parts of an intrinsically valuable whole, the sacred dance, and (2) internally, from the point of view of other participants, because, analogous to the way that family members deserve respect from each other, we are all part of the same family. In this model, equality derives from our common membership and from our equal potential to achieve excellence within our own particular circumstances. Although it is possible to conceptualize a dance, like ballet, in terms of mutual rights and duties that dancers have to one another, it is an odd way of thinking about what they are doing. Furthermore it is unnecessary. Far from being central, rights seem at best peripheral to, and at worst, at odds with the objectives of the dance.

This admittedly sketchy picture should help to show that even though Confucianism makes no mention of rights, it has a significant and interesting conception of human equality and human worth. Respect for persons and proper pride might plausibly be thought to arise out of these human capacities and their exercise, even though they are not grounded on being potential makers of claims.

Is this Confucian conception of human worth a satisfactory alternative to Feinberg's rights-based conception? If the question is "Can a Confucian conception of human beings provide an interesting and not implausible basis for people to have feelings of self-respect, human dignity, human worth, proper pride, equality, and respect for others?" then the answer seems clearly affirmative.

If the question is "Can a Confucian conception of human being give rise to precisely *the very same* conceptions as those based on the notion of being an individual rights-bearer?" the answer is much more doubtful. But even if it cannot, this in itself is not sufficient to condemn the Confucian view unless we already agree that the rights-based conceptions are the only ones acceptable and that persons must be conceived as individual rights-bearers. Taking this view requires that we accept something like the view that persons are essentially individuals whose humanity is defined by rationality and autonomy, the honoring of which requires acknowledging the demands that one individual can make against others.

But putting the focus on the individual, her rationality and autonomy, and the demands that she can make is a peculiarly Western concern. Traditional societies, like those based on Confucianism, and even pre-Enlightenment Western societies, clearly understand being human in other terms. Feinberg could simply assert that such views are mistaken, and that the rights view is correct, but doing so seems presumptuous.

Throughout, Feinberg argues that we can have no concept of human dignity without the concept of rights. To a large measure this depends on what is meant by "human dignity." In one plausible interpretation, human dignity can be understood as the recognition that human beings have an intrinsic value qua human beings, which is of a different order than the value of mere objects. Understood this way, Confucian and other traditional cultures without the concept of rights have a conception of human dignity insofar as they have their own conception of human value, which is, to use Kant's terminology, beyond mere price.

However, if human dignity must be analyzed in terms of the individual and her rights, or in terms of human autonomy and rationality, then Confucian and other traditions may indeed not have a conception of human dignity, but may be none the worse for that. In other words, if Feinberg is arguing that we cannot have the correct conception of human dignity unless it is grounded on a conception of persons as rights-bearers, then, if this is to be more than a trivial analytic claim, he must first define more clearly the conditions an acceptable conception of dignity must meet and provide more arguments to the effect that only this conception will do.

As we can see, the question of whether the Confucian conception of human worth might be a satisfactory alternative to a rights-based conception of persons is a very difficult one, because any answer would seem to beg the question by presupposing some evaluative perspective. From the point of view of a Confucian, the answer is, obviously, affirmative. From the point of view of someone in the individual rights tradition, probably not. A third alternative, working for some transcultural agreement, is probably a long way off. If so, the only reasonable course may be not to reject any moral system that recognizes human worth, even if that worth is grounded on a different conception of human beings and not on individual rights.

To summarize this criticism of Feinberg's second claim: I have not argued that being a rights holder cannot be *a way* of establishing and maintaining a sense of human worth in our diverse and fragmented modern world.[22] What I think is false, and what I have argued against, is the view that conceiving of oneself and others as having rights is the *only way* to have a sense of human equality, dignity, self-respect, and the rest. What I have suggested is that other moral theories might plausibly be thought to support a sense of human dignity and do not rely on the conception of individual rights to do so.

VI. THE VALUE OF INDIVIDUAL RIGHTS

In this concluding section I would like to pursue a line of speculation about what the value of individual rights might in fact be. To do this, again consider the sport of basketball. In basketball, talk of rules is important, but talk of individual rights is unusual and unnecessary. It is not, however, impossible. I grant that we could introduce rights into basketball. Why don't we do this, and under what circumstances might we want to do so?

One suggestion is that we don't need to initiate talk of rights when the players, coaches, fans, or referees can be relied on to do their best to identify and rectify rule or role violations. Conferring any kind of privileged position on the one who most directly suffers the consequences of the rule or role breaking (e.g., a player who is fouled while taking a shot) is unnecessary because it is unlikely to increase the fairness of the game. The shooter is not likely to be objective or reliable.

What are we trying to protect in this situation? Rules are designed both to constitute the game and to improve it by making it more competitive, and thereby more exciting and enjoyable. Essential to achieving these objectives is the maintenance of fair competition, including, especially, the fair application of the rules.

Perhaps this gives us a clue to rights talk and its importance. If one important aspect of morality is to manage competition, especially a competition between individuals, then it becomes very important to protect the competitors from unfair treatment. On the one hand, if one can assume a basic cooperativeness and honesty or, as in basketball, some reliable and impartial authority or mechanism, then conceptualizing the game in terms of individual rights, and conferring special abilities to make claims on individuals, may be less important or altogether unnecessary. On the other hand, if one cannot, then investing individuals with the ability to have and to press their own claims may be vitally important.

Perhaps another image, other than the one of competition, might be useful. Consider a company or a family where a cooperative whole is constituted through the fulfillment of role responsibilities. When a group is a kind of community working toward a common goal, talk of rights is neither necessary nor appropriate. In fact, it can be deleterious. Respect, equality, and dignity are all understood in terms of being a contributing member of the community. There will still be rules and boundaries, not because individuals in the community have rights, but because roles have to be defined for the community to work effectively and to progress. On the other hand, when a community breaks down, when there is no common goal, and when the desire for individual advancement or other forms of competition dominate, then each person will want and need individual safeguards or rights.

Now it is sometimes claimed, especially in the case of dysfunctional families, that family members had rights all along, but that when families are working well those rights are all being recognized and therefore do not need to be mentioned. Although this is one way of conceptualizing the situation, it is just as easy, and perhaps simpler and significantly less fraught with metaphysical assumptions, to maintain that rights within a family, say children's rights, are social constructs created for the purpose of adjudicating the differences that exist in dysfunctional families. It is not that children have always had rights, but that they come to do so in societies where many families are seriously dysfunctional. It is sometimes useful to regard children as having rights once families no longer perform the job of caring for children as they should. What is basic is how children should be treated. Whether establishing rights will further that end depends on how well the families are operating.

What I have maintained is that it is possible for people to ensure rule/role compliance and to have a sense of human dignity and worth without having the concept of individual rights. In my view, individual rights are valuable when having them can improve on other impartial mechanisms geared to ensure rule/role observance, or to adjudicate conflict, or to protect persons against those, including the state, who refuse to fulfill their responsibilities. In any team game, such as basketball, if players were less biased and better situated than referees to identify rule violations against them, it might make sense to give their complaints special weight by letting them identify infractions that could then be adjudicated by some other procedure. If referees were known to have less than impartial attitudes toward teams or players, individual rights might be a way of correcting that bias. If families degenerate to a point where one cannot count on parental affection, then instituting talk of children's rights may be an unhappy necessity.

One problem with our increasingly diverse and complex society may be that we are so fragmented that we apparently can no longer count on interests other than self-interests, and we cannot rely on informal protections such as community pressure to protect those interests. Attribution of rights, that is, giving individuals special status within the institution, is one way to ensure that individual interests will be taken into account and that rule violations will be identified and pursued in a vigorous manner. If this is correct, we can see why the notion of a right can be such a useful one in certain contemporary contexts. Rights can give unique weight to the claims of individuals; and in the case of human rights it gives the individual an importance that extends beyond specific sociopolitical structures.

In my analysis, whether it makes sense to promote the idea of individual rights depends on whether giving special weight to individual claims is called for by a specific set of circumstances. It should not be promoted if moral systems that do not invoke the notion of individual rights can serve as well or better.

Given our culturally diverse modern world, it is not difficult to see why many claim that traditional moral systems such as Confucianism are impractical. But even if they are correct, not being practical in the modern world is far from being morally unacceptable in the way Feinberg and others charge.[23]

Notes

An NEH Summer Seminar and its director, Prof. Thomas E. Hill, contributed significantly to the development of this chapter, as did the comments of many individuals present at readings of earlier drafts at the UCLA Law and Philosophy Reading Group, Moral and Political Philosophers of Orange County, the Pacific Division of the APA, and the Second Annual East Meets West Conference in Long Beach, California, as well as at University of Redlands, Chapman University, and my own campus, University of California, Fullerton. In particular I am indebted to the work of Henry Rosemont for many of the fundamental ideas presented here, and especially to Seung-hwan Lee for stimulating my thoughts on these issues. I have also received significant feedback and support from Kwong-loi Shun, David B. Wong, Paul Kjellberg, Carl F. Cranor, and anonymous reviewers for Cambridge University Press.

1. Alasdair MacIntyre, *After Virtue* (Notre Dame, IN: University of Notre Dame Press, 1981), pp. 175ff.
2. See Tu Wei-Ming, "Li as Process of Humanization" and "The Confucian Perception of Adulthood," in *Humanity and Self-Cultivation: Essays in Confucian Thought* (Berkeley, CA: Asian Humanities Press, 1979), pp. 27, 54 (n. 23) and Henry Rosemont, Jr., "Why Take Rights Seriously? A Confucian Critique" in Leroy S. Rouner ed., *Human Rights and the World's Religions* (Notre Dame, IN: University of Notre Dame Press, 1988), pp. 167–182; Roger T. Ames, "Rites as Rights: The Confucian Alternative" in Leroy S. Rouner ed., *Human Rights and the World's Religions* (Notre Dame, IN: University of Notre Dame Press, 1988), pp. 199–216; Chad Hansen, "Punishment and Dignity in China" in Donald Munro ed., *Individualism and Holism* (Ann Arbor: University of Michigan Center for Chinese Studies, 1985), p. 360.
3. The claim is not simply that there is no concept of *human* rights in Confucianism, but there is no concept of rights at all.
4. Seung-hwan Lee, "Was There a Concept of Rights in Confucian Virtue-Based Morality?" *The Journal of Chinese Philosophy*, vol. 19 (1992), pp. 241–61.
5. Ronald Dworkin, *Taking Rights Seriously* (Cambridge, MA: Harvard University Press, 1977); Alan Gewirth, *Reason and Morality* (Chicago: University of Chicago Press, 1978); Judith Jarvis Thomson, *The Realm of Rights* (Cambridge, MA: Harvard University Press, 1990); J. L. Mackie, *Ethics: Inventing Right and Wrong* (New York: Penguin Books, 1977); A. I. Meldon, *Rights and Persons* (Berkeley: University of California Press, 1980); Joel Feinberg, "The Nature and Value of Rights," *The Journal of Value Inquiry*, vol. 4 (1970), pp. 243–7.
6. Alan Gewirth, "Why Rights Are Indispensible," *Mind*, vol. 95 (1986), p. 343.
7. Feinberg, op. cit., pp. 243–7.
8. Although Feinberg and others use the term "rights" simpliciter, I maintain that their arguments are normally about the rights of individuals. More on this later.
9. Feinberg, op. cit., pp. 243–7.
10. Ibid., p. 249. This emphasis on claiming reflects Feinberg's specific conception of rights. He specifically distinguishes his notion of claim rights from

other Hohfeldian conceptions of rights such as liberties, immunities, and powers: "claim rights are distinguished from the mere liberties, immunities, and powers, also sometimes called 'rights,' (and) with which they are easily confused" (p. 249). For purposes of this chapter, I adopt Feinberg's conception of rights understood as valid claims.

11. Ibid., p. 251.

12. Obviously what Feinberg says about legal claiming is much more clear and forceful than those extrapolated to moral claiming.

13. Feinberg, op. cit., pp. 252–3.

14. Ibid., p. 249.

15. Ibid., p. 247.

16. I assume it is implausible that the runner has a right against the batter to lay down a bunt. At most the runner might be said to have a right *to expect* the batter to try and lay down the bunt, but such a right is epistemological, not a claim right. That is to say, it is a right based on having information that makes it reasonable to believe the batter will try to bunt (e.g., a bunt sign the runner sees the coach give the batter). It is not based on promises or commitments of any kind by the batter to the runner.

17. Feinberg, op. cit., p. 252.

18. It strikes me that even those, like Seung-hwan Lee, who argue that there is a concept of rights in Confucianism agree that those rights have been seriously deemphasized. If so, and if the Western authors cited at the beginning are correct, then Confucian ethics is seriously defective for never giving rights and claiming their proper role.

19. For a discussion of the Confucian conception of human equality, see Donald Munro, *The Concept of Man in Early China* (Stanford, CA: Stanford University Press, 1967).

20. Herbert Fingarette, *Confucius: The Secular as Sacred* (New York: Harper Torchbooks, 1972).

21. Ibid., pp. 71–9.

22. There is also a case to be made, though I have only suggested it in this essay, that excessive individualism can undermine self-respect by, for example, depriving human beings of a social context within which actions have meaning. (I owe this point to Paul Kjellberg.)

23. Admittedly this analysis of rights argues for the importance of rights, but only under certain specific social conditions. This is in contrast with Feinberg and others who seem to argue for its importance without qualification. However, the view I present is not simply a utilitarian or even consequentialist conception of rights, since, as presented, it is compatible with a Rawlsian constructivism. In it, compatible with Rawls, rights can be understood as part of a reasonable solution to certain choice situations partly determined by specific social circumstances such as the lack of any shared conception of the good, and need not be conceptualized as an essential part of any morally acceptable system.

2

Rights and Community in Confucianism

David B. Wong

I. INTRODUCTION

There is an interesting turn toward Confucianism in much U.S. scholarship on Chinese philosophy. Heiner Roetz, in a recent book on Confucian ethics, detects certain frequently recurring themes in this scholarship. Quoting and paraphrasing from authors such as Herbert Fingarette, Henry Rosemont, David Hall, and Roger Ames, Roetz summarizes the themes in the following way:[1]

China can teach us to recognize that the mentality of self, autonomy, and freedom has run its course. Together with the Chinese, we should recall our "communal rituals, customs, and traditions"[2] and "inherited forms of life."[3] We should abandon the "myth of objective knowledge," and adopt a "thinking that avoids the disjunction of normative and spontaneous thought."[4] Confucius especially presents us with a model which for our world is perhaps "more relevant, more timely, more urgent" than it has been even in China herself.[5]

Roetz criticizes the line of thought he finds in these authors for its apparent paradoxicality: the criticism of negative developments within Western society presupposes general normative criteria, yet the allegedly better model – Confucianism – is deployed to argue for a "contextualism which is no longer interested in questions of right and wrong, or relativity and objectivity."[6] Furthermore, Roetz argues that context and tradition sanctified foot-binding in China, widow burning in India, and slavery in the United States. Roetz asks, "How can we criticize the unspeakable injustice inflicted upon man in the name of traditions and contexts if we leave the final say to both and abandon any ethical reserve?"[7] Roetz goes on to argue for an interpretation of Confucianism that finds within it important universalistic ethical themes relating to Habermasian and Kohlbergian conceptions of moral development.

Now I am not certain that the authors Roetz mentions would agree that they hold the particular combination of views he attributes to them.[8] But on the other hand, it is not unusual to find this combination of views in Westerners who react favorably to Confucianism – both the view that Confucianism reveals something important that one's own tradition has neglected or underemphasized and the view that it is wrongheaded to search for some transcendent truth about which tradition is objectively superior to others. I suspect that many of us who do comparative ethics get caught in the tension between these two views. In this essay I want to explain a way to live with both. I stake out a position between the new contextualist and postmodernist approaches to Confucianism, on the one hand, and the universalist approach that can find insight or injustice in Confucianism.

I want to focus on the question of whether moralities ought to recognize individual rights and in particular the rights to speech and dissent. The common view, one to which I have contributed in the past, is that rights do not find a congenial home in Confucianism because of its emphasis on community. In this essay I want to take a more complex position. I still maintain that there is a significant difference between typical rights-centered moralities and the community-centered morality of Confucianism. I will argue for a pluralism that accepts both rights-centered and Confucian moralities, and in that respect I am with the contextualists and postmodernists. On the other hand, I also will argue that there are universal constraints on morality rooted in the human condition and human nature, and that these constraints push Confucianism and rights-centered moralities closer together through the recognition of the interdependence of rights and community. To lay the groundwork for this argument, let me re-introduce the ways in which I have distinguished Confucianism from rights-centered moralities.

II. COMMUNITY-CENTERED AND RIGHTS-CENTERED MORALITIES

In previous work, I have characterized Confucianism as a virtue-centered morality with the core value of a common good at its center. This common good consists in a shared life as defined by a network of roles specifying the contribution of each member to the sustenance of that life. This communally oriented morality contrasts with a rights-centered morality, which gives no comparable emphasis to a common good. Rather it emphasizes what each individual, qua individual, is entitled to claim from other members. Rights-centered moralities spring from a recognition of the moral worth of individuals independently of their roles in community.

It now seems necessary to qualify my original distinction in several ways. First, I need to distinguish at least in theory between virtue-centered and community-centered moralities. I originally identified the two types because they have been historically linked through the concept of a virtue as a quality needed by members to contribute to the common good of community. However, it now seems to me at least theoretically possible that virtues can become uncoupled from a common good and be deemed desirable qualities on some basis other than their necessity for a shared life.[9] Having said this, let me stipulate that my focus shall be on community-centered moralities in which the concept of virtue *is* associated with the qualities necessary for sustaining the common good of a shared life.

Second, I now want to emphasize that my conception of a rights-centered morality includes a conception of the characteristic ground for the recognition of individual rights, as well as a generic conception of rights. We may think of the individual's moral rights as that to which the individual is legitimately entitled to claim against others as her moral entitlement. But a rights-centered morality typically assumes as a basis for such entitlements that the individual has substantial domain of morally legitimate personal interests that may conflict with the goal of promoting public or collective goods. Rights constitute constraints or limits on the extent that individual personal interests may be sacrificed for the sake of public or collective goods. Let me call this kind of ground for the recognition of rights "the autonomy ground." I do not want to claim that this is the only ground for rights recognized in the modern Western democratic tradition, but I do think it is probably the most recognized ground in that tradition and that it is the predominant ground in terms of its widespread acceptance and the degree of importance attached to it.

Third, I want to identify another possible ground for the recognition of rights that may exist alongside the autonomy ground. Rights may be recognized on the basis of their necessity for promoting the common good. Community-centered moralities, I shall argue, can and should recognize this sort of "communal ground" for rights. Rights-centered and community-centered moralities, then, need not differ because one recognizes rights while the other does not. They must differ in the sort of basis they offer for the recognition of rights.

III. THE COMMUNAL GROUND FOR RIGHTS

Seung-hwan Lee has argued[10] that the Confucian virtues do involve rights, if rights are conceived as enabling persons to make justified claims against others whose duty it is to fulfill them. This is in effect what I want to call the "generic" conception of rights, and Lee goes on to point out that in Mencius in particular there is a conception of rights in this sense. The Mencian virtue of righteousness (*yi*) involves "dutifulness in discharging of one's obligation, rightfulness in respecting other's due, and righteousness in recognizing the limit of one's own desert."[11] In the case of rites and propriety (*li*), Lee points out that the rules governing duties between people standing in the cardinal relationships, such as father and son, can be conceived as rules specifying correlative rights and duties.

But Lee warns us not to equate the rights found in Confucianism with the type of "individualistic" rights found in Western traditions. And one major reason for his warning is that "the Confucian ideal of a communitarian society in which good of the community always precedes individual good tends to devaluate individualistic assertion of one's rights against the common good."[12] This is connected, Lee argues, with the Confucian conception of the human being as a relational being. In terms of my framework, Lee is according a communal ground to the generic conception of rights, not an autonomy ground.

So conceived, Confucian rights do not seem to offer much aid and comfort to those Chinese intellectuals and reformers who see a need for rights of dissent, of free speech, and of the democratic election of leaders in a multiparty political system. Lee seems to conclude as much, arguing that Chinese society needs a dose of Western individualism in order to counter an "excessive emphasis on the collectivist conception of the common good," in the name of which "people's assertions of basic rights and freedom have been neglected."[13] However, I think the turn to an autonomy ground for rights may be premature. We need to see what rights a communal ground can yield.

Roetz, for example, calls for a "nonregressive appropriation of tradition" that "combines the interpretation and adaptation" of the Confucian heritage with "the modern demands for democracy and change."[14] He points to themes in the Confucian canon that seem especially relevant to rights to dissent and freedom of speech. Consider the following passage from the *Zidao (The Way of the Son)*, chapter 29 of the *Xunzi*.

Zigong said, "If a son follows the order of the father, this is already filial piety. And if a subject follows the order of the ruler, this is already loyalty. But what is the answer of my teacher?"

Confucius said, "What a mean man you are! You do not know that in antiquity, if there were four frank ministers in a state with ten thousand war-chariots, its territory was never diminished. If there were three frank ministers in a state with a thousand war-chariots, that state was never endangered. And if there were two frank subordinates in a clan with one hundred war-chariots, its ancestral temple was never destroyed. If a father has a frank son, he will not do anything that contradicts propriety. If a scholar has a frank friend, he will not do anything unjust. *How, then, could a son be filial if he follows the order of his father? And how could a subject be loyal if he follows the order of the ruler? One can only speak of filial piety and loyalty after one has examined the reasons why they follow the order.*"[15]

The implication of this passage is that one has a duty to speak frankly when the violation of propriety and justice is in question, even if it is the ruler who is about to violate them. The basis for such a duty to speak is the sort of communal ground I have been describing. It is in the interests of having a community that realizes propriety and justice that a minister or a son speaks out. It might be thought that the duty to speak frankly implies as a necessary correlate the right to speak. After all, if one has a duty to speak, should one be allowed to speak and in fact be protected from interference through force and coercion?

It is important to recognize the ways in which Xunzi's argument has a more limited scope than we might assume. For one thing, Xunzi would not have thought the duty to frank speech applied to *daughters* in relation to their fathers, nor is it clear that he meant the duty to frankly speak to one's king to apply to everyone in the empire below the rank of minister. Xunzi's duty does not correspond to a modern, liberal democratic right to free speech held by all citizens. Furthermore, it is at least logically possible that the duty to speak as Xunzi conceived was not even associated with any *right* to speak. As I indicated previously, one could begin to make an argument for a right to speak only if relevant others have a duty to let one speak. But the fact that a minister or a son may have a duty to speak frankly does not necessarily imply that a king or a father has a general duty to let him.[16] Indeed, if one keeps in mind Xunzi's abiding and deep concern for political and moral order and the way that order is under constant threat from an anarchic and self-serving human nature, one could imagine him holding that the king or father may have a duty to punish the minister or son for speaking out if it threatens the political and moral order within the kingdom or the family. This duty to punish may hold even if the minister or son has spoken truly and appropriately.

There is another ground for blocking the inference of a *general* right to speak from Xunzi's argument. This argument is consistent with the possibility that a minister or son has a general prima facie duty to follow orders from his king or father *without* questioning them in frank speech. Xunzi may have been saying that such a duty can be overridden, say, if it is needed to correct some especially grave error in these orders. On this interpretation, the duty to speak would be one that arises on specific and relatively infrequent occasions. Under these assumptions, there could not be a general right to speech corresponding to the duty to speak, since such a duty would arise only under specific and infrequent circumstances.[17]

So I do not mean to suggest that one finds in the Chinese classical tradition anything like a full-blown argument for a right to free speech. What I do mean to suggest is that we do have the *germ* of an argument in the idea that the common good is sustained by recognition of a duty to speak. The full-blown argument requires further substantial claims that are broadly empirical and that are, I shall argue, consistent with a communal ground for the right. Some of the issues involve criticism of traditional hierarchies that accord more powers and privileges to ministers and sons than to other subordinates and daughters. I have made such arguments elsewhere so I will not do so here. I do want to address here the issues of whether one can have a duty to speak without others having a duty to let one speak and whether there really is a good argument for a general prima facie duty to obey the orders of political authorities without frank questioning. I intend to dispute that the common good is actually promoted by failing to recognize a duty to let others speak or by limiting the duty to dissent to especially grave and infrequent occasions.

Let me start with an argument Allen Buchanan gives in the context of the contemporary Western debate between communitarian and rights-centered theorists. As a theorist who bases rights on the autonomy ground, Buchanan addresses communitarians on their own ground when he writes that

individual rights can play a valuable role even in societies in which there is unanimous agreement as to what the common good is and a universal commitment to pursuing it. For even in such a society there could be serious, indeed violent, disagreements either about how the common good is to be specified concretely and in detail or about the proper means and strategies for achieving it. Individual rights, especially rights of political participation, freedom of expression, and association can serve to contain and channel such disagreements and to preserve community in spite of their presence.[18]

It seems to me pretty plausible that the sort of disagreements Buchanan mentions are a regular and constant feature of human societies, and that therefore the "need to protect and allow for the peaceful transformations of communities"[19] requires regular and institutionalized channels for dissent, not simply the occasional recognition of a duty to frank speech in specific and infrequent circumstances. Such regularized channels of dissent would require the recognition of duties to let others speak and more positively to protect them in speech from threat and coercion by others. It is to allow those who would speak to publicly hold others to this duty to allow and to protect their speech, something that is involved in being able to claim something as one's right. Once we have such duties, I think we are pretty close to something like a modern democratic right to speak.

Indeed, a communal grounding for a right to speech could be made within a contextualist and postmodernist interpretation of Confucianism, provided that such an interpretation still leaves room for criticism of the tradition. Hall and Ames, well known for their postmodernist interpretation of Confucius and for their vigorous defense of him, nevertheless observe that "The most serious failings of Confucius's philosophy are due to the provincialism and parochialism that seem inevitably to result from the institutionalization of his thinking." This parochialism, they charge, retards "cross-cultural communication" and fosters abuses that cross the "fine line that keeps social order beginning at home separate from nepotism, personal loyalties from special privilege, deference to excellence from elitism, appropriate respect from graft," and, finally, "appropriate deference to the tradition and a cultural dogmatism that has too frequently been in the interests of particular groups."[20] In the spirit of such criticism, one could argue that an appropriate remedy for these failings is recognition and vigorous protection of rights to free speech and dissent.

The argument thus far weighs in favor of recognizing various duties to allow and to protect dissenting speech. Implicit in this argument is an assumption worth making explicit: dissenting speech will not be heard often enough to serve the common good if it is not allowed and protected from interference. This assumption may appear trivially true, but if so, it is so only to us. As I indicated earlier, Xunzi probably recognized a duty to frank speech while denying a duty to allow it. He was theoretically consistent, but in practice, I want to argue, inconsistent.

The recognition that speech and dissent must be publicly recognized and protected in order for it to serve its function in promoting the common good is a lesson that some Chinese thinkers learned from Chinese history. Andrew Nathan has identified a succession of Chinese intellectuals in the early part of the twentieth century who argued for democratic rights on the ground that China's problems in modernizing stemmed from the "systematic overconcentration of power" and its abuse. At the same time, Nathan points out that these intellectuals very rarely put forward a line of reasoning central to the Western democratic tradition: "that the individual's interests are separate from the group's, that certain of them are so basic as to have the status of 'rights,' and that democracy is first of all a system that protects these rights."[21] Implicit in this characterization of Chinese democratic thought, I claim, is a communal grounding for rights of speech and dissent.

To give another example of this sort of grounding in the Chinese tradition, seven eminent intellectuals led by the historian Xu Liangying recently protested a series of arrests of dissidents by connecting human rights with modernization:

To talk about modernization without mentioning human rights is like climbing a tree to catch a fish. Two hundred and five years ago, the French Declaration of the Rights of Man stated clearly that being ignorant, neglectful and disdainful of human rights is the sole cause of the general public's misfortunes and corruption in government. China's history and reality have verified that longstanding truth.[22]

If one could make the case for substantial rights to free speech and dissent in this way, as I believe one can, what are the implications for the debate between universalism and postmodernist contextualism? It suggests to me that there are human tendencies that span very different cultures, tendencies that render community-centered moralities subject to certain kinds of liabilities. These liabilities need not be judged in Western terms, and not specifically in terms of a moral perspective that places a premium on the value of individual autonomy. Rather, the liabilities are failures to realize the ideal of the common good itself. If, as Buchanan suggests, communitarian traditions frequently give rise to serious and even violent disagreements over questions as to how concretely to realize a common good, democratic rights may be necessary to ensure the peaceful resolution of such disagreements. If, as Hall and Ames suggest, and as many generations of Chinese intellectuals and reformers have concluded, centralized authority unchecked by dissenting voices from below tends toward abuse of power, nepotism, and isolation and ignorance of what those below really do need, democratic rights may be part of the required remedy, if not the entire remedy.

Having roughly outlined the case for the possibility of communally grounded democratic rights, let me note that a communal grounding is different from a utilitarian grounding for rights, though both groundings are consequentialist in character. A utilitarian grounding of rights would make the case for their utility, where the sum total of utility is a function of the welfare of individuals. For most utilitarians, anyway, the character of the relations between individuals does not in itself necessarily count as part of the total good to be promoted.[23] But it is precisely the character of the relations between individuals that is the primary focus of community-centered moralities. Underlying this focus is a normative and descriptive conception of the person as constituted by her relationships to others and whose good is constituted by relationships that fulfill a moral ideal of appropriate respect and mutual concern. A community-centered morality must, of course, concern itself with some of the same goods with which utilitarianism is concerned. Both Mencius and Xunzi, for example, knew full well that their moral ideals of community could not begin to be fulfilled without a minimal level of material security for the people. And that has remained a preoccupation for Confucians up to the present. But a community-centered morality locates the importance of individual welfare within the larger context of a common good. In fact, the individual's good and the common good are inextricably linked.

IV. THE DIFFERENT OUTCOMES OF THE COMMUNITY AND AUTONOMY GROUNDS

Having noted the possibility of providing a communal ground for rights, however, we must note what such a ground does not provide. The scope of rights grounded in community will not be the same as the scope of rights grounded in autonomy. As Buchanan notes, if one were to justify individual rights only by reference to the moral requirement of autonomy, one might justify a "rather broad, virtually unrestricted right to freedom of expression." If, however, we allow the value of community "independent weight as a factor in determining the scope of the right of freedom of expression, we might find that only a more restricted right of freedom of expression can be justified." Therefore, concludes Buchanan, "In the justification of individual rights, the traditional liberal and the [rights-minded] communitarian may travel the same path for some time, but eventually the path may fork and they may be forced to part company."[24]

Indeed, it might be that the rights-minded communitarian and the traditional liberal will part sooner rather than later, and quite dramatically, depending on what the communitarian perceives as necessary for the common good. Nathan's historical study of Chinese conceptions of democracy reveals the fragility of rights when seen solely as instrumental to collective goods such as prosperity and modernization. Time and again, rights championed as necessary for the common good have been suspended or curtailed because of fear of chaos and national weakness.

Such an observation will lead to the conclusion that a significant difference between community-centered and rights-centered moralities remains, even if both kinds of moralities are constrained by the need for rights to dissenting speech. On the one hand, human nature and the human condition place common constraints on what could count as an adequate morality. Human beings in power tend often enough to abuse that power or to confuse the personal interests served by their exercise of power with the ethical interests of their communities, and therefore need to be checked through the protected use of dissenting speech. Even if a morality provides no autonomy ground for rights to dissenting speech, it must provide for some version of those rights. However, significant moral differences are consistent with such common constraints. Not only do the two types of morality endorse democratic rights for different reasons, the scope of the rights endorsed and their relative immunity to being overridden by other considerations may differ significantly.

V. WORRIES ABOUT THE COMMUNAL GROUND FOR RIGHTS

However, a worry arises from reflection on the ways in which communally grounded rights within the Chinese tradition have easily given way to fear of chaos and national weakness. The concept of communally grounded rights may be too weak an instrument for combating the liabilities of community-centered traditions. Especially instructive in this regard is Nathan's account of the way that the Communist Party, from Mao onward, moved toward the idea of free speech and dissent, only to withdraw support for it when it threatened to undermine the equation between the interests of the party and those of the people.[25]

This worry may remind us of the familiar charge against consequentialist groundings of rights: that they provide an uncertain and inconstant grounding for them.[26] In one sense, of course, the community-centered moralist must admit this charge. As noted previously, rights with a communal grounding will never be as wide in scope or as secure from being overridden by other moral considerations as they would be with an autonomy grounding. From the perspective of the community-centered moralist, this is how it should be. But such a moralist still has reason to worry because she may wonder whether *the common good* is harmed when rights to speech and dissent are as insecure as they have been in the Chinese tradition.

The recognition of rights by itself will be ineffectual when the decision to override them for the sake of the common good is in the hands of a class that is motivated to identify its interests, and not necessarily morally legitimate ones, with the common good. But to say that the real problem may be an overcentralization of power is not to say what should take its place. The facile answer is to propose a transplanting of Western democratic machinery and to suppose that will take care of the problem. A real solution to the insecure grounding of rights within communal traditions, I suggest, must look to the character of civil society and not solely to democratic machinery.

William de Bary has recently identified two reasons for the failure of Confucianism to be more influential than it has been in its native country: first, an inability to realize its ideal of education for all people which would infuse a unified national consciousness, and second, a failure to mobilize the people as a politically active body, capable of supporting its initiatives and proposed reforms. The second failure, suggests de Bary, was linked to the lack of an infrastructure of politically effective associations that could serve as channels of communication and influence between the family and local forms of community on the one hand, and the ruling elite on the other.[27] A major concern of some democratic theorists in this country is the possible disappearance or eroding authority of precisely such an intermediate infrastructure. These theorists see Tocqueville as prescient about the dangers of an atomistic individualism that leaves citizens isolated, pursuing their purely private interests, and quite ineffective in making their voices heard in the political sphere because their voices are single. Now I am uncertain as to whether our intermediate institutions have gotten weaker or fewer, as these theorists worry, or whether these institutions have always been as sporadically effective as they seem to be now. In either case, I believe there is justifiable concern. The common element of concern in both scenarios is that there is not enough community (whether it is less community than in the past or not) to support effective democracy.

VI. THE INTERDEPENDENCE OF RIGHTS AND COMMUNITY

A common problem for both the Chinese and American democratic traditions, I suggest, is that they have not possessed enough community, at least enough community at levels above the family and local community. The problem for the American tradition goes beyond alienation from the political process for average citizens. Consider Tocqueville's definition of individualism as a "calm and considered feeling which disposes each citizen to isolate himself from the mass of his fellows and withdraw into the circle of family and friends," such that "with this little society formed to his taste he gladly leaves the greater society to look after itself." Such people, Tocqueville observed, form "the habit of thinking of themselves in isolation and imagine that their whole destiny is in their hands." They come to "forget their ancestors" and also their descendants, as well as isolating themselves from their contemporaries. "Each man is forever thrown back on himself alone, and there is danger that he may be shut up in the solitude of his own heart."[28]

Tocqueville's warning about isolation from our contemporaries and our descendants is reflected in the persistent and large inequalities of income and wealth in this country and in a shamefully high proportion of our children who are growing up in poverty; most importantly, it is reflected in the national inability or unwillingness to address these problems. And this brings me to the other side of the coin: if community-centered moralities should move closer to rights-centered moralities, at least in recognizing some of the most fundamental democratic rights, so too must rights-centered moralities recognize the indispensability of community for the realization of democratic values of self-governance and social justice. That is why I suggested at the beginning of this essay that rights and community are interdependent.

The lesson, to return to the issue of universalism versus postmodern contextualism with which I began, is that adequate moral traditions need both community and rights. Rights-centered traditions require a range of viable communities to nurture effective moral agency (a requirement of which Confucianism is well aware) and to make for the effective use of democratic machinery. They require viable communities to foster the sense of common project and fellowship that in turn promotes real and effective concern for meaningful equality among all citizens. Community-centered traditions need rights for the moral renewal of community and their peaceful transformation through the many disagreements it will experience over the common good. These necessities are grounded in our human nature. This is the sense in which I side with the universalists. However, this does not mean that rights and community must have precisely the same content across traditions, nor does it mean that they have to be given the same emphasis and the same rationale. This is the sense in which I side with the postmodernists.

VII. A FURTHER COMPLICATION

Rights-centered theorists have resisted appeals for community because they resist the ideal of a shared vision of a common good. I believe that they are right to do so if this ideal involves the impossible ideal of unanimity of belief about what the common good is, but I also believe that it is an error to reject community as a necessary moral ideal. The sort of community needed by both kinds of tradition must accommodate considerably more diversity of views on the common good than is commonly recognized by the more simplistic forms of communitarianism. Such forms typically envision their ideal communities as centered on some shared and unambiguous conception of the common good. Yet if we look at actual communities, even those with strong traditions of belief in a common good, we find continual disagreement and conflict over the common good. In part, this is the result of the complex nature of the common good. It is not one good, but an array of goods. These goods can be mutually supporting but also in tension with one another.

We can see this clearly in the Confucian tradition. If filial piety and brotherly respect are the root of *ren* or comprehensive moral virtue,[29] it also may conflict with other aspects of moral virtue, such as our concern for others outside the family. If loyalty to family nurtures a respect for authority not based on coercion, and if this respect is absolutely necessary for the cultivation of public virtue,[30] it may also encourage a partiality for one's own that is damaging to public virtue. Confucian ethics, as Hall and Ames have observed, is liable to continuous disagreement as to when the line between a rightful loyalty to family has crossed the line into nepotism and special privilege. And lest we take this as an occasion for condescending condemnation of Confucianism, let us recall that from different parts of the political spectrum in this country there has arisen a regret for the passing of the big city political machines. Back then, "taking care of one's own" was at least taking care of *someone well,* and the average person on the street could feel capable of real influence on political decision making.

My point then is not to condemn Confucianism for this difficulty but to take it as indicative of the tensions between the goods that make up the complex whole called the common good. Or to take another issue that very much bears on present-day China: the provision of material security for all may be necessary for the moral flourishing of Chinese society, as Mencius and Xunzi rightly observed, but at the same time the necessary means for development and modernization in the future can have enormously destructive effects on the moral quality of a society in the present. I have in mind the extremely coercive one-child policy and the growing gap that modernization and a measure of capitalism have produced between an impoverished countryside and some relatively affluent classes in cities.

Because the common good is a complex whole including a plurality of goods and within which these different goods may come into conflict, there always will be some disagreement over which goods are included and the most reasonable way to deal with conflicts between the goods that are included. The vision of a society united around a shared and unambiguous vision of a common good is dangerously simplistic and, moreover, ignores bases for community other than such a shared conception of the common good. Actual communities are based not only on some degree of agreement in moral belief but also on a shared history, often of struggle and internal conflict, ties of affection or loyalty, or on a limited set of common goals that may be educational, artistic, political, or economic in nature.

Given the inevitability of serious disagreement within all kinds of moral traditions that have any degree of complexity, a particular sort of ethical value becomes especially important for the stability and integrity of these traditions and societies. Let me call this value "accommodation."[31] To have this value involves commitment to supporting noncoercive and constructive relations with others even though they have ethical beliefs that conflict with one's own. Why is this value important? From the standpoint of the integrity and stability of a society, this value is important given the regularity of occurrence of serious ethical disagreement. If such disagreement always threatened to become the source of schism, no society could survive for very long without brutal repression.

To conclude, both rights-centered and community-centered traditions need a conception of community that is not based on an unattainable ideal of a shared vision of the common good. This new conception must accept significant diversity and disagreement and must maintain community in spite of that disagreement – not only through the recognition of rights but also through acceptance of the value of accommodation. To accept this value is to seek to find creative ways for conflicting sides within a community to stay within a community and yet not yield entirely to the other. If democratic virtues are needed here, it is not so much the ability to insist on one's rights, but the creative ability to negotiate, to give and to take, to create solutions that fully satisfy neither side in a conflict but that allow both sides to "save face."

This value has a basis in the Confucian tradition. Consider Antonio Cua's interpretation of the Confucian virtue of *ren*. This virtue, he says, involves an attitude toward human conflicts as subjects of "arbitration" rather than "adjudication." Arbitration is an attempted resolution of disputes oriented toward the reconciliation of the contending parties. The arbitrator is "concerned with repairing the rupture of human relationship rather than with deciding the rights or wrongs of the parties" [which is adjudication] and accordingly attempts to shape "the expectations of the contending parties along the line of mutual concern, to get them to appreciate one another as interacting members in a community."[32] Now I think Cua's interpretation underemphasizes real themes of "adjudication" to be found in Confucius, Mencius, and Xunzi,[33] but it does capture a theme of accommodation and reconciliation in Confucianism[34] that could have received greater emphasis than it did in the tradition as it actually evolved.

Unfortunately, the way in which Confucianism became institutionalized resulted in a deemphasis of this theme and in a corresponding greater emphasis on agreement in conception of the common good. For example, Nathan identifies a crucial assumption running throughout the advocacy of democratic rights by Chinese intellectuals. The assumption is that such rights would tap the energies of the people, check abuses of the ruling elite, further development, *and produce harmony in the sense of all sharing the same ideals.*[35] It is this last element of the assumption that is fatal.

Nathan unfortunately tends to draw the wrong lesson from his observation. He equates this aversion to disagreement with the assumption that the legitimate personal interests of the individual must ultimately harmonize with the common good.[36] This is a natural assumption for a Westerner to make: to deemphasize the legitimacy of disagreement and conflict is to deemphasize the legitimacy of conflicts between individuals and their communities. But conflict and disagreement can come from differences over conceptions of the common good. And because the common good of a complex society will include the goods of different communities contained within that society, there will be conflict between the goods and the communities. Mozi had a better insight into the source of disagreement and conflict in community-centered traditions: he recognized that much conflict can arise from people's *social* identities, from their identifications with family that lead to conflict with other families, from their identifications with their states that lead to conflict with other states.[37]

I believe there is sufficient plasticity in human nature so that people in community-centered traditions have to a greater degree relational identities. I believe that a life lived in accordance with such an identity can have great satisfactions. It of course can have deep frustrations, as do lives lived in accordance with identities that are much less relational in nature. The problem with Confucianism has not lain in its claim that a life shared and lived in relation with others is a morally flourishing life. The problem has lain in its assumption that the different aspects of a person's social identity, which correspond to the different goods that go into the common good, can all somehow be subsumed and ordered under some grand harmonizing principle. Here, perhaps, we might have wished not only that institutionalized Confucianism had taken rights more seriously, but also for a greater synthesis of Confucianism and Daoism, and more specifically, Zhuangzi's appreciation for difference and the multiplicity of perspectives.[38]

Notes

1. Heiner Roetz, *Confucian Ethics of the Axial Age: A Reconstruction under the Aspect of the Breakthrough toward Postconventional Thinking* (Albany: State University of New York Press, 1993), p. 2.
2. Roetz here refers to Henry Rosemont, Jr., "Kierkegaard and Confucius: On Finding the Way," *Philosophy East and West*, vol. 36 (1986), pp. 208–9.
3. The reference here is to Herbert Fingarette, *Confucius: The Secular as Sacred* (New York: Harper, 1972), p. 69.
4. The reference here is to David Hall and Roger Ames, *Thinking Through Confucius* (Albany: State University of New York Press, 1987), pp. 73, 43.
5. Fingarette, op. cit., p. 72.
6. Roetz, op. cit., p. 2.

7. Ibid., p. 3.

8. For example, I am uncertain that Fingarette has rejected "the myth of objective knowledge" in favor of a radical contextualism. On the contrary in *Confucius: The Secular as Sacred*, he seems to argue that Confucianism has merits that Westerners ought to recognize and, to the extent possible, incorporate into their own traditions, and that it has certain lacks that perhaps ought to be recognized by everyone as such. Roetz, of course, accuses these authors of a kind of self-contradiction, both proclaiming the objective merits of Confucianism and of decrying the myth of objective knowledge. In the case of Fingarette, however, I see little discussion of objective knowledge or its impossibility.

9. Amélie Rorty brought this point to my attention some years ago.

10. Seung-hwan Lee, "Was There a Concept of Rights in Confucian Virtue-Based Morality?" *Journal of Chinese Philosophy*, vol. 19 (1992), pp. 241–61.

11. Ibid., p. 249.

12. Ibid., p. 250.

13. Ibid., p. 257.

14. Roetz, op. cit., p. 5.

15. Xunzi, Wang Xianqian, *Xunzi jijie*, chapter 29, in *Zhuzi jicheng*, vol. 2 (Hong Kong: Zhonghua, 1978), pp. 347–8; translated by Roetz, op. cit., pp. 63–4.

16. This point was first brought to my attention by a university administrator, interestingly enough.

17. I gratefully acknowledge Uma Narayan's help in making this point to me in correspondence.

18. Allen E. Buchanan, "Assessing the Communitarian Critique of Liberalism," *Ethics*, vol. 99 (1989), p. 877.

19. Ibid., p. 881.

20. Hall and Ames, pp. 308–9, 310.

21. Andrew J. Nathan, *Chinese Democracy* (Berkeley: University of California Press, 1985), p. 104.

22. *New York Times*, Friday, March 11, 1994, p. A10.

23. An exception would be the "ideal" form of utilitarianism such as G. E. Moore held. This form counts certain states of affairs or relationships of a certain character as part of the total good to be promoted. More recently, Peter Railton has developed a theory that in some respects resembles Moore's ideal utilitarianism, in that he also counts certain kinds of relationships as part of the good. See his "Alienation, Consequentialism and Morality," *Philosophy and Public Affairs*, vol. 13 (1984), p. 159.

24. Buchanan, op. cit., p. 881.

25. See, for example, Nathan's characterization (op. cit., p. 72) of Mao's attack on party bureaucrats, leading to the "Hundred Flowers" movement to subject them to public criticism. The response was so unexpectedly harsh that it was suppressed by designating hundreds of thousands of critics as "rightists." By way of caution, I should point out that I certainly do not mean to equate Confucianism with Chinese communism. I mean to point out only one sort of parallel to Confucianism: that the *institutionalized* forms of state

Confucianism have often suspended rights to speech too quickly and for insufficient reason or for the wrong sort of reason.

26. John Rawls, in *A Theory of Justice* (Cambridge, MA: Harvard University Press, 1971), has articulated the most influential expression of this charge.

27. William Theodore de Bary, *The Trouble with Confucianism* (Cambridge, MA: Harvard University Press, 1991), pp. 87–103.

28. Alexis de Tocqueville, *Democracy in America*, George Lawrence trans., J. P. Mayer ed. (New York: Doubleday, 1969), pp. 506, 508.

29. *Analects* 1:2.

30. Benjamin Schwartz, *The World of Thought in Ancient China* (Cambridge, MA: Belknap Press, 1985), p. 70.

31. For more on this value, see my "Coping with Moral Conflict and Ambiguity," *Ethics*, vol. 102 (1992), pp. 763–84.

32. Antonio Cua, "The Status of Principles in Confucian Ethics," *Journal of Chinese Philosophy*, vol. 16 (1989), p. 281.

33. It would seem that the very concepts of *yi* (righteousness) and *ren* (when it connotes the necessity of expressing respect and concern for others) would have to involve a judgment that certain kinds of actions are simply *wrong* – that an action done purely from profit and purely to humiliate another person is simply wrong, for instance.

34. For example, see the *Analects*, 2:14 and 13:23. Arthur Waley, in *The Analects of Confucius* (New York: Random House, 1938), translates 13:23 as: "The true gentleman is conciliatory but not accommodating. Common people are accommodating but not conciliatory." However, *t'ung*, which he translates as accommodating, means sacrificing principle for agreement, as in *kou t'ung* (agreeing somehow or other, at all costs). On my meaning, accommodation is a moral principle itself that embodies the value of staying in constructive relations with others despite serious disagreement with them.

35. See, for example, Nathan, op. cit., p. 84, where he quotes Li Jiahua of the Enlightenment group. Democracy, Li said, "is the recipe for curing the Chinese nation of its age-old sickness." Without it, "people . . . cannot contribute their ability and wisdom to society." In a democracy, he went on, people "will share the same views . . . and have identical ideals."

36. See Nathan, op. cit., pp. 104–5.

37. See the *Mozi*, chapter 15, "Universal Love," part 2, in *Basic Writings of Mo Tzu, Hsün Tzu, and Han Fei Tzu*, trans. Burton Watson (New York: Columbia University Press, 1964).

38. This essay was originally written for a symposium on rights in Chinese thought that was organized by Kwong-loi Shun for the Pacific meetings of the American Philosophical Association in 1994. I am grateful to Shun and to Chad Hansen and Craig Ihara, who also participated in the symposium, for comments. I also received extensive and helpful comments from Uma Narayan.

3

Whose Democracy? Which Rights?

A Confucian Critique of Modern Western Liberalism

Henry Rosemont, Jr.

I. INTRODUCTION

One of the major reasons for engaging in comparative philosophical research is to make a small contribution to the intercultural dialogues that
are becoming a more prominent part of international affairs, especially
those dialogues that take up basic human issues such as democracy, human rights, and global justice – with the ultimate goal of these dialogues
being to increase the probability that the over six billion human citizens
of the global community will live more peaceably with one another in the
twenty-first century than they did in the twentieth.

If this ultimate goal is to be realized, it is essential that the dialogues
be genuine dialogues, with give and take, and with all sides being willing
to entertain seriously the possibility that their own moral and political
theories might not capture the essence of what it is to be a human being.[1]
The necessity of the dialogues being genuine is of especial importance
to citizens of the United States, for it is clearly the most powerful voice
in virtually every international gathering; the World Court would be a far
more effective institution if the United States would agree to abide by its
decisions, our oceans would be much more ecologically sound if it would
sign the Law of the Sea, and the world would be safer if it would agree
to the Comprehensive Test Ban Treaty it urges other nations to ratify.
But if the United States is to become more internationally responsible,
its regnant ideology must be challenged. We certainly have a monopoly
on power, but once the political rhetoric is seen for what it is, it is by no
means clear that we occupy a similar position with respect to concepts of
truth, beauty, justice, or the good.

49

The regnant ideology I wish to challenge may be loosely but usefully referred to as "modern Western liberalism," meaning by the expression support for a partial welfare state so long as it does not conflict with the basic concern of classical liberalism, namely, to protect individual freedom against the power of the state.[2] But challenges will come to naught if they are based on premises or presuppositions that are either factually mistaken, or embody basic values that modern liberalism finds abhorrent. Thus it will do no good to defend, for example, female genital circumcision solely on the grounds that it is embedded in a culture different from the West's but with its own integrity, and hence should be left alone to evolve in accordance with its own dynamics. Similarly, Western liberals – and many others – are rightfully skeptical of arguments that a particular people aren't ready for democracy yet, or that rights are a luxury the peoples of poor nations cannot afford. I wish, in other words, to question the conceptual framework of liberalism, but at the same time believe that those who accept the framework nevertheless have moral instincts that closely approximate my own.

To be at all useful then, a challenge to modern Western liberalism will have to show that certain values central to the Western intellectual tradition cannot be realized so long as other values championed by modern liberalism dominate our moral and political discourse, and that a rival tradition – in the present case, classical Confucianism – is superior to liberalism in this regard.

It is for this reason that I have entitled my paper to signal an indebtedness to the writings of Alasdair MacIntyre.[3] MacIntyre is, of course, as deeply suspicious of modern Western liberalism as I am. He is usually portrayed as an arch-conservative, fully committed to a modern version of Aristotelian Thomism. But he is not a relativist – pragmatic or otherwise – and unlike the great majority of "liberal" philosophers and political theorists, he takes Confucianism seriously as a genuine rival moral tradition.[4] Perhaps most important, he has argued well that incommensurable discourses between rival traditions can be made commensurable if certain conditions are met, and thus genuine dialogue can indeed take place. In his own words:

[T]he only way to approach a point at which our own [moral] standpoint could be vindicated against some rival is to understand our own standpoint in a way that renders it from our own point of view as problematic as possible and therefore as maximally vulnerable as possible to defeat by that rival. We can only learn what intellectual and moral resources our own standpoint, our own tradition of theoretical and practical inquiry possesses, as well as what intellectual and moral resources its rivals may possess, when we have understood our own point of view in a way that takes with full seriousness the possibility that we may in the end, as rational beings, have to abandon that point of view. This admission of fallibilism need not entail any present lack of certitude, but it is a condition of worthwhile conversation with equally certain antagonists.[5]

Most philosophical conversations of this kind, because of historical determinants, are being conducted in English, as are the great majority of the intercultural dialogues on human rights, democracy, and justice. This linguistic hegemony, if such it is, is not merely owing to the economic and military superiority of the West, for which English is now the lingua franca. It is deeply embedded in and has established the agenda for the intercultural dialogues themselves. There are no traditional close semantic equivalents for "democracy," "justice," or "rights" in most of the world's languages; these are Western. The former two have their origins in Greek *demos* and *dike*, and "rights" we owe largely to the writings of John Locke, with conceptual roots that may go back to the *sokes* and *sakes* of late medieval England, and perhaps earlier.[6]

Thus, if we are to follow MacIntyre methodologically, we must allow the other their otherness, and, without in any way surrendering rationality, nevertheless allow for the possibility not only that we don't have all the answers, but also that we may not have been asking all the questions in as universal a vocabulary as has hitherto been presupposed. Specifically for the early Confucians, there are, in addition to "rights," "democracy," and "justice," no analogous lexical items for most of the modern Western basic vocabulary for developing moral and political theories: "autonomy," "choice," "private," "public," "dilemma," and – perhaps most eerie of all for a modern Western moral theorist – no term corresponding to English "ought," prudential or obligatory.[7] Thus the comparativist must be especially sensitive to the choice of terms employed in dialogue, so as not to beg the questions, for or against, the views under analysis and evaluation.

Another narrative difficulty facing the comparative philosopher is that the hypothetico-deductive, adversarial style of discourse common in Western analytic philosophical work is not found in most non-Western philosophical writings (which is why a great many analytically trained Western philosophers do not take the non-Western writings seriously).

Still another narrative difficulty facing comparativists is that the texts they study do not as tidily separate metaphysical, moral, religious, political, and aesthetic human concerns as do their Western counterparts. This problem is painfully acute for a student of classical Confucianism for, as I shall be suggesting in some of the pages to follow, much of the persuasiveness of the Confucian vision lies in its *integrating* these basic human concerns, rather than seeing them as disparate spheres of human life. But in order to make such a case, I would have to take up each of these areas (each treated in specialized journals) in the depth they deserve, resulting in this essay becoming much longer than the entire anthology of which it supposed to be only a small part.

A final narrative difficulty facing (at least) the classical Chinese comparativist is that in the texts more purely philosophical statements are closely interwoven with judgments about current events in the lives of the writers, a style I shall follow, even though it is altogether alien to the modern Western philosophical tradition of discourse. (How much of the horror of the Thirty Year Wars is discernible in Descartes' *Meditations?*)[8]

As a consequence of all of these methodological difficulties attendant on engaging in comparative philosophical dialogue, comparativists must steer between the Scylla of distorting the views, and the manner in which those views are presented, in the non-Western texts they study and the Charybdis of making those views, and the manner in which they are presented, appear to be no more than a sociopolitical screed, and/or philosophically naive to the analytically trained Western philosopher. Briefly, what follows is Confucian in narrative flavor (I think) but, for all that, rational (I hope). My focus will be on the concept of what it is to be a human being, with special reference to human rights, and, to a lesser extent, to democracy. Current events loom large in my narration, I will employ the technical philosophical vocabulary of contemporary English as little as possible, and I will run together the aesthetic, the political, the moral, and the spiritual in using a hurried sketch of the early Confucian vision to challenge modern Western liberalism in its variant philosophical guises, the challenge itself occupying center stage throughout.

II. CONCEPTUAL BACKGROUND

Although the scholarly study of Confucianism in the West looks very different today than when it began with the first Jesuit mission to China, at least one feature of those studies has remained constant: Western investigators have sought similarities and differences between Confucian principles and those principles embedded in their own Western conceptual framework.

Originally that framework was Christianity, and beginning with Father Ricci, running through Leibniz, and even extending in some circles to the present, many scholars have declared Confucianism, in either its classical or Song formulations or both, to be compatible with basic Christian

principles and beliefs.[9] Other scholars, beginning with Ricci's succes-
sor Nicolo Longobardi, running through Malebranche, and again even
extending to the present, found Confucian principles and beliefs sufficiently unChristian to necessitate their rejection as a precondition for
conversion.[10] But however much these two groups differed in their analyses and evaluations, they shared the same presupposition, namely, that
the fundamental principles and beliefs of Christianity were universal,
and, therefore, binding on all peoples.

To be sure, not all Christians agreed on what the fundamental principles and beliefs of their faith were, or ought to be; there was much
room for theological and metaphysical debate. But at least a few beliefs
were indeed fundamental, paramount among them being the Passion of
Christ from which much else of Christianity follows.

A somewhat different conceptual framework is employed by contemporary students of Confucianism. Most Western scholars – and not a few
Chinese – now seek similarities and differences between Confucian moral
and political principles and beliefs and those embedded in a conceptual
framework that clusters around the concepts of democracy and human
rights. While Christian concerns may still underlie some research, they
no longer have pride of place in the great bulk of comparative studies.[11]

This change has been significant, and it is equally significant, I believe,
that many scholars have argued cogently that much of Confucianism
is compatible with the modern Western moral and political principles
and beliefs centered in the concept of human rights, and democracy.[12]
What has not changed, however (or so it seems to me), is that almost
all contemporary scholars share a common presupposition, in this case
the presupposition that the rights-based Western conceptual framework
is universal, and therefore binding on all peoples.

To be sure, within this conceptual framework of rights, there is room
for legitimate disagreement (just as in the framework of Christianity).
For those who embrace deontological moral and political theories, especially of a Kantian sort, rights are absolutely central; whereas for most
consequentialists, they are more adjunctive. But again, some things are
fundamental, paramount among them being that human beings are, or
ought to be, seen as free, autonomous individuals. If, for Matteo Ricci
and his colleagues, the rejection of the Passion of Christ was tantamount
to turning the world over to the Devil, so today the rejection of the
free, autonomous individual seems tantamount to turning the world
over to repressive governments and other terriorist organizations. But
just as one can be skeptical of Christian theology without endorsing Old
Scratch, so too, I believe, one can be skeptical of a rights-based conceptual

framework, and a uniquely American notion of democracy, without giving any aid or comfort to the Husseins, Milosevics, or Li Pengs of this world.

In other writings, I have taken into account differences between rights theorists on such issues as natural rights, absolute rights, rights as "trumps," defeasible rights, and so forth, but herein I want to concentrate on what binds them together (and binds them as well to most social scientists, especially economists): the vision of human beings as free, autonomous individuals, rational and self-interested.[13] For myself, the study of classical Confucianism has suggested that rights-oriented moral and political theories based on this vision are flawed, and that a different vocabulary for moral and political discourse is needed. The concept of human rights, and related concepts clustered around it like liberty, the individual, property, autonomy, freedom, reason, and choice, do not capture what it is we believe to be a human being, have served to obscure the wrongness of the radical maldistribution of the world's wealth – both intra- and internationally – and, even more fundamentally, cannot, I believe, be employed to produce a coherent and consistent theory, much less a theory that is in accord with our basic moral intuitions, intuitions that have been obscured by concepts such as "human rights" and "democracy" as these have been defined for us in the contemporary capitalist West. Other definitions are possible.

III. WHOSE DEMOCRACY?

The basic moral ideal that underlies our espousal of democracy is, I suggest, that all rational human beings should have a significant and equal voice in arriving at decisions that directly affect their own lives.[14] This is indeed an ideal, for it does not seem to ever have been realized even approximately in any nation-state, with the possible exception of Catalonia for a few months in early 1937 before the Communists and the Falange combined to crush the anarchist cooperatives established there.[15]

If this be granted, it follows that all ostensible democracies are flawed, and consequently must be evaluated along a continuum of more or less. A basic criterion used in the evaluation will of course be how much freedom any government grants its citizens. By this criterion the so-called democratic republics of Vietnam, North Korea, and the Congo fare very poorly, and the United States ranks high.

But while a healthy measure of freedom is necessary for considering a state democratic, it cannot be sufficient. By many standards, the citizens of the United States enjoy a very large amount of freedom. But an increasing majority of those citizens have virtually no control over the impersonal forces – economic and otherwise – that directly affect their lives, and they are becoming increasingly apolitical. They have a sense of powerlessness, with good reason: democracy has been pretty much reduced to the ritual of going to the democracy temples once every four years to pull a lever for Tweedledee or Tweedledum, cynically expressed in the saying "If voting could really change things, the government would make it illegal."[16]

My point here, however, is not simply to criticize the United States for the present sorry state of democracy within its borders. Rather the criticism is based on the slow evolution of the democratic ideal since 1789. The United States has always been a flawed democracy – slavery, institutionalized racism, lack of women's suffrage, and so on – but it was a fledgling democracy at least; most white males had some voice in political decisions that directly affected their lives. And of course democracy developed: slavery was abolished, women got the vote, and institutional racism was dismantled. Most of these evolutionary changes did not, however, come about by voting; slavery was effectively abolished on the battlefields of Shiloh, Antietam, and Gettysburg, not at the ballot box, and it was the courts that initiated the breakdown of the institutional racism it had earlier strengthened when *Dred Scott* and *Plessy v. Ferguson* were replaced by *Brown v. Board of Education*. And the rights of women, and all working people (now being lost), were obtained by their own militant organizing efforts.[17]

Given then that the U.S. form of democratic government has been in existence for over two hundred years, how much has been accomplished toward realizing the democratic ideal? That is to say, another criterion we must employ in evaluating nation-states with respect to democracy is the extent to which they nourish those qualities of character that enable their citizens to be self-governing, and sustain those institutions intermediate between the individual and the state (schools, local government, churches, unions, etc.), which are necessary for self-government to be effective, and hence for democracy to flourish.[18]

By these lights, the United States may well not be evaluated as at the higher end of the democratic scale, as the modern liberal tradition would have it. To see this point another way, let us contrast the United States with a very different contemporary state.

Malaysia's Prime Minister, Mahathir Mohamad, along with Singapore's Lee Kuan Yew, are usually portrayed in the West as advocating "Asian authoritarianism" – more or less Confucian inspired – as against the liberal democratic tradition of the West. And Mahathir surely has been vocal in criticizing Western social, economic, and political institutions, as has Lee. But then what are we to make of Mahathir's Asian authoritarianism when he says:

> When Malaya became independent in 1957, our per capita income was lower than that of Haiti. Haiti did not take the path of democracy. We did. Haiti today is the poorest country in all the Americas. We now have a standard of living higher than any major economy in the Americas, save only the United States and Canada. We could not have achieved what we have achieved without democracy.[19]

Moreover, Mahathir has publicly criticized China for its policies on Tibet, the Indonesian government for its atrocities in East Timor, and the Burmese generals for their ill-treatment of Muslims; and of course there are contested elections in Malaysia: the opposition party Pas currently governs two provinces.[20] What, then, might Asian authoritarianism mean, other than as a shibboleth?

If we assume that Mahathir was sincere in his statement, then we might see the policies of his "National Front" government as designed to foster self-government, and to foster many basic human rights as well. Malaysia – like Singapore and many other nation-states rich and poor – is multiethnic, and the avowed goal of the government was to achieve a strong measure of economic equity between the ethnic groupings so as to minimize communalist ethnic strife. Further, while Malaysia allows market forces to operate, the government requires major corporations to measure their success largely in terms of production and employment, rather than the way U.S. corporations measure their success in the market (i.e., by consumption and return on investment).

Malaysia remains a flawed democracy; its citizens are not as free as their U.S. counterparts: free speech has been restricted in the past on university campuses, and the government's prosecution of Anwar Ibrahim is surely deplorable. But it has given its citizens the franchise, and tolerated criticism, as has Singapore, despite its caning practices, and ban on gum chewing. Given how little a democratic base the Malaysian government had in 1957 (and Singapore in 1961), these countries have indeed come a long way socially, politically, and economically by their focus on equity across ethnic and religious boundaries and have equally been encouraging of self-government within and between those communalist groupings. (In both countries today, and in Hong Kong, Taiwan, South Korea and Japan, there are strong and vocal opposition political parties, all of which criticize governmental policies.)

If this be so, and when it is realized how many young nation-states are multiethnic today, then an argument can be made for Asian authoritarianism perhaps being not altogether authoritarian, but rather sensitive to cultural influences historically, yet supportive of a democratic ideal,[21] perhaps a better one than is insisted upon by the United States. And if this argument has merit, it will follow in turn that the fledgling democracies of East and Southeast Asia might provide a better model for the evolution of self-government than the U.S. model proffered by modern Western liberalism, and it may well fall to these Asian countries to be the true champions of democracy and human rights in the twenty-first century. This is precisely the claim – startling as it initially appears – made by political scientist Edward Friedman in an incisive recent article:

> Since it is difficult to long maintain a fledgling democracy without economic growth ... dynamic Asian societies are seeking communalist equity.... [I]f the economic pie does not expand, then the only way the previously excluded can get their fair share of the pie is to take a big bite out of what established elites already have.... Lacking the benefits of East Asia's more dynamic, statist and equitable path to growth, a polarizing democracy elsewhere, in neo-liberalist guise, can quickly seem the enemy of most of the people. This has been the case with numerous new democracies in both Latin America and Eastern Europe.
>
> At the end of the twentieth century ... pure market economics further polarizes a society. What is emphasized in the post-Keynesian orthodoxy is containing inflation. What is rewarded is creating a climate welcomed by free-floating capital. The concerns of the marginalized, the poor, and the unemployed are not high on this agenda.... State intervention on behalf of equity – as with the way Singapore tries to make housing available to all, as with Malaysia's success with state aid to rural dwellers – is far more likely to sustain democratic institutionalization.[22]

Without idealizing the governments of East and Southeast Asian fledgling democracies – some defenders of Asian authoritarianism are indeed authoritarian and hostile to democracy – it remains that countries like Malaysia – and to a lesser extent, Singapore and the five "mini-dragons" – have come a fair distance in nourishing self-government, and their record is especially impressive when compared to that of the United States: they began with much less, both economically and politically, and they have achieved much, both economically and politically, in only one-fifth of the time the United States has been at it.

To deepen our analysis of this state of affairs, and to bring the Confucian persuasion more directly to bear on the analysis, we turn now from this woefully brief consideration of democracy to the other issue central to intercultural dialogue today: human rights.

IV. WHICH RIGHTS?

A global concern for human rights has grown appreciably since the U.N. Declaration of 1948, with human rights activists found in every country, sufficient in quality and quantity as to render flatly wrong the view that human rights – and democracy – are simply Western conceits. There is increasing international insistence that human rights be respected, and democracy encouraged.[23]

In the course of these dialogues, and in recent political and moral theory, rights have been roughly placed in three categories: civil and political, social and economic, and solidarity rights. It is usually understood that each succeeding set of rights is a natural progression from the preceding set, evidenced in the terms by which we refer to them: first-, second-, and third-generation rights.[24]

Unfortunately, upon closer examination, it becomes less obvious that second-generation rights are a natural conceptual progression from first-generation rights. And if we are to understand the early Confucians, we must first come to appreciate the difference between the two.

For Locke, civil and political rights accrued to human beings as gifts from their Creator. But God is seldom invoked today to justify first-generation rights. Instead, they are grounded in the view that human beings are basically autonomous individuals.[25] And if I am indeed essentially an autonomous individual, it is easy to understand and appreciate my demands that *ceteris paribus* neither the state nor anyone else abridge my freedom to choose my own ends and means, so long as I similarly respect the civil and political rights of all others. But on what grounds can autonomous individuals demand a job, or health care, or an education – the second-generation rights – from other autonomous individuals? There is a logical gap here, which no one has successfully bridged yet: from the mere premise of being an autonomous individual, no conclusion can follow that I have a right to employment. Something more is needed, but it is by no means clear what that something might be, unless it conflicted with the view of human beings as basically autonomous individuals.

Put another way, jobs, adequate housing, schools, health care, and so on, do not fall from the sky. They are human creations, and no one has been able to show how I can demand that other human beings create these goods for me without their surrendering some significant portion of their first-generation rights, which accrue to them by virtue of their being autonomous individuals, free to pursue their own projects rather than being obliged to assist me with mine.

That I, too, can claim second-generation rights to such goods is of no consequence if I believe I can secure them on my own, or in free association with a few others, and thereby keep secure my civil and political rights. It is equally irrelevant that I can rationally and freely choose to assist you in securing those goods on my own initiative for this would be an act of charity, not an acknowledgment of your rights to those goods.

To see the logical gap between first- and second-generation rights in another way, consider this difference between them: 99 percent of the time I can fully respect your civil and political rights merely by ignoring you. (You certainly have the right to speak, but no right to make me listen.) If you have legitimate social and economic rights, on the other hand, then I have responsibilities to act on your behalf, and not ignore you. And what would it take for your social and economic rights claims to be legitimately binding on me? Basically what is required is that I see neither you nor myself as an autonomous individual, but rather see both of us as more fundamentally comembers of a human community. No one would insist, of course, that we are either solely autonomous individuals or solely social beings. But if we believe we are fundamentally first and foremost autonomous individuals, then our basic moral obligation in the political realm will be to (passively) respect the first-generation rights of all others. If we are first and foremost comembers of a community, on the other hand, our moral obligation to (actively) respect the second-generation rights of all others will be binding – as it would be for Confucians.

V. A CONFUCIAN RESPONSE

Against this background let me quickly sketch my answer to the question of whether precursors of the concept of human rights – and derivatively, democracy – may be found in classical Confucianism. Unsurprisingly, my answer is "yes and no." It is "no" if the most basic rights are seen as civil and political, grounded in the view that we are autonomous individuals, but it is "yes" if our most basic rights stem from membership in a community, with each member assuming a measure of responsibility for the welfare of all other members.

I do not believe much argumentation is necessary to establish that the classical Confucians did not focus on the individualism of human beings. *Ren*, the highest human excellence, must be given expression in interpersonal endeavors. Rituals (*li*), necessary for self-cultivation and the ordering of society, are communal activities. In order to exercise *xiao*, I must have parents, or at least their memory. This point is virtually a truism: in order to give human expression to the qualities inherent in being a friend, spouse, sibling, or neighbor, I must *have* a friend, spouse, sibling and neighbor, and these all-too-human interactions are not an accidental or incidental part of my life, for a Confucian; on the contrary, they are absolutely essential if I am to achieve any significant measure of human flourishing.[26]

It is not merely that we are obliged, of necessity, to interact with others; we must care about them as well, and this caring, while it begins with the family, must nevertheless extend beyond it. The obligation to be attentive to the needs of all others in the community – large or small – can be traced as far back as the *Shu Jing*, in the well-known passage that "*Tian* hears and sees as our people hear and see."[27]

This same theme permeates the *Lun Yu*, with Confucius insisting that even the humblest peasant was entitled to his opinions – which deserved attention – and insisting as well that the first responsibility of an official was to see that the people under his jurisdiction were well fed, with the attendant disgrace if he should be well fed when the people were not; and after they have been fed, they should be educated.[28] And that is exactly what is also required for generating those qualities of character that lead to public self-government – the democratic ideal. Moreover, think of how often the disciples ask socially oriented questions: about government, about filial piety, about rituals, and so on. A very common question, of course, concerns the qualities of the *jun zi*. In the overwhelming majority of cases, the Master places his response in a social setting: in the presence of superiors, the *jun zi* does X; in the presence of friends, Y, and in the presence of *xiao ren*, Z.[29]

Albeit in a semantically camouflaged way, Mencius justifies regicide when the ruler does not care for his people, and places him at the bottom of the moral hierarchy even when he does.[30] At a much more profound philosophical level, Mencius maintains that this caring for others is, to borrow Irene Bloom's felicitous term, a "foundational intuition"[31] in humans, as the child/well "gedanke experiment" is designed to establish.[32] And of course the "man in the street can become a Yao or a Shun."[33]

Moreover, this caring for all others was not to be only a personal excellence to be nurtured but to be institutionalized as well. Xunzi's *Wang Zhi Pian* makes this point explicitly. To take only one example, after insisting that the ruler appoint ministers on the basis of their moral qualities rather than on the basis of lineage or wealth, he goes on to say:

When it comes to men of perverse words and theories, perverse undertakings and talents, or to people who are slippery and vagrant, they should be given tasks to do, taught what is right, and allowed a period of trial. . . . In the case of the Five incapacitated groups, the government should gather them together, look after them, and give them whatever work they are able to do. Employ them, provide them with food and clothing, and take care to see that none are left out. . . . [L]ook after widows and orphans, and assist the poor.[34]

This remarkable passage – and there are many others in a similar vein in the *Wang Zhi Pian* – requires comment. First, despite a number of semiauthoritarian pronouncements in this and other chapters, Xunzi is clearly advocating the functional equivalent of job training programs, Aid to Families with Dependent Children, welfare, and Medicare for the Chinese peoples; on this score he is far to the left of either Republicans or Democrats in the United States. What makes this advocacy all the more impressive is that it requires the state to provide many goods and services to groups of people who cannot possibly pose a threat to that state's power; Machiavellian it is not.

Second, it is significant that Xunzi's concern for the well-being of the sick, the poor, the marginalized, and the unlettered is not mirrored in the political treatises composed by his near-contemporaries on the other side of the globe; we will read Plato's *Republic* and the *Laws*, and Aristotle's *Politics* in vain if what we wish to learn is the obligations of the state toward its neediest members.

Third, and perhaps most important in attending to this passage, to the several others cited previously, and to a great many others in the classical Confucian corpus, is it not possible to discern not only a sense of self-governance, but a sense of the importance of nurturing self-governance in others as well? Might we here be seeing a genesis for the development of social and economic rights, and for democracy? The answer, of course, is "no," if our model of democracy is autonomous individuals freely exercising their franchise at the voting booth. Xunzi's view of government is surely of the people and for the people, but not explicitly by the people. But bracket Lincoln and the United States, and return for a moment to Mahathir Mohamad's Malaysia and Lee Kuan Yew's Singapore. If we agree that these countries, warts and all, are nevertheless fledgling democracies, whose theoretical perspective more significantly underlies the social, economic, and political progress that has been made, Xunzi's or John Locke's?

As a final example of the Confucian claim that we cannot merely dwell among the birds and beasts (i.e., we are not autonomous individuals) and at the same time meet the common objection that Confucian community norms are highly particularistic, let us examine a very familiar passage from the *Da Xue* for a moment. There is a strong spiritual dimension to this text, signaled by the large number of times worlds like "repose," "tranquility," "peace," and "the highest good" – *ding, jing, an,* and *zhi shan,* respectively – appear in it.[35]

Its religious message is, however, singular; I know of no close parallel to it in other traditions. To find peace and to dwell in the highest good, as defined by the West, for example, we are uniformly instructed to look inward: to know our selves, as Socrates put it, or to know ourselves in relation to deity, as the texts of the three Abrahamic religions make clear. In the *Da Xue,* on the other hand, looking inward and coming to know our selves is more of a means than the ultimate end toward which we must strive. That goal is to augment *tian xia,* which may fairly be translated as "the world community," despite the monocultural orientation of the Han author(s) of the text. And we reach this goal by first shrinking our perspectives and activities from *tian xia* through the state, the clan, the family, and then to our own heart-mind. But once this task is accomplished, we must then begin to expand our perspectives and activities outward again, until they eventually encompass the world community.[36] Herein lies the highest good, to "serve the people" (*wei ren min*), Mao's abuse of the expression two millennia later notwithstanding.

There is a great deal more I could say to justify the claim that a sound conceptual basis for second-generation rights, grounded in membership in a community, is contained in both the letter and the spirit of the classical Confucian writings. And I will go further, to also claim that if we can learn to read those writings against a global background that goes beyond modern Western liberalism, we may also see a basis for the development of democracies that is of direct relevance today. I am not suggesting that "Alle Menschen werden Bruder" is reflected in the classical corpus; to my knowledge, Zhang Cai's beautiful *Xi Ming* is the first text to do that. But "No man is an Island" thoroughly permeates classical Confucianism, and very probably we must fully appreciate Donne's vision before we can embrace Schiller's.

In sum, Confucian selves are much less autonomous individuals than they are relational persons, persons leading lives integrated morally, aesthetically, politically, and spiritually; and they lead these lives in a human community. As Confucius said:

> We cannot run with the birds and beasts
> Am I not one among the people of this world?
> If not them, with whom should I associate?[37]

All of the specific human relations of which we are a part, interacting with the dead as well as the living, will be mediated by the courtesy, customs, rituals, and traditions we come to share as our inextricably linked histories unfold (the *li*). By fulfilling the obligations defined by these relationships, we are, for early Confucians, following the human way. It is a comprehensive way. By the manner in which we interact with others our lives will clearly have moral and political dimensions infusing *all*, not just some, of our conduct. By the ways in which this ethical interpersonal conduct is effected, with reciprocity, and governed by civility, respect, affection, custom, ritual, and tradition, our lives will also have an aesthetic dimension for ourselves and for others. And by specifically meeting our defining traditional obligations to our elders and ancestors on the one hand, and to our contemporaries and descendants on the other, the early Confucians offer an uncommon, but nevertheless spiritually authentic form of transcendence, a human capacity to go beyond the specific spatiotemporal circumstances in which we exist, giving our personhood the sense of humanity shared in common, and thereby a sense of strong continuity with what has gone before and what will come later, and a concomitant commitment to leave this earth in a better condition than we found it. There being no question for the early Confucians of the meaning *of* life, we may nevertheless see that their view of what it is to be a human being provided for every person to find meaning *in* life.[38]

This, then, is an all-too-brief sketch of the conceptual framework of Confucianism, wherein rights-talk was not spoken, and within which I am not basically a free, autonomous individual. I am a son, husband, father, grandfather, neighbor, colleague, student, teacher, citizen, friend. I have a very large number of relational obligations and responsibilities, which severely constrain my choices of what to do. These responsibilities occasionally frustrate or annoy, they more often are satisfying, and they are always binding. If we are going to use words like "freedom" here, it must be seen as an achievement, not a stative term, as Confucius suggests in describing the milestones of his life. And my individuality, if anyone wishes to keep the concept, will come from the specific actions I take in meeting my relational responsibilities. There are many ways to be a good teacher, spouse, sibling, friend, and so forth; if Confucian persons aren't free, autonomous individuals, they aren't dull, faceless automatons either. As Herbert Fingarette has noted well, for the Confucians there must be at least two human beings before there can be any human beings.[39]

Furthermore, the language of Confucian discourse is rich and varied, permitting me to eulogize a Martin Luther King; it allows me a full lexicon to inveigh against the Chinese government for its treatment of Han Dongfang, Falun Gong members, and others and against the Indonesian government for the horrors visited on the East Timorese people. I not only can express outrage at the rape of Bosnian women and the NATO/U.S. bombing of Kosovo and Serbia but also petition the Governor of Pennsylvania to grant a new trial to Mumia Abu Jamal. I can, in sum, fully express my moral sentiments in any democracy without ever invoking the language of first-generation human rights.

Perhaps then, we should study Confucianism as a genuine alternative to modern Western theories of rights (and democracy), rather than merely as an implicit early version of them. When it is remembered that three-quarters of the world's peoples have, and continue to define themselves in terms of kinship and community rather than as rights-bearers, we may come to entertain seriously the possibility that if the search for universal moral and political principles – and a universally acceptable language for expressing these principles – are worthwhile endeavors, we might find more of a philosophical grounding for those principles, beliefs, and language in the writings of Confucius, Mengzi, and Xunzi than those of John Locke, Adam Smith, and their successors. To emphasize this argument, let us return to the contemporary world.

VI. BEYOND THE LIBERAL TRADITION

The best way to go beyond modern Western liberalism in a global context is, I believe, to focus on economics. Large corporations are increasingly unrestrained in their behaviors both intra- and internationally, in an increasingly relentless drive for greater profits. The adverse social effects of this drive are obvious, yet we seem incapable of changing things; why?

One major reason, I submit, is that the Western – now international – legal system that is designed to protect the first-generation civil and political rights of autonomous individuals equally protects the rights of autonomous individual corporations to do pretty much as they please, and the so-called democratic process, especially in the United States, is so money-driven that those corporations can usually choose whichever candidates please them.

Consider a statement from Robert Reich, the former Secretary of Labor. Upon being challenged for expressing a measure of unhappiness at AT&T's recent decision to lay off 40,000 workers after declaring near-record dividends, he responded:

> I don't question the morality of AT&T. In fact, I am very much against villainizing any of these people. And with regard to whether they did it wisely – the share price went up. By some measures, AT&T did precisely what it ought to have done. But the fundamental question is whether society is better off.[40]

This is an astonishing statement. If society is better off for AT&T's action, then it would *prima facie* suggest the action was moral; and if society is worse off, then immoral. How, then, could Reich not wish to question the morality of AT&T's action? Worse, the answer to the "fundamental question" he asks surely appears to be that U.S. society is worse off for the job losses, even when we take shareholder gains into account: a great many AT&T shares are owned by a very few people.

In this light, we may better appreciate why the governments of the fledgling democracies in East Asia are so often called "authoritarian": they enact laws prohibiting major corporations from laying off large numbers of workers in order to secure greater profits, and in this way, those governments restrict "free trade."

Japan, too, restricts free trade, which is at least partially responsible for the "Asian authoritarian" label continuing to be affixed to the way the country is run. The curmudgeonly economist and political analyst Edward Luttwak has brought home succinctly the difference between a restrictive Japan and a free United States:

> When I go to my gas station in Japan, five young men wearing uniforms jump on my car. They not only check the oil but also wash the tires and wash the lights. Why is that? Because government doesn't allow oil companies to compete by price, and therefore they have to compete by service. They're still trying to maximize shareholder value, but they hire the young men. I pay a lot of money for the gas.
>
> Then I come to Washington, and in Washington gas is much cheaper. Nobody washes the tires, nobody does anything for me, but here, too, there are five young men. The five young men who in Japan are employed to wash my car are, here, standing around, unemployed, waiting to rob my car. I still have to pay for them, through my taxes, through imprisonment, through a failed welfare system. I still have to pay for them. But in Japan at least they clean my car.[41]

Similarly, Clinton defended the North American Free Trade Agreement by claiming that it would raise the Gross National Product and create more hi-tech jobs. But as Luttwak also noted, the United States already has the highest GNP in the world, and it is not important, for the vast majority of U.S. citizens, to give great weight to increasing it further. And to ascertain just how badly we need a lot more hi-tech jobs, just ask virtually any recent college graduate. What we do need is more decent-paying semiskilled jobs for those five young men waiting to steal Luttwak's car, and for millions more young men and women just like them.

Perhaps I am mistaken here, we might indeed need to increase GNP and secure more hi-tech jobs. That is not my point. Rather I wish to suggest a question: why is it in this most free of all nations, we freely choosing autonomous individuals have no democratic choice about whether we want to spend our money having our windshields washed or building more prisons?

More directly: the anti–World Trade Organization demonstrations in Seattle made clear that many U.S. citizens would like to abolish the organization. Yet the four major candiates for the presidency early in the year 2000 – Gore, Bradley, Bush, and McCain – all supported the WTO, as do the corporations that finance their campaigns; for whom can the Seattle demonstrators and other like-minded citizens vote to represent them in this "democracy"?

Consider the results of a poll conducted by the Preamble Center for Public Policy (completed shortly before President Clinton signed the end-of-welfare bill): 70 percent of 800 registered voters believed corporate greed, not the global economy, was responsible for downsizing; and an equal number supported increased governmental action to curb that greed and promote socially responsible conduct. Almost 80 percent favored obliging large employers to provide health benefits and pension plans, and equally favored "living wage" laws.[42]

As indicated earlier, one reason we have little or no real choice in such matters is that our legal system, significantly designed to protect and enhance the first-generation rights of autonomous individuals, equally protects and enhances those rights for large corporations.[43]

A related reason is a cardinal tenet of modern Western liberalism: the government, being public, must say nothing of the highest good; that is a private matter, for each autonomous individual to choose freely for him/herself. The state cannot legislate morality (which is why Secretary Reich did not wish to question AT&T's actions).

This is a powerful point, which contributes greatly to the support we are inclined to give to modern Western liberalism: we – especially we intellectuals – do want to be free to choose our own ends; we each have our individual hopes and dreams, and do not want our manner of expressing them dictated or altered by others. Herein lies, I believe, the basic appeal of the concept of civil and political rights for autonomous individuals.

But as Michael Sandel has argued in a recent work:

By insisting that we are bound only by ends and roles we choose for ourselves, [modern Western liberalism] denies that we can ever be claimed by ends we have not chosen – ends given by nature or God, for example, or by our identities as members of families, peoples, cultures, or traditions.[44]

For the Confucians, this liberal denial is flatly mistaken at best, self-serving at worst, for human beings do indeed, they insist, have ends they have not chosen, ends given by nature and by their roles in families, as members of communities, and as inheritors of tradition. The highest good is not many; it is one, no matter how difficult to ascertain, and it is communally realized in an intergenerational context. Confucius himself was absolutely clear on this point, for when a disciple asked him what he would most enjoy doing, he said:

I would like to bring peace and contentment to the aged, share relationships of trust and confidence with friends, and love and protect the young.[45]

This, then, in far too brief a compass, is a sketch of a challenge to modern Western liberalism from a Confucian perspective. I believe I have met MacIntyre's criteria for intercultural discourse, for I have attempted to challenge contemporary Western liberalism largely on its own grounds, without recourse to any views liberals would claim to be patently false, and by appeal to a number of basic values the majority of liberals would endorse. And I have also attempted to show how those basic values cannot be realized in the modern liberal tradition owing to endorsing other values, namely, those that attach directly to autonomous individuals – and transnational corporations.

If my challenge is at all sustainable, it suggests that either (1) the liberal or some other tradition must conceptually reconcile first- and second-generation rights claims much more clearly in the future than has been done in the past; or (2) we must give pride of place to second-, and third-generation rights in future intercultural dialogues on the subject, and future dialogues on democracy and justice as well; or (3) we might abandon the language of rights altogether and seek a more appropriate language for expressing our moral and political concerns cross-culturally. But if either of the latter, it must follow that these dialogues can no more be value-neutral than can the governments of fledgling democracies in East and Southeast Asia or in not-so-fledgling democracies like the United States.

The spell of the concept of autonomous individuals – once a needed bulwark perhaps against totalitarian regimes – is not confined to the economic and political dimensions of our (increasingly disjointed) lives; it affects us metaphysically and spiritually as well, which Aldous Huxley has well captured succinctly:

We live together, we act on, and react to, one another; but always and in all circumstance we are by ourselves. The martyrs go hand in hand into the arena; they are crucified alone.[46]

Or as A. E. Housman put it:

> I, a stranger and afraid
> In a world I never made[47]

Much as I admire Huxley and Housman, this is a frightening universalist view to foist on the global community, and as most U.S. citizens and third-world peoples are beginning to understand, has the quality of being a self-fulfilling prophecy. Thus it seems imperative to challenge U.S. ideology at its moral, political, and metaphysical roots, both for the sake of its citizens and for the sake of the rest of the world, whose peoples share the burden of having to live with the untoward consequences of U.S. foreign policies defended by reference to that ideology.

There are alternatives to the Western liberal tradition, alternative visions that just might be endorsed by all people of good will, no matter what their cultural background.

There is nothing wrong with seeking universalist values; indeed, that search must go forward if we are ever to see an end to the ethnic, racial, religious, and sexual violence that has so thoroughly splattered the pages of human history with blood and gore since the Enlightenment. Rather does the wrongness lie in the belief that we – or any single culture – are already fully in possession of those values, and therefore feel justified, backed by superior economic and military threats, in foisting those values on everyone else.

Classical Confucianism proffers an alternative.[48]

Notes

1. I appreciate that "essence" is a buzzword in most postmodern discourse today. For details, see my "Against Relativism" in G. Larson and E. Deutsch eds., *Interpreting Across Boundaries* (Princeton, NJ: Princeton University Press, 1987).

2. The basic concern of John Rawls in his *A Theory of Justice* (Cambridge, MA: Harvard University Press, 1970), most of the writings of Richard Rorty since 1980, Ronald Dworkin's *Taking Rights Seriously* (Cambridge, MA: Harvard University Press, 1977), plus all the commentaries on these and related works over the years. My loose definition parallels Michael Sandel's in "America's Search for a New Public Philosophy," *The Atlantic Monthly* (March 1996), which is a lengthy excerpt from his book *Democracy's Discontent* (Cambridge, MA: Harvard University Press, 1996).

3. See especially his *After Virtue, Whose Justice? Which Rationality?* and *Three Rival Versions of Moral Enquiry* (Notre Dame, IN: University of Notre Dame Press, 1981, 1988, and 1990, respectively). [Editor's note: When he wrote this essay, Rosemont did not know that MacIntyre was to write the commentary essay.]

4. "Incommensurability, Truth, and the Conversation Between Confucians and Aristotelians about the Virtues" in Eliot Deutsch ed., *Culture and Modernity*, (Honolulu: University of Hawaii Press, 1991).

5. Ibid., p. 121.

6. Others would trace the concept of rights to even earlier periods. See, for example, Brian Tierney, "Origins of Natural Rights Language: Texts and Contexts, 1150–1250," *History of Political Thought*, vol. X, no. 4 (Winter 1989), pp. 615–46; or Fred D. Miller, Jr., *Nature, Justice, and Rights in Aristotle's Politics* (Oxford: Clarendon Press, 1995).

7. I have argued this point in "Is There a Primordial Tradition in Ethics?" in Arvind Sharma ed., *Fragments of Infinity* (Dorset, UK: Prism Press, 1991).

8. For properly contextualizing the cultural and historical milieu in which Descartes philosophized – or, more acurately, conducted his scientific work – I am indebted to Stephen Toulmin's *Cosmopolis* (New York: Free Press, 1990). And the importance of current moral issues occupying an intellectual is not confined to the Confucians. Perhaps the greatest intellectual the United States has contributed to the world in the second half of this closing century of the millenium has said: "The responsibility of the writer as a *moral agent* is to try to bring the truth about *matters of human significance* to *an audience that can do something about them.*" [Italics in the original.] Noam Chomsky, *Powers and Prospects* (Boston: South End Press, 1996), p. 59.

9. See the "Introduction" to *Leibniz: Writings on China*, Daniel J. Cook and Henry Rosemont, Jr., trans. (Chicago: Open Court Publishing Company, 1994).

10. Ibid.

11. An exception is Julia Ching's *Chinese Religions* (New York: Orbis Books, 1993).

12. William T. deBary and Tu Weiming eds., *Confucianism & Human Rights* (New York: Columbia University Press, 1998).

13. "Rights-Bearing Individuals and Role-Bearing Persons" in Mary I. Bockover ed., *Rules, Rituals, and Responsibility*, (Chicago: Open Court Publishing Company, 1991); "Why Take Rights Seriously? A Confucian Critique" in Leroy Rouner ed., *Human Rights and the World's Religions*, (Notre Dame, IN: University of Notre Dame Press, 1988), pp. 167–82. For an analysis of the role of individualism in modern Western philosophy, see C. B. McPherson, *The Political Theory of Possessive Individualism* (Oxford: Oxford University Press, 1962).

14. Following Sandel, "America's Search for a New Public Philosophy," *Atlantic Monthly*, vol. 277 (1996), pp. 45–58.
15. See Noam Chomsky, "The Responsibility of Intellectuals" in his *American Power and the New Mandarins* (New York: Vintage Press, 1969).
16. A bumper sticker put out by the Charles F. Kerr Publishing Company.
17. Some sources for these claims: P. Buhle and A. Dawley eds., *Working for Democracy* (Champaign: University of Illinois Press, 1985); Mari J. Buhle et al. eds., *Encyclopaedia of the American Left* (Champaign: University of Illinois Press, 1992); Howard Zinn, *A People's History of the United States, 1492–1992*, rev. ed. (New York: Harper Collins, 1995).
18. See n. 14.
19. Quoted in Edward Friedman, "What Asia Will or Won't Stand For: Globalizing Human Rights and Democracy," *Osaka Journal of Foreign Studies* (1996).
20. Kelantan has been in opposition hands for some time now, and in the recent (November 1999) elections, its eastern neighbor Teregganu also voted the Pas into power. It is equally important to note that despite his treatment of Awar, Mahathir's National Front government won 56 percent of the popular vote. See the *Far Eastern Economic Review*, vol. 163 (12/9/99) for details.
21. Although the ideal may have originally had economic more than moral and political roots. See my "Why the Chinese Economic Miracle Isn't One," *Z Magazine* (October 1995).
22. See n. 19.
23. For an excellent survey, see Sumner B. Twiss, "Comparative Ethics and Intercultural Human Rights Dialogue: A Programmatic Inquiry" in William T. deBary and Tu Wei-Ming eds., *Confucianism & Human Rights* (New York: Columbia University Press, 1998).
24. Ibid., especially pp. 17–19, for discussion and additional citations.
25. For discussion, see my "Who Chooses?" in Henry Rosemont, Jr., ed., *Chinese Texts and Philosophical Contexts* (Chicago: Open Court Publishing Company, 1991).
26. A point now fairly well agreed upon in Confucian scholarship. See, for example, Tu Weiming's *Humanity and Self-Cultivation: Essays in Confucian Thought* (Berkeley, CA: Asian Humanities Press, 1979) or David L. Hall and Roger T. Ames, *Thinking Through Confucius* (Albany: SUNY Press, 1987), especially chapters IV and V.
27. James Legge, trans., *The Chinese Classics* (Hong Kong: University of Hong Kong, reprint of the 1894 edition), volume III, *The Shoo King*, pp. 74, 292.
28. Some examples from the *Lun Yu* on these themes: 1:14, 1:15, 12:5, 12:7, 13:9. All citations are taken from *The Analects of Confucius*, Roger T. Ames and Henry Rosemont, Jr., trans. (New York: Ballantine Books, 1998).
29. See ibid., pp. 48–65, for discussion.
30. *Mencius*, D. C. Lau, trans. (Penguin Books, 1970). On regicide, see 1B8; on the moral hierarchy, 7A14.
31. As employed in her contribution, "Mencius and Human Rights," to deBary and Tu Wei-Ming eds., *Confucianism & Human Rights*, pp. 94–116.

32. *Mencius*, op. cit., 2A6.
33. Ibid., 6B2.
34. *Hsün Tzu: Basic Writings*, Burton Watson trans. (New York: Columbia University Press, 1963), pp. 34, 37.
35. Legge, op. cit., vol. I, pp. 357 ff.
36. Ibid.
37. *Lun Yu*, 18:6.
38. This paragraph is taken from my contribution to deBary and Wei-Ming eds., *Confucianism & Human Rights*, op. cit., pp. 54–67. The distinction between the meaning of life and meaning in life was first drawn by Kurt Baier in "The Meaning of Life" in Morris Weitz ed., *20th Century Philosophy: The Analytic Tradition* (New York: Prentice-Hall, 1966).
39. "The Music of Humanity in the Conversations of Confucius," *Journal of Chinese Philosophy*, vol. 10 (1983), pp. 331–56.
40. "Does America Still Work?" *Harper's Magazine* (May 1996), p. 38.
41. Ibid., p. 47.
42. Cited in the *Nation* (Aug. 26/Sept. 2, 1996), p. 5.
43. Mancur Olson makes clear the relation between the political and the economic with respect to first-generation rights: "A thriving market economy requires, among other things, institutions that provide secure individual rights. The incentives to save, to invest, to produce, and to engage in mutually advantageous trade depend particularly upon individual rights to marketable assets – on property rights. / Similarly, ... [i]f there is no right to create legally secure corporations, the private economy cannot properly exploit... productive opportunities." "Development Depends on Institutions," *College Park International* (April 1996), p. 2.
44. Sandel, op cit., p. 70.
45. *Lun Yu*, 5:26.
46. *The Doors of Perception* (New York: Penguin, 1963), p. 12.
47. In my original manuscript I slightly misquoted these lines, having forgotten the source in which I first read them long ago. I am thus grateful to Mr. Andrew Terjesen for the correct wording, and for locating the source, which is Poem XII from *Last Poems* (H. Holt & Company, 1922).
48. Some of the arguments advanced in this essay were first presented at the Second Conference on Confucian and Human Rights at the East-West Center, May 22–24, 1996.

4

The Normative Impact of Comparative Ethics

Human Rights

Chad Hansen

In this chapter, I address human rights as an illustration of the role of comparative ethics in normative reasoning. In Section I, I distinguish comparative ethics from related intellectual enterprises inside and outside philosophy and discuss the difficulties of a comparative conception of morality. In Section II, I argue that the normative relevance of comparative studies is subtle and indirect. It flows out of three conditions of normative respect. I argue that these apply in the case of a Chinese–Western comparison but do not warrant treating all traditions as equals. These conditions underlie the appeal of a "synthesis of East and West" and illustrate the limited normative relevance of comparative ethics. I argue that any envisioned synthesis must come from continued moral discourse within the distinct normative traditions themselves. Comparativists may inform the traditions about each other and thus stimulate moral discourse but may not otherwise "guide" or adjudicate the shape of the final synthesis. In Section III, I apply the methodology to some forms of the argument that human rights do not apply to China. Then in Section IV, I briefly develop why comparative arguments purporting to justify excepting China from the realm of human rights subvert their own role by undermining or ignoring the crucial conditions of normative respect.

I. INTRODUCTION: COMPARATIVE ETHICS AND CHINESE PHILOSOPHY

We distinguish comparative ethics from anthropology or history on broadly normative grounds. It addresses philosophical "value."

Anthropology, by contrast, would normally address actual patterns of behavior or a description of "ordinary" attitudes. Philosophical comparison evaluates the normative doctrines of a society's "philosophers." Historical and religious studies may also focus more on "elite" written sources than does anthropology, but they still adopt a descriptive "scientific" posture in presenting the content of the doctrines they study.

Comparative ethics does not merely catalogue moral attitudes and motivations; it evaluates the proffered supporting doctrines and implicit underlying reasoning. Philosophers may take note of actual attitudes and behavior within the community, but they should not merely cite those attitudes or describe the behavior. The dimension of their evaluation, however, is seldom the simple truth of the ethical positions presented. Another dominant philosophical value is epistemic – the comparative justification of moral attitudes.[1] Philosophers should also be sensitive to other elements of a broad conception of epistemic values (e.g., problem-solving ability, ease of use, reliability as a shared guide, stimulation to further progress from a prior basis, novelty or difference).

Philosophical values center on coherence. This makes study of comparative moral psychology and metaethics important in evaluating normative positions. Indeed, philosophers evaluate the motivation or warrant of different normative positions against the background of the entire philosophical and conceptual system. Clearly, an individualist epistemology, semantics, and metaphysics would be relevant to a coherent understanding of Western normative individualism.[2]

Comparative philosophers thus naturally tend to focus on cultures with a rich tradition of normative theorizing – a philosophical tradition. China is a natural target for such philosophical study. It has a rich and distinctive philosophical heritage in which ethical issues are a central concern. A robust moral tradition normally has lively internal debates among various rival theories. Philosophical study focuses on interpretive hypotheses about the assumptions driving the debate. They would seek to reconstruct any shared commitment to higher-level standards and norms guiding that reasoning and argument about moral attitudes.[3]

Philosophers may draw on anthropological and religious studies as well as other attitudes (e.g., aesthetics) in their evaluation. Still their focus should be on theoretical evaluation, not mere description. Within philosophy, comparative ethics has a complex and controversial relation to antecedent metaethics and normative theory. I will look first at metaethics and then normative theory.[4]

A. Metaethical Issues: The Definition of "Morality"

The initial step in comparison raises a metaethical issue. A comparative analysis requires some account of "morality" that is general enough to structure our comparison. Henry Rosemont has argued that some differences between two cultures' beliefs could rule out comparative morality. For example, they may lead us to conclude that one culture has no concept of morality at all. We should not then say that they have a different morality.[5] They have a different kind of normative structure (dao^{guide}).

A sound metaethics need not conclude that all communities have a morality. It hardly follows from the meaning of "moral," and evolutionary considerations are inconclusive. A community might survive with reasonable harmony with a social dao^{guide} combining etiquette, law, and positive or conventional mores. On the other hand, a sound metaethics should be sensitive to the range of moral systems in actual cultures. It should count against a metaethical theory that its conception of morality entails that only Western Europe has morality!

Metaethics regularly intrudes in normative disputes. Some familiar Kantian arguments, for example, adopt narrow metaethical conceptions that rule out familiar theories like utilitarianism as viable candidates for the moral. Other conceptions render "ethical egoism" an oxymoron. The comparativist's goal of understanding different moral systems would find content-based accounts counterproductive. If, for example, we require that a culture have a conception of "laws of pure reason" to count as having a concept of morality, the result (that Chinese philosophy has no moral theory) will convey only negative (and misleading) information. Even a broader content criterion, like "morality consists of the rules or principles that govern interpersonal actions" may rule out a moral system (or a conception of one) that describes morality solely in terms of inner virtues rather than rules.

Still, it may be hard to find a suitably neutral conception that is broad enough to allow us to speak of a Western-Chinese moral comparison. For comparison purposes, I propose to finesse some metaethical issues. We should make the relatively uncontroversial contrasts we normally do with morality. That is, we want to distinguish morality from etiquette, religious piety, positive mores, fashion, and taste. These inferential contrasts are arguably "part of the meaning" of the term.[6] Provisionally, I propose we assume a conception that makes these "canonical" distinctions but does not put any controversial normative restrictions on what counts as a morality.

B. *Morality as a Hierarchy of Standards*

The urgent issue now is to clarify what implications comparative morality has for straightforward normative moral theory. We should distinguish the two at the outset. Comparative inquiry need carry no implication of normative moral relativism. We deal with normative questions (e.g., whether Chinese humans have human rights) in the usual noncomparative way. Does the correct morality justify a scheme of human rights for Asians or Chinese? Whether Chinese morality itself justifies such a conception is technically irrelevant to the first-order normative issue. Comparative study presupposes neither that no correct moral theory exists nor that Chinese moral theory is correct relative to "Chinese realities."

Still, I hope to explain why we naturally tend to treat comparative morality as relevant in some way to normative questions. Here I will defend a severely limited normative role for comparative morality.

I have proposed using a metaethical criterion that does allow the Chinese–Western moral comparison. As I hinted in my worries about narrower conceptions, ancient Chinese normative thought does not use any *close* counterpart of human "reason."[7] However, we can describe a substitute to underwrite a principled evaluative comparison. To do this, we generalize "reasoning" to make it apply to using any systematic hierarchy of standards of warrant to guide deliberation and discourse. It counts as a hierarchy as long as it includes higher-level deliberating about the standards for accepting and rejecting lower-level judgments. When debates ascend to address the norms for settling first-order debates, we can mark it as a reflective tradition, even when we are suspicious of the norms used. We need make no other controversial claims about the content of reasons as long as the social discourse has this internal mechanism of self-evaluation and self-correction.

A system of norms that forms a complex hierarchy is just the sort of thing a philosopher values. Let us distinguish "morality" as that system of social discourse that exhibits such a complexity. The scheme of social discourse starts from first-level evaluations – praising, blaming, excusing, feeling guilty or angry, and so on.[8] When the justification of these is treated as appropriately raising further questions about norms of evaluation, we are dealing with *critical morality* in contrast with mere *mores* or *etiquette*.

Although we do not postulate an autonomous rational standard, we can now partly explain the rationalist intuition that morality per se is autonomous. We have implicitly distinguished moral systems from positive mores and etiquette. A moral system is one whose highest standards of evaluation do not rest unquestionably on simple conformity with traditional or customary social practice.

We still conceive of a community's morality as a social practice, but distinguish it from other social practices. The norms of moral discourse allow discussants to question and reject the simple appeal to a social practice as a justification. A social practice that did rest on such "factual" appeals would not be a morality as opposed to mores, conventions, or manners. It might still have a complex structure (as law does). However, if it endorsed ultimate appeal to the bald sociological fact that *these* are the laws then it would not be autonomous in the crucial way we think morality is autonomous.

II. NORMATIVE IMPLICATIONS

Consider how this metaethical conception bears on human rights. We treat the claim of a special Chinese or Asian conception of human rights as a normative claim, not a descriptive one. The actual prevalence of a different Asian attitude toward individual liberty would not determine the normative status of rights in Chinese morality. No existing moral attitudes or tradition would directly justify breaching or ignoring human rights. A morality would reject that any bald appeal to tradition justifies such a thing. Those who reject human rights citing only the ground that such is their tradition would violate their own community's moral tradition.[9]

In adopting this stance, we are appealing to a procedural conception of rationality, not presupposing any transcendent rational content or moral principle. This judgment would be equally available to competent members of the local moral-linguistic community. We are treating a moral tradition as one that rejects the simple authority of dominant judgments. As Dworkin[10] puts it, we imagine a community's morality, as having a complexity such that the members of that community may all be wrong about what it requires and forbids.

In any rich moral system, the appeal to standards usually turns out to be highly complex. It is unlikely that any particular thinker will have correctly formulated her culture's ultimate standards.[11] Any explicit standard that one raises in moral discourse could be a target of further standard-based evaluation.

The implicit standards of a community are the idealized outcome of open-ended, norm-guided discussion within that moral community.[12] We engage in discourse together about ways (*daos*) to evaluate and guide action. We naturally adjust our attitudes to harmonize with those of others in our community. The community's morality "evolves" (emerges?) via internal discourse.

A. *Subjective Responsibility and Excuses*

This brings us to a valid normative dimension of a comparative study. We can understand the normative relevance of comparative ethics on the analogy of an excuse. Western moral reasoning commonly distinguishes between "objective" and "subjective" rightness. Briefly, for something to be objectively right is for it to be what we should do given the way the world actually goes. "Subjectively right" refers to what we should do given our epistemic situation.

We normally do not blame people for objectively wrong actions if they acted in good faith and on the best information available to them. This consideration may even incline us to praise subjectively right actions (i.e., to judge that the person acted rightly, while still finding the action "objectively tragic").

Once we have the conception of a valid justification of moral attitudes, we can extend this analysis from factual beliefs to evaluations. If Anson Chan (Hong Kong's chief secretary) acts on the best information of both types available to her, we can judge her as being subjectively right even if we disagree with her actions. We may even think more highly of her when she conforms to the best evaluation available to her than we would if she were merely to ape British ethical standards.

We may excuse an action without making any stronger judgment that the actor acted rightly, that is, we may reasonably conclude that it would be wrong to punish but stop short of praising the actor as subjectively right. In other cases, we are willing to praise an actor for good intentions and principled behavior even though we find the action tragically wrong. Let us call this positive excusing in contrast to the more normal case where we simply withhold blame or punishment – negative excusing.

Positive excusing is essentially approving of the epistemic "responsibility" of an actor. It is enough for negative excusing to have made a "normal" mistake. For positive excusing, we look for evidence that the actor reasoned carefully and correctly (i.e., responsibly). We would be disinclined to praise an excusable action that did not show sufficient effort to reflect on and evaluate one's sincerely held moral attitudes and principles. We expect one responsibly to address the considerations that are available given one's norms of moral discourse.

Both Chinese and Western moral conceptions envision a common moral goal. Their norms should yield general agreement in attitudes and reactions about behavior and feelings. When the application of standards is controversial within a community, we normally expect to engage in further moral discourse, to advocate our different moral attitudes, and to seek to convince each other. We would not positively excuse a judgment that did not both take rival arguments on board and seriously address them.

Ethical argument and persuasion are activities that make sense only when communities do not assume the dominant or majority view determines what is right. The practice signals a "regulative ideal" that discourse in the community seeks an autonomous "right." It signals that any currently dominant attitude may be wrong.

B. *Widening Moral Community*

Here we address an even more perplexing normative issue. Remember that comparative ethics need not make us dismiss morality as relative. Awareness of different moral systems with different moral beliefs warrants a mild degree of skepticism but does not undermine the reasonableness of making any evaluation.

Both Chinese and Western traditions take the target audience of potential moral agreement to be humans in general. We implicitly address our moral appeals to all of humanity and our regulative ideal is that moral discourse among humans tends toward that agreement. Comparative studies need not undermine *either* culture's conception of this universal scope of the intended recipients of morality – all of humanity. Both implicitly entertain this universalism and nothing so far shows that this aspiration is wrong. (A great deal, however, suggests that it is both a difficult and distant goal!)

One result of comparative ethics is that we implicitly come to recognize ours as one of a group of alternative, distinctive moral systems. We learn a new way of seeing ourselves as others see us. Comparative exposure will make us less dogmatic or mildly skeptical about our attitudes. We see our considered first-level judgments as contingent on prior higher-order judgments for which we may not have full reflective justifications, which no one ever challenged before. However, this insight into the plurality of normative systems is perfectly general. We have no reason either to adopt the alternative or to stop making all our normative judgments as best we can.[13] Our insights require discussants from neither moral tradition to abandon their system of moral justification wholesale for a thought experiment with a rival tradition.

The Western advocate of individual liberty is not irrational in continuing to adopt the result of her "reflective moral equilibrium" merely on being told that Confucian moral sensibilities are different. A Chinese conservative, on similar grounds, may correctly dismiss the appeal to "international moral standards" in favor of the sincere application of his existing norms of reason. Both continue to address the question of what is objectively right for everyone and both approach it with the best information and norms of reasoning available. Even when aware of the moral conflict, each can make such judgments with intellectual integrity and a commitment to the formal autonomy of morality. Neither, that is, justifies their judgments by appealing to the bald fact that the judgment is his or belongs to his tradition.

The normative relevance of comparative studies arises for each discussant in a more indirect way. The set of beliefs among which she must now achieve reflective equilibrium includes a belief about another morality. Our awareness of a rival moral perspective does mildly destabilize our moral confidence when it meets three conditions:

1. The rival moral tradition is significantly different in its conceptual or theoretical approach.
2. It is an intellectually rich, reflective, hierarchical system of norms.
3. It satisfies some plausible condition for substantive rightness (e.g., has been historically successful or leads to correct moral judgments).

We may provisionally read the latter judgment as "yields moral insights that impress us from our present moral point of view." To the degree that we become aware that a significant conceptual rival is comparable in reflective coherence and cultural success, we may rationally come to adopt a mildly skeptical attitude toward our own morality.[14]

The first condition suggests a difference between moral disagreement among significant rival moral communities and disagreements within our own community. We may view this as merely a matter of degree. We share many assumptions, standards of reasoning, and so forth in normal disagreements, but any domestic disagreement may turn on norms as well as facts. The difference would then concern mainly the degree of similarity of our respective norms guiding moral reasoning.

Still, the broad and deep conceptual nature of the differences may contribute to a kind of "intuitive" respect. The fascination with "different ways of thinking" about life and ethics prompts a deeper recognition of the range of unreflective assumptions we must make in moral reasoning.

Westerners commonly exhibit a more "receptive" attitude toward the differences they find in Chinese morality than to those of India or the Middle East. Charges of "orientalism" are louder and angrier from writers in those areas than from Japan and China. One reason for the difference might be that initially, the Indo-European link marks a less significant conceptual departure. In the "near" east cases, Westerners sense the comparatively greater historical, religious, and conceptual background. Moral disagreement is more likely to strike them as less profound, as simply extensions of disagreements internal to their own community.

The third condition may also be at work in this contrast in Western attitudes toward the Middle and Far East. Westerners may feel a greater alienation from the orthodox results of a Middle Eastern moral outlook than they would those of the Far East (China). They would find the arguments for the attitudes resemble rather disreputable arguments from within their own tradition – those for sexism and class discrimination. Given our settled judgment of these similar attitudes supported by similar arguments in similar conceptual and cultural contexts, such practices in a closely related culture will not justify the mild skepticism required. More "distant" India prompts more fascination but still with a sense of a common base. We plausibly link differences in moral judgments to religious or "factual" beliefs (e.g., reincarnation), which are accessible and familiar to us. Since, however, we have already come to find them rationally suspect, we may not imagine the resulting moral disagreement is a deeply normative one.

This initial reaction may vanish with greater insight, of course, but it is prima facie consistent with the conditions of moral tradition respect. Westerners have a greater fascination with Chinese ethics because they sense it to be reflectively rich, radically different tradition that generates moral attitudes they instinctively respect. The differences still seem mistakes, of course, but seldom simply cruel or dogmatically prejudiced. Taking such an attitude does not entail taking an equal interest in the teachings of a Navaho shaman or the polygamous prophet of some rural mountain community. The mere existence of an alternative moral community need not induce the same skepticism.[15]

Where we find that a rival tradition meets the three conditions (significant difference in approach, rich reflective development, and compatible or successful outcomes) our norms suggest an equilibrium-disturbing possibility. The rival scheme of norms may justify sound moral insights that one's home system has missed. We rationally begin to suspect that our moral view is complete or comprehensive. Autonomous thinkers from mutually respecting communities can then entertain a common possibility induced by their similar regulative ideals. Some conceivable moral system may do better than either rival does. For example, one that successfully synthesized the insights of both rival traditions would seem superior to either.

The implicit assumption behind discussion and persuasion is that the correct moral standards can move others. Failure to get that agreement from an otherwise rational interlocutor normally prompts more moral discourse. We implicitly suppose that repeated first-order debates within and between the mutual cultures would tend to converge. I think such concrete, day-to-day discussion is the plausible route to the cherished "synthesis of East and West." I doubt that comparative philosophers can achieve it by acting as moral prophets or as counterparts of Mill's beings who by virtue of being "competently acquainted with both" can declare which is better.[16]

As I imagine it, the move to synthesis must take place as each moral community gradually shifts. It would have to be motivated mainly by its own norms with the addition only of the mild skepticism induced by granting moral tradition respect to the other. In effect, it would have to be bottom-up, gradual change. That is, a Chinese theorist would have to make arguments that convince other Chinese given their existing norms, experiences, and assumptions. Similarly, a Western advocate has to make first-order normative arguments along with other normative ethical theorists.

Let us suppose that each is aware of and appreciates the other moral tradition. Still, I suggest, it is improbable that these comparativists will successfully convince other members of their home community to reject an existing moral attitude simply by citing its status in the foreign scheme. That may count as a reason for initiating a moral debate about it, but not a reason for accepting the moral attitude in question.

When a comparative philosopher, for example, argues that we should adopt Confucianism's "virtue ethics," we legitimately may wonder how the fact that Confucius believed it is relevant to any rational moral decision we are facing. Virtue ethicists regularly cite Aristotle as a model, but if appeal to *that* authority is insufficient to convince doubters, it is hardly likely that an appeal to Mencius will do better.

Similar points apply to the liberal–communitarian debate. Whatever reasons a Westerner might have for adopting communitarian attitudes, they become no stronger if it is true that Confucians are communitarians. If the argument given by the other culture's philosopher is a good one when translated to the local language and context, then the argument, not the guru source, justifies the new belief.

So, while the regulative ideal of a wider moral community is implicit in both traditions, it is not clear how to derive any more specific normative relevance for comparative ethics. Its main role is inducing moral tradition respect and warranting a kind of excuse (tolerance) for continued disagreement. I know of no argument for any disputed feature of either ethical system that would come directly from comparative premises.[17] The normative relevance of comparative ethics ends when we have made the case for moral tradition respect. Its role, then, is the rather "academic" one of exhibiting and illuminating the rich complexity and coherence of the background assumptions, concepts, and norms of reflection. In this way, it justifies some skepticism at home and openness to possible moral reform and study of the other tradition. From that point, normal, first-order moral discourse must take over.

C. Summary of Normative Relevance

We have uncovered two ways comparative philosophy can have normative relevance: by using positive excusing and by motivating the ideal of a moral synthesis. Of course, we would already have good reasons to value openness, moral curiosity, and so on, and we have good practical reasons to find modes of harmonious coexistence with other cultures. These values need not depend on the claims of the reflective coherence of the other tradition.

Let us now see how the three criteria of normative respect bear on the "Asian values" debate. First, we can agree that the West should avoid any imperious, lecturing attitude toward any Asian culture when we can justify moral tradition respect. The "should" here is not merely diplomatic, but a requirement of our own norms of reasoning about morality. We are not being moral relativists when we adopt this attitude – just the opposite. The only relativism required is the familiar type that results from applying the principle of epistemic responsibility to different situations.

It does not follow, however, that we need eschew open and frank moral discourse and disagreement. We still should express our strong moral attitudes to each other and offer our best reasoning in the expectation the other community will see its moral relevance. We should then be willing to carry the moral discourse to higher levels and confront the differences in norms or warrants – assumptions about human nature and so forth. Failing to be open, frank, and principled in our moral objections may signal the very lack of normative respect due a coequal moral discussant. It would signal that we do not consider them as potential collaborators in a wider moral community.

Western advocates should provide a reflective, normative argument, not appeal to any alleged "international consensus." Neither side is entitled merely to cite the "dominance" of their favored view in their home tradition. Each should elucidate in detail the assumptions and higher norms supporting their judgment. This reflects an attitude of treating each other as potential members of a wider moral community.

Westerners should expect and accept no less from the Chinese side. They should not allow the simple, unelaborated assertion of "traditional differences" to end the exchange. If that is what Asian values advocates offer, then they treat their own moral community as unreflective and undermine the justification of moral tradition respect. What higher values and assumptions of the Chinese perspective warrant the different moral judgment? Moral tradition respect should inspire interest in whether deeper and higher norms warrant Confucian moral attitudes. This is especially important since other sectors of the Chinese moral community actively dispute Confucian intuitions. If rival, reflective Chinese moral theorists question Confucian attitudes then Confucian moral prejudices can only play approximately the role of Catholic dogma in the Western abortion debate.

In this normative justification project, of course, comparative philosophers have an important role to play that draws on the distinction between philosophy and anthropology, history, and the like. We may excuse political leaders from the philosophical task of formulating the assumptions, higher norms, and so forth. If we are to inspire moral tradition respect, we rely on comparative moral philosophers to explore and spell out these deeper justifications. Both cultures need access to the reasoning, which is a crucial precondition of moral tradition respect.

III. CHINA AND THE HUMAN RIGHTS DEBATE

Given my argument up to this point, I now formally abandon the posture of discussing Asian values in general. I suspect this slogan is a political, not a philosophical invention. The moral communities that make up Asia lack the kind of philosophical coherence required for comparative philosophy to treat them as one. This is certainly the case, as I argued earlier, for South Asia and the Middle East. I limit myself formally now to elucidating the clearly equilibrium-challenging Chinese comparison.

A. *Initial Problems for Chinese Theories of Rights*

We should first distinguish between conceptual and value issues surrounding human rights claims. The alleged lack of an ancient or traditional rights concept has limited relevance. It would bar certain ways of making and justifying the claims, but we can formulate most moral issues in alternative language. The absence of a concept of a right bars a Chinese male from asserting a right to beat his wife as much as it does from asserting that he has a right to political and civil liberty.

Our concern is obviously with the content of the two rights. We can usually restate any normative issue in terms that do not require that specialized Western vocabulary. For example, *should* the Chinese political structure give individuals a larger and more stable set of basic liberties? We need not argue that it should adopt the language of rights in doing so. Conceptual issues are relevant, however, since the availability of certain ways of framing an issue may influence the answers a reasonable discourse within a community draws for guiding their moral attitudes.[18] I have suggested there are other such differences in the classical Chinese perspective in several papers. My conclusions were that there might, but that study was limited to pre-Buddhist China. Pre-Han (c. 200 B.C.) Chinese thought lacked not only "rights" but also strict counterparts of "duty," "ought" and "reason."

So, again, the case that Chinese political structures should give individuals a larger and more stable set of basic liberties would not justify doing so by appealing to the inherent dignity of the individual as a rational being. We may find no counterpart of the conception of individual moral agents as rational. The familiar cluster of metaphysical and epistemological doctrines (e.g., the private mind as the locus of meaning) that ground the Western intuition about the primacy and dignity of the individual may all be quite alien to the classical tradition. These considerations explain why the kinds of considerations Europeans address to each other in justifying individual rights would not "make contact" with the considered views of a responsible Chinese thinker.

Many other seemingly nonethical features of the two traditions of philosophy may also yield coherence-based partial explanations of our divergent moral attitudes. No doubt, Western doctrines of metaphysical and methodological individualism would buttress the Western intuition of the moral primacy of human individuals. Western theorists mostly understand the world as being made up of particular objects. Chinese metaphysical theory tends to analyze objects as parts of a larger, more basic whole.

Western folk psychology and philosophy of mind postulated a private, individualized mind as the locus of meaning, thought, and reason. Chinese thinkers viewed meaning as stemming from conformity to conventions of terminology that derived from the culture heroes who invented language (writing). It places fluid dispositions to language use in the place of sentential belief, assertability in the place of truth, and different schemes of distinctions in the place of rival theories. It has no clear counterpart of a proof or human faculty for assessing validity – reason.

Western epistemology attends to the ways we go from the private, subjective, individualized beliefs to an abstract, objective knowledge. Western thought typically bypasses and denigrates social conventions as "conventional wisdom." Chinese epistemology focuses on how we take guiding discourse (a *dao*^{guide}) and apply it in real-world conditions. It had, until the Cultural Revolution, a long tradition of considering history as a treasure trove of practical guidance.

Chinese theories locate meaning in social conventions. Where Western folk theory postulates a language of private symbols (ideas or mental ideograms), Chinese folk theory places conventional public symbols (ideograms). Western mental ideograms are distributed through the individual minds of the community. They arise from each individual's personal history of contact with objects. The Chinese folk theory also makes a story about historical contact with objects relevant to the meaning of the symbols. However, theirs is a story of contact by ancient culture heroes (sage kings) who created the ideograms. Meaning does not depend on private, individual experience. Language has meaning because we conform to a shared tradition. Knowledge is primarily knowledge of a *dao* – a social guiding discourse.

Classical Chinese thinkers framed the central normative question as a social one. What content should a community's moral discourse have? Socrates, famously, posed the question as a more individual one. What parts of the community morality should one rationally accept? The differences influencing Chinese and Western moral reasoning are both broad and deep.

The observation of all these kinds of difference, however, yields only a limited "negative" point. It merely shows how some coherence considerations that inform Western European attitudes toward individual freedom would be absent from Chinese reasoning. At best, it may help explain why the Chinese community has not yet overwhelmingly concluded that individual liberty and democracy are important political value (i.e., why today the issue is an ongoing and controversial one in China).

These considerations, however, cannot block genuinely culturally Chinese participants in moral discourse from giving sound and convincing arguments for greater and more stable liberty. Why would a comparative ethicist treat them as doing so? I suspect it is because he assumes that *only* the line of thought that leads to Western proliberty attitudes could lead to a similar Chinese conclusion. The tendency to magnify the implications of the differences noted may stem from John Rawls's treatment of Utilitarianism.

In Rawls's classic presentation of his "liberty principle," he argued that it best accounts for all of our considered judgments about justice. He traces the principles to a Kantian attitude of fundamental respect for the individual reasoning moral agent. Utilitarian reasoning, he argued, would not justify the principles *in ways* that coincide with all *our* considered judgments (intuitions). Utilitarianism, he concluded, applies to a whole society a mode of reasoning appropriate for the individual. It thus does not take seriously the difference among individuals.[19]

Rawls's subtlety here is easily missed (even assuming his argument is sound). He does not say that utilitarian considerations cannot justify a conception of justice in which liberty and equality are important values. He argues that utilitarian arguments do not do justice to our intuitions about the ontological and practical status of individuals.[20] Our respective moral attitudes, our moral "intuitions," are not isolated judgments. We ground them on a comprehensive philosophical outlook – a view of ourselves, of society and of the world. That view, Rawls argues, is not utilitarian.

B. Chinese Classical Moral Discourse

Now, of what relevance are these kinds of considerations to any live practical issue in China? Let us take the question of whether the executive branch of the Hong Kong Special Administrative Region should allow Hong Kong citizens to exercise substantial individual liberty. Further, let us imagine the debate is one carried on mainly within the local community. The preceding ancient conceptual issues, I suggest, are simply irrelevant, historical curiosities. Given the contemporary complexity of the Chinese moral community, these anachronistic considerations are distractions from the real issue.

Any living member of a Chinese moral community has much more to draw on in aiming for reflective equilibrium than merely the classical Chinese ethics. We may appropriately notice that internal political debate includes frequent rhetorical appeal to what is "purely Chinese." Traditional affiliation retains a powerful emotional pull within Chinese communities. The most common manifestation is the accusation that reformers are "Westernized" or aping Western ways.[21]

Historically, Chinese liberals have felt and arguably still feel the necessity to buttress their other arguments by showing that the reforms they advocate have a traditional base. Obvious examples include Kang Yuwei, Liang Qiqiao, and Hu Shi. Clearly, however, other "reformers" have felt quite comfortable with far more radical antitraditional advocacy. So it surely is not a shared discourse requirement of the entire moral community that their political ideas should have a pure, traditional Chinese base.

I do not endorse its normative relevance, but the question of the compatibility of classical thought and political liberalism is an interesting intellectual issue. Many in the community regard it as relevant to the debate about human rights. Could a reflective, coherent, pre-Buddhist Chinese philosopher appreciate an argument for individual liberty? The question should not be "could Confucianism be coherent with liberty?" The limitation to Confucianism is a common error of comparative ethicists.[22] Nothing I have said warrants respect for Confucianism in particular as opposed to Chinese moral discourse in general.

The religious, as opposed to philosophical, attachment to Confucianism may be an important causal factor in Chinese politics, but it has no logical or epistemic importance in answering our straightforward normative question. Like a comparable focus on Catholicism in discussions about abortion in the West, attention to Confucianism may have predictive or explanatory value, but is normatively inert. A modern Chinese moral thinker has no more reason to conform to traditional Confucian beliefs than a modern European has to conform to the moral judgments of Thomas Aquinas.[23]

I need not deny that Confucianism is one authentic expression of the Chinese tradition. However, the "pure" tradition is not Confucian, even if, by the pure tradition, we mean the native philosophical basis set during the pre-Buddhist, classical period. That is the period of a "hundred philosophers." What if those Chinese philosophers who thought carefully about higher norms of moral reasoning mostly regarded Confucianism as a "soft target"?

Modern Confucians work hard to dispel these suspicions, but they are not merely Western skepticism or bias. Historically, from the dawn of Chinese thought to the modern period, Chinese thinkers have raised similar doubts. One does not have to step outside of the Chinese community to hear devastating criticisms of the deleterious effects of Confucian education and indoctrination on Chinese culture! In the face of these suspicions, arguments that limit themselves to reciting Confucian views get their conclusion at the cost of any plausible normative relevance.

Confucian apologists note that despite the criticism from other Chinese thinkers, Confucianism has become the dominant ideology in China, *and that gives it a kind of normative authority.* No one denies the antecedent (at least for medieval China), but it is not obvious that the normative conclusion follows.[24] Prima facie, Chinese political history provides excellent grounds for doubt that Confucianism's historical dominance is a product of anything like reflective coherence. It was not a spontaneous social choice following a reflection and open, free competitive discourse. By focusing on Confucianism, they may have implicitly substituted a political orthodoxy chosen by an emperor for its worth in sustaining his and his family's dynasty, not a morality based on sound application of Chinese norms of moral reasoning. Arguably, precisely what appealed to early political authorities was Confucianism's reflective naiveté. That modern autocrats still draw comfort from the way it encourages submissiveness to authority is no surprise.

Any account of pure Chinese attitudes and norms for argument must take account of all the thinkers in Classical China who engaged in systematic and higher-level reflection about ethics. Studying the philosophical content of much pro-Confucian writing, one may justifiably suspect that being trained as a Confucian may be precisely the kind of indoctrination that would block or undermine the three bases of moral respect. I have argued that prominent Confucian thinkers were not adept in the techniques of critical moral reflection developed by other native Chinese thinkers.[25] If we conclude either that modern Confucianism is essentially a scholastic tradition (one that accords authoritative religious status to classical scriptures) or that political factors won it the cultural dominance it enjoyed, then its cultural importance will be irrelevant to morality. It will not warrant moral tradition respect. Only evidence that shared Chinese assumptions and norms of reasoning warrant its conclusions can justify moral tradition respect.

I see no clear route to justifying moral tradition respect for Confucianism per se. The justification I outline here works only for a broadly defined moral community with all its divisions and disagreements. Any argument for Confucian values must first confront and respond adequately to the doubts historically (and currently) expressed by Daoists, Mohists, Buddhists, Legalists, Muslims, Christians, and liberals from within the Chinese community. There were Chinese on both ends of the guns in Tiananmen Square.

For one illustration of such criticism from the pure classical period, let us briefly consider Mohism. It was a highly influential school from that period and it "lost out" shortly after the establishment of imperial Chinese authority "buried" philosophy. Chinese conservatives tend to castigate Mohism as Western or Western-style thinking. Alternately, they characterize it as "plebeian," "shallow," or "lacking in style." I have argued elsewhere that these aspersions are baseless.[26] What is of interest here is their transparent irrelevance. It illustrates a lingering Confucian reluctance to deal openly and fairly with criticism and objections to their ethical theories.

The philosophical quality, in context, is hard to dispute. Mozi was the first "master" after Confucius and he gave Chinese philosophy an impressively rich and sophisticated beginning – especially given the notorious nonphilosophical character of Confucius' teachings. Mozi's teachings included a distinctly Chinese version of utilitarianism, a counterpart of a contract theory of government, and a pragmatic theory of language. He virtually "invented" the argumentative essay as a literary style. His doctrines stimulated Confucianism to philosophical reflection and led eventually to Daoism and Legalism. The debate between Mohism and Confucianism became a paradigm for Chinese metaethics – for higher-level reflection on ethics.

For our purposes, the single most important feature of Mohism is that it gave an argument for rejecting the authority of tradition. From that point on, no Confucian felt comfortable appealing as simply to moral tradition as Confucius had.[27] Obviously other rival schools (particularly Daoist or Legalist) eschewed such appeal to the authority of tradition. Mencius, following Mozi, explicitly sought to give a nontraditional justification of Confucian rites. Xunzi, too, constructs elaborate pragmatic justifications of tradition. Once Confucianism steps into Mozi's arena, the question simply shifts to whether their arguments are sound or not. Hence, as

I remarked earlier, when Chinese advocates of Asian values imply that traditional values justify ignoring human rights, they scorn a certifiably traditional Chinese value.

Mencius, given his enormous historical influence, is relevant to the Asian values debate in other ways. Besides confirming that Chinese moral reasoning rejects bald appeal to tradition, his attempts to give a metajustification of tradition introduce strikingly "democratic" lines of thought. He shows a distinct tendency to interpret the Confucian "mandate of Heaven" based on the mechanism of popular acceptance.[28] His moral psychology (still a subject of great dispute) appears to provide a viable base for arguments assuming an in-principle equal respect and concern for all humans.

IV. COMPARATIVE NORMATIVE CONCLUSIONS: SOME FAMILIAR FALLACIES

When comparativists hold Chinese philosophy out as a model for Western moral reform, they run the risk of undermining the basis for normative respect for the Chinese tradition. Bryan Van Norden's tantalizing title "What Should Western Philosophy Learn from Chinese Philosophy?" illustrates the problem.[29] Despite the provocative title, Van Norden's position is that one would find the study of Chinese philosophy worthwhile only if one already had two related beliefs:

1. Some belief about the problem(s) with ("the crisis in") Western philosophy, and
2. Some belief about the degree of difference between Western and Chinese philosophy.

The former belief comes from internal Western critics.[30] The second is clearly too weak. To judge Chinese thought "worthy" of study, one needs an evaluative, not a descriptive view of Chinese thought. Mere difference (or similarity) would not justify studying it. Comparativists need to show not that it is either similar or different, but that it warrants moral tradition respect. Merely asserting its worth undermines rather than promotes such respect.

Van Norden implies that Chinese philosophy strengthens the case for a virtue ethics reform of Western tradition, so one might expect to find in his article an argument from Chinese philosophy that shows Western ethics needs such a change. Instead, he cites works that compare Chinese thinkers to Western philosophers who espouse virtue ethics. These comparisons focus on Confucian doctrines.[31]

Since the debate about the advantages and disadvantages of virtue ethics is an ongoing one in Western thought, it is unclear what normative relevance we should assign to the mere fact that some ancient Chinese had opted for that approach. I have argued that of classical Chinese philosophers, Mencius is the most plausible example of such a path to ethical reflection.[32] Other thinkers produced some powerful criticisms of the position.[33] When accompanied with the tacit admission that they confronted challenges from rival ethical approaches within their own tradition and never really formulated or addressed the current Western alternative – duty ethics – it is hard to see what normative relevance Confucian conclusions have.

Van Norden allows in passing that "other Chinese intellectual movements are . . . worthy of study" and observes that they resemble Western thinkers. This dismissive characterization, however, completely misses the point. The question is "Do non-Confucian thinkers challenge Confucian virtue ethics?" If they do, we can ask, "Given those challenges, how do Chinese virtue ethicists respond?" If Chinese norms of reasoning warrant their responses, we can ask, "Are Chinese norms of reasoning such that these responses would also be warranted in the West?" If the challenges and answers are warranted by both Western and Chinese standards *and* if Western defenders of virtue ethics have not yet noticed the responses, then Western philosophy can indeed learn something from Chinese philosophy. However, it will be irrelevant that it comes from a Chinese thinker. The argument itself will be relevant within a Westerner's own norms or inference. We would acknowledge the thinker who originated just as we acknowledge Western historical antecedents.

If there are some deep differences among the concepts, background theories of moral psychology and the like, or norms or warrant for ethical claims, then we can still justify moral tradition respect even as we disagree with the "winning" Chinese position. We would note that the Chinese virtue ethicist's response to their contemporary critics is sound *by their lights* though not by ours. Having granted moral tradition respect, we then may imagine the possibility of some possible synthesis but still have no way to move directly to such a synthesis. If the native contemporary Chinese critics object to the same weaknesses in Confucian theory that we are inclined to, then we have no reason to think that Confucianism represents anything more than a Chinese way of going wrong.

Chad Hansen

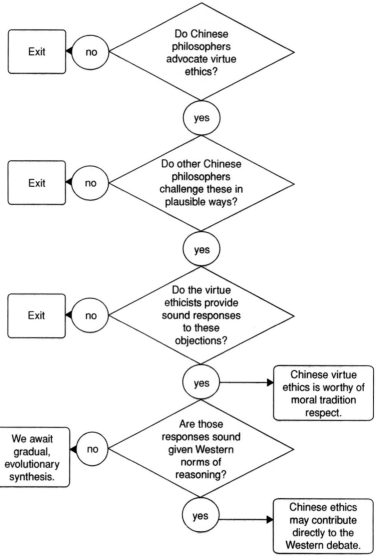

How is Confucian advocacy of virtue ethics nomatively relevant?

Van Norden's authorities have only argued for the first step in this process of evaluation. His treating Confucian critics as merely "worthy objects of study" misses their crucial role in justifying moral tradition respect. The advocate of Western learning from Chinese philosophy needs to show that Confucians responded well to their own critics. Merely reciting the Confucian case and giving modern arguments for it does nothing to warrant moral tradition respect. This is a particularly crucial point since Van Norden is dismissive of scholars who criticize Confucian reasoning. Such "sincere" advocacy, as we noted earlier, simply undermines the comparativist's own credibility.

A parallel challenge faces the familiar appeal to Chinese attitudes to commend communitarianism.[34] First, communitarian attitudes are controversial within the Chinese tradition (again associated mainly with Confucianism). Notoriously, Daoism tended toward anarchism and included a tradition of hermitage.[35] Some read Mohism as adopting a contract theory that implies they are individualists.[36] Mencius characterizes Yangism as a doctrine of egoism. It would require much more careful argument than I have seen to show that the higher norms that governed the debate in ancient China clearly entailed communitarianism. If they did, the reasoning might still be unconvincing from a Western point of view, except for justifying moral tradition respect. Nothing follows from the mere observation that some (or even most) Confucians have de facto communitarian attitudes.

I do agree that some features of ancient Chinese (e.g., some I discussed earlier in Section III.A) made the appeal of more communitarian attitudes "natural" in ancient China. Conversely, some features I discussed make individualism as a moral perspective rather less likely. This predictive conclusion, however, has no bearing on the normative question of whether Chinese should now have human rights. Given how a modern Chinese or Westerner poses a question, it calls for a normative argument, and all the arguments for both sides that I know of could be fully understood by both modern audiences.

Again, the liberal–communitarian debate is a live and vibrant one within modern ethics. In that context, it is far from clear how the alleged fact of Chinese preference for one is relevant to the debate. If one is inclined to value the communitarian perspective, then she might express the predictive conclusion as a Chinese receptivity to the value of communitarian attitudes. If one is inclined to value individualism, it might be expressed as a susceptibility to the blandishments and illusion of normative relevance of empty and uncontroversial observations about human social nature.[37]

Most attempts at argument amount to implicit apologetics for Chinese government attitudes toward human rights.[38] They imply that rights follow only from Rawlsian assumptions. However, as we saw, nothing Rawls says bars the possibility of justifying a stable scheme of individual liberty from communitarian assumptions. John Dewey and Philip Pettit, for example, both show how such a justification of individualism from communitarian assumptions could go.[39]

I have suggested a conception of morality that could justify some normative relevance for comparative ethics. It would do this by justifying moral tradition respect. This analysis explains why direct appeals to allegedly dominant Chinese attitudes have no normative relevance. Rather than seeking in Chinese thought for short-cut answers to contemporary Western controversies, comparativists should focus on tracing the background assumptions and higher norms of warrant that underlie all sides of Chinese ethical debates. This will give us an appreciation for how another reflective moral culture frames the question. Comparative ethics could be directly relevant if it uncovers "foreign" arguments that our own discussants have failed to notice. These arguments must be accessible (in translation) and warranted given our present norms of reasoning.

The idea of a moral synthesis is a powerful and natural one when a culture meets the conditions of normative respect. The nature of moral discourse and reasoning, however, may mean that both communities could experience ongoing progress and development in moral attitudes and yet never meet.

Notes

1. One early philosophical study had an "anthropological" character and clearly illustrates the distinction. Richard Brandt studied Hopi ethics. Richard B. Brandt, *Hopi Ethics: A Theoretical Analysis* (Chicago: University of Chicago Press, 1954). His method approximated "field work," but Brandt's interests were in the *principles* that intellectual leaders of the Hopi used in *justifying* their different doctrines and behaviors.

2. The contrast between *narrow* and *wide* "reflective equilibrium" motivates this observation. We understand moral reflection as the attempt to harmonize our "considered judgments," but not only our moral judgments. The entire range of beliefs about human nature, society, and the world can be evaluated for coherence. On reflective equilibrium, see John Rawls, *A Theory of Justice* (Cambridge, MA: Harvard University Press, 1971); Margaret Holmgren, "The Wide and Narrow of Reflective Equilibrium," *Canadian Journal of Philosophy*, vol. 19, no. 1 (1989), pp. 43–60; and Richard B. Brandt, "The Science of Man and Wide Reflective Equilibrium," *Ethics*, vol. 100, no. 1 (1990), pp. 259–78.

3. Explaining contrast or similarities in actual moral attitudes need not be the main interest of a philosophical study. A philosopher may be as interested in how *similar* moral attitudes can emerge from a culture with different conceptual structure and background philosophical doctrines.

4. I have little to say here about comparative moral psychology aside from evaluating the coherence of psychological theories and normative attitudes. That is, I do not speculate, here, about the possible truth of rival theories of moral psychology. This might be relevant for claims that Chinese ethics may work better for Chinese people as a distinct psychological type. It is conceivable that different nationalities might have different psychologies, or even that a theory's wide acceptance of a moral psychology might become a "self-fulfilling prophecy." Modern Europeans, shaped by institutions constructed on the assumption that we are psychological egoists, may become more "selfish" than Chinese. However, the empirical grounds for such a claim remain weak.

5. Henry Rosemont, Jr., "Why Take Rights Seriously? A Confucian Critique" in Leroy S. Rouner ed., *Human Rights and the World's Religions* (Notre Dame, IN: Notre Dame University Press, 1988), pp. 167–82. Rosemont suggests that China may be such a case. He draws on Fingarette's analysis of Confucian ethics as lacking a concept of choice and that differences in Chinese views on human behavior cannot underwrite issues about moral relativity. Rosemont's argument is interesting, in part, for his suggesting that the alternative is possibly *better* than a morality. I comment indirectly on this argument in Chad Hansen, *A Daoist Theory of Chinese Thought* (New York: Oxford University Press, 1992), pp. 81–3.

6. Probably less because it attaches to the term than because, as Saussure and Derrida remind us, meaning is a function of difference. It is because we normally contrast morality with conventions and religious rules. Conversely, we normally refer to utilitarianism as a moral theory even when we think it wrong. In any case, philosophers will have less interest in (place less value on) communities that advance only revelation, instinct or traditional authority as standards for evaluative judgments.

7. Hansen, ibid., pp. 140–3; Chad Hansen, "Should the Ancient Masters Value Reason?" in Henry Rosemont, Jr. ed., *Chinese Texts and Philosophical Contexts: Essays Dedicated to A. C. Graham* (La Salle, IL: Open Court. 1991), pp. 179–209; and Chad Hansen, "Individualism in Chinese Thought" in Donald J. Munro ed., *Individualism and Holism: Studies in Confucian and Taoist Values* (Ann Arbor: University of Michigan Press, 1995), pp. 35–56.

8. I am guided here by Alan Gibbard, *Wise Choices, Apt Feelings: A Theory of Normative Judgment* (Oxford: Clarendon Press, 1990). He elucidates the claim that an ethical judgment is rational as expressing and endorsing a system of norms from which it follows.

9. This is only one of the puzzles facing naïve appeals to tradition of this sort. Another would be that the Chinese critic of human rights could not justify his critical attitude. He implicitly allows that Western tradition is different so he must judge that it is right for Westerners to advocate human rights and to push them on Asian societies as well. That is what, he supposes, Western moral tradition tells them to do.

10. Ronald Dworkin, *Taking Rights Seriously* (Cambridge, MA: Harvard University Press, 1977).

11. This need not be because they are mystical like Plato's good. A more likely explanation is because the system of standards will form a coherent scheme. The justification of any standard will depend on its coherence with the others in the community's overall system. There will be rival ways of achieving this coherence, and they will inform and shape moral disagreement and debate in the community.
12. See Gibbard, op. cit.
13. See Thomas Nagel, *The Last Word* (New York: Oxford University Press, 1997).
14. Notice that Rosemont's thesis that we should not regard Chinese normative thinking as a morality may block this line of thought. If it is not moral thinking but some other kind of normative activity, then we need not conclude that the resultant norm systems are in conflict. The conflict comes from the assumption that both traditions are formally autonomous and thus think of moral judgments as other than merely traditional and as applying universally. These conditions would then motivate respect, but not necessarily any ideal of a synthesis.
15. Westerners may still be cynical about Chinese morality where they sense familiar appeals. For example, the argument that we should restrict liberty for administrative or economic advantage is so familiar in Western political discourse they need find it no more impressive in the mouth of a Chinese ruler.
16. John Stuart Mill, *Utilitarianism* (London: World Library, 1863), chapter 2.
17. Many familiar premises used in moral argument could be rebutted by comparativists (e.g., assertions that such and such moral attitudes are "universally acknowledged").
18. Certain features of translation might also contribute to the difficulty in presenting certain moral views. See Roger Ames, "Rites as Rights: The Confucian Alternative" in Leroy S. Rouner ed., *Human Rights and the World's Religions* (Notre Dame, IN: Notre Dame University Press, 1988), pp. 199–214.
19. Rawls, op. cit., p. 27.
20. I do not mean to suggest that the difference would not have normative implications. The differences arise from narrow as well as wide reflective equilibrium. The shape of a Chinese "utilitarian" conception of individual liberty may differ from a Western one.
21. One may worry that giving arguments showing that classical thought is consistent with human rights gives reformers a response to the unfortunate rhetorical context but also implicitly endorses and strengthens it. Should we on principle insist *only* on the normative irrelevance of descriptive classical thought – which may give the (mistaken) impression that conservatives win the point? Some Chinese conservatives even hint that Mozi, the nearest contemporary of Confucius and a strong critic, was a "Western" thinker.
22. Rosemont, op. cit., pp. 167–82. Most of the contributions mainly address Confucianism. Rosemont limits his claims to Confucius himself and does so with a clearer awareness of their relevance. He treats it as an *interesting* intellectual enterprise. Would there be a way to show Confucius (or one of his disciples) that his conception was wrong and that it should include elements of human rights? I think Rosemont knows that it is strictly irrelevant

to the normative issue itself – for which he offers separate argument. The question, however, loses most of its philosophical interest when personalized or relativized to an individual. It would be too easy to find *a* philosopher in both traditions whose thought was inimical to individual rights. One might easily doubt that Confucius counted as a moral *philosopher* in the sense of a thinker who reflected on and questioned his *own* standards of judgment. Many have expressed such skepticism, so in the absence of evidence of such higher-level reflection, Confucius' actual beliefs and tendencies to believe are of interest mainly to those with a religious attachment to Confucianism. Confucius' views may have been the result of his psychological peculiarities or his ignorance or inattention to lines of thought that were available in his contemporary culture. See Hansen, *A Daoist Theory of Chinese Thought*, op. cit., pp. 112–15.

23. And, of course, no less. One may reflectively judge that Aquinas' moral position is correct or the best available. See the discussion in Alasdair MacIntyre, *Whose Justice? Which Rationality?* (Notre Dame, IN: Notre Dame University Press, 1988). But to make the case hold, the defender of Confucian ethics has to make a case, as MacIntyre does, not merely appeal to Confucianism's Chineseness. Whether the case is a good one or not is a matter of norms, not history or tradition.

24. Scholars seldom defend this assumption in print, but when I have put the point to my comparative colleagues, they offer various ways of preserving it. Some imply that the political decision itself shows the "naturalness" or "fit" of Confucianism for the Chinese "mind." Others claim that the fact that it could be imposed and "work" demonstrates this and finally that the fact that it was imposed and worked effected a gradual (hereditary) change so that Chinese minds are *now* effectively shaped by that decision.

25. Earlier, I would have excluded Xunzi (298–238 B.C.E.) from this negative judgment of theoretical sophistication. I do still think there are some signs of theoretical strength and originality; however, his position as a whole now strikes me as either uncomprehending or disingenuous. See my discussion in Hansen, *A Daoist Theory of Chinese Thought*, op. cit., pp. 307–43.

I thank an anonymous referee of this volume for reminding me to address the widespread perception that my interpretation of Confucians is "uncharitable." I certainly acknowledge that such is a common view of my account, and I do explicitly set out to tell a story from a perspective that is different from the usual Confucian perspective on the classical period. My negative evaluation of Confucian thinking may be controversial on various grounds, but I think it is a confusion to describe it as "uncharitable" without substantial further argument. First, I explicitly disavow the strict principle of charity in favor of the principle of humanity. I argue extensively for this choice in my work and the grounds include that selecting translation manuals that maximize the "truth" of the consequent belief systems invites us to confuse understanding with agreement. Critics should, in fairness (in charity?) at least note that before making such a charge.

Even were I to appeal to charity in interpretation, I think this criticism confuses my open expression of disagreement and other negative judgments as the sign of failure of interpretive charity. Charity lies in making the best sense of a community's discourse, not in limning incoherent or simple-minded accounts of it with fulsome praise. Further, I explicitly argue in my work such interpretive principles should apply to the whole discourse community, not to a single book, writer, or school. I explicitly argue that if the cost of giving a charitable reading to Confucians is that one must make naïve simpletons of all their native critics then the principles weigh *against* that interpretation.

Even given that limitation, I would dispute that my analysis of Confucians themselves makes less rational sense of their doctrine than do the traditional alternatives. I find their explanations of Confucianism do not make sense despite the frequent use of adjectives like "brilliant" and "penetrating" or the introduction of their alleged doctrines with verbs like "sees that" and "understands that." I am happy to invite neutral observers to judge whether I have contributed more or less to making Confucian theorizing more intelligible in its context than do these treatments that include such praise. My separate judgment that Confucians fail to provide adequate answers to their native contemporary critics is a case where I am answerable only to my own philosophical integrity. I am happy similarly to invite readers also to consult their best philosophical judgment and draw their own conclusions. However, these judgments are largely independent of the question of the theoretical value of my interpretative innovations.

26. See Hansen, *A Daoist Theory of Chinese Thought*, op. cit., pp. 95–152, especially 95–8.

27. The "simply" is important because Xunzi did have access to and used several arguments for tradition. Some of the deeper bases of his argument included intuition, evaluation of name use, and pragmatic considerations.

28. He does not, however, accept a purely procedural account of democratic legitimacy. The targeted selection was the wisest and best, and the implicit method was more like popular acclaim than voting. The democratic feature was intertwined with a natural meritocracy. Both points suggest Mohist inspiration (as does Mencius' doctrine of benevolence). The Mohists probably elected their leaders democratically.

29. See Bryan Van Norden, "What Should Western Philosophy Learn from Chinese Philosophy?" in Philip J. Ivanhoe ed., *Chinese Language, Thought and Culture: Nivison and His Critics* (Chicago: Open Court, 1996), pp. 224–49.

30. Van Norden cites names and works but does not provide any arguments. The authorities he cites for the view that Western philosophy is in crisis include no obvious comparativists.

31. Van Norden cites other thinkers (e.g., Hall and Ames) who also concentrate on Confucianism.

32. This is, obviously, an interpretive claim with which Van Norden may well disagree. Still, it seems such interpretive issues must be settled before we can give any normative force to the claim. I argue for the claim that only Mencius seems to adopt a straightforward virtue ethics in my article in the same volume. Chad Hansen, "Duty and Virtue" in Philip J. Ivanhoe ed., *Chinese Language, Thought and Culture: Nivison and His Critics* (Chicago: Open Court, 1996), pp. 173–92.

33. Im Manyul, "Emotional Control and Virtue in the Mencius," *Philosophy East and West*, vol. 49, no. 1 (1999), pp. 1–27, argues against the standard reading of Mencius as a virtue ethicist at least if one takes Aristotle as a paradigm.

34. See for example, Daniel Bell, "A Communitarian Critique of Authoritarianism," *Society*, vol. 32, no. 5 (1995), pp. 38–44; Daniel Bell, "The East Asian Challenge to Human Rights: Reflections on an East West Dialogue," *Human Rights Quarterly*, vol. 18, no. 3 (1996), pp. 641–68; Daniel Bell, "A Communitarian Critique of Authoritarianism," *Political Theory*, vol. 25, no. 1 (1997), pp. 6–33; and Daniel Bell, "What Does Confucius Add to Human Rights?" *Times Literary Supplement* (January 1, 1999), pp. 6–13.

35. Some have argued that Daoism provides a basis for the liberal value of equal respect. See David Wong, "Taoism and the Problem of Equal Respect," *Journal of Chinese Philosophy*, vol. 11 (1984), pp. 165–83.

36. See Benjamin Schwartz, *The World of Thought in Ancient China* (Cambridge, MA: Harvard University Press. 1985), p. 142. I respond in Hansen, *A Daoist Theory of Chinese Thought*, op. cit., pp. 132–3. I doubt that Mohists were egoists – either psychological or ethical. I do, however, think that they were moral reformers who thought that we collectively can reflect on how to change our moral *dao*.

37. Even this, notice, assumes the cultural dominance of Confucianism is a product of its natural appeal as opposed to political imposition of an orthodox morality as a condition of employment. If we have reason to suspect the latter, then the prominence of communitarian attitudes in China will be utterly irrelevant.

38. See for example, Bell, "The East Asian Challenge to Human Rights," op. cit.

39. See Philip Pettit, *The Common Mind: An Essay on Psychology, Society and Politics* (Oxford: Oxford University Press, 1993), and John Dewey, *Freedom and Culture* (New York: Capricorn Books, 1939), p. 6.

II

SELF AND SELF-CULTIVATION

5

Tradition and Community in the Formation of Character and Self

Joel J. Kupperman

Call the world if you Please "The vale of Soul-making." ... There may be intelligences or sparks of the divinity in millions – but they are not Souls till they acquire identities, till each one is personally itself.

John Keats (1970, pp. 249–50), from a letter to his brother and sister-in-law in Kentucky, 1819

This chapter will explore the role of tradition and community in the process in which a human being becomes "personally itself." The argument will be (1) that tradition and community are constitutive as well as causal factors, so that they will contribute to elements of the soul or self that is formed, (2) that how they do this has a great deal to do with the excellence of the result, and (3) that Confucius gives an exceptionally good account of this in the stages corresponding to advanced education.

Our exploration will begin with the early stages and the development in childhood of the foundation of self. Then we will examine the development in teenage and early adult years, and how someone becomes a really good person. Finally, we need to pay some attention to general issues concerning the unity of the self and also creativity. To become personally oneself is an exceptionally important activity and, if done well, can be a creative achievement; we will need to examine the role of tradition and community in creativity generally.

I. THE DEVELOPMENT IN CHILDHOOD OF THE FOUNDATION OF SELF

Erik Erikson (1968, p. 160) has observed that "the community often underestimates to what extent a long intricate childhood history has

restricted a youth's further choice of identity change." Aristotle would
not have been surprised by this observation. The *Nicomachean Ethics* is
full of comments on the ethical importance of early upbringing and on
how it should be managed. The *Analects* in contrast has relatively little
that is explicitly on the subject. If we ask why this is so, when Confucius
has so much to say about the advanced stages of ethical development,
a variety of answers suggest themselves. One is that teachers and writers, including philosophers, often do not say what does not need to be
said: what it can be assumed that virtually everyone in the audience already knows. It simply may be that early upbringing had become more
problematic in Aristotle's Greece than it was in Confucius' China. Also,
Confucius himself functioned primarily as an educator, all the while in
search of other roles. His students were no longer small children when
they arrived, and it would be natural for him to have much more to say
about the stage of their ethical development in which he had a major role
than about much earlier stages. Finally, it is natural to regard early childhood ethical development as the province of the family. Confucius has a
great deal to say on the subject of family life and its importance. But this
is compatible with regarding some matters as best left to the judgment of
parents.

The broad outlines of what Confucius and his circle thought family
relations should be are evident, as are the social ramifications of proper
family structure. The *Analects* quotes Master Yu as saying, "Those who in
private life behave well towards their parents and elder brothers, in public
life seldom show a disposition to resist the authority of their superiors"
(Book I, 2, p. 83). Proper family attitudes are the trunk of goodness.

Aristotle is far more specific on early childhood training techniques.
"We ought to be brought up in a particular way from our very youth,
as Plato says, so as to delight in and to be pained by the things that we
ought" (Book II, 3, p. 1744). Our more mature delight and pain are the
result of childhood management (by parents and others) of pleasure and
pain, which in a rather Pavlovian manner establishes predispositions to
feel pleasure and pain at certain things or thoughts. This is central to
early childhood education. "In educating the young we steer them by the
rudders of pleasure and pain" (Book X, 1, p. 1852).

This is linked to an emphasis on habit as a factor in the foundation of
goodness. In much of our adult life we behave characteristically, expressing established predispositions. As Aristotle says (Book II, 4, p. 1745), we
become just by doing just acts and temperate by doing temperate ones.
Childhood patterning reinforced by pleasure and pain is crucial.

It would be tempting to regard the right set of habits as the core, and perhaps nearly the whole, of personal goodness. But Aristotle knew that this would be an exaggeration, for two reasons. One is that even someone who is a creature of habits can encounter major temptations, in which habit-violating actions promise great pleasure (or at least the thought of them is very pleasant). Even Pavlov's dogs might well break their training under such circumstances. One element of protection in Aristotle's view seems to be a habit of associating incontinent or antisocial behavior with pain, which can add a painful element to what would otherwise be pleasant thoughts of habit-violating behavior. Plainly this element can be supplied by persistent measures that make incontinent or antisocial behavior in early childhood come out to be, on balance, painful, thus creating a habit of painful thoughts to be associated with it. This is the most plausible explanation of what Aristotle has in mind by the "rudder of pain."

A second reason why habits, including habits of connecting painful thoughts with certain kinds of transgressions, can never be entirely protective is that they will have power chiefly when someone is faced with familiar options in familiar kinds of circumstance. Their power, conversely, will be limited when the choice is among alternatives that may not be readily classifiable (so that someone may not identify what he or she is about to do as a transgression), or when the agent is disoriented by unusual circumstances in which the choice is presented. Familiar modern examples are choices made during wartime, or after social upheavals, or by people who have moved into occupations whose rules are not clear. Various psychological experiments, the most famous of which are the ones initiated by Stanley Milgram, have shown that a majority of people (most of whom must be presumed to have been moderately decent in ordinary life) will do appalling things in circumstances so unusual that ordinary standards might seem not to apply, especially if someone who seems reliable suggests to them that what they are about to do is really quite normal (see Milgram 1974; also Haney et al. 1973). The desire to ingratiate oneself, to be agreeable, appears to play a part in these cases. Perhaps this kind of thing is part of what Confucius had in mind in his observation (Book XVII, 13, p. 213) that "The 'honest villager' spoils true virtue"? To be reliably good in familiar everyday situations is not necessarily to be a genuinely good person.

Aristotle certainly would have been familiar with Plato's thought experiment in the Myth of Er of Book X of the *Republic* (St. 619, p. 877). Er is reported to have had a near-death experience in which he saw the spirits of the dead, in the underworld, choosing new lives. One, who had completed a decent life in a well-regulated city, chose the life of a tyrant. Yielding to this glittering (and ruinous) temptation might seem inexplicable; but Plato remarks of the man, "His virtue was a matter of habit only, and he had no philosophy." There is nothing to suggest that Aristotle differs from Plato on this issue. A good set of habits, including the habit of having painful thoughts on appropriate occasions, will constitute the foundation of personal goodness in Aristotle's view and will not constitute goodness itself. The habits are a prelude to philosophy and are required in order to hear the philosophy in the right spirit.

Aristotle's last word on the subject in the *Nicomachean Ethics* lays this out. "The soul of the student must first have been cultivated by means of habits for noble joy and noble hatred, like earth which is to nourish the seed. . . . The character, then must somehow be there already with a kinship to excellence" (Book X, 9, p. 1864). The phrase "kinship to excellence" is meant, I think, to do justice to the phenomenon of the very good child, who has not fully become a very good person, but who is clearly on her or his way and already has qualities that resemble those of a very good person.

How do we create such very good children? It is here that Aristotle deviates most sharply from what Confucius almost certainly would have said. He insists that what are required are right *laws*. Sparta is referred to as a place where they take these things seriously, rather than allowing (as in most states) each man to live "as he pleases, Cyclops-fashion, 'to his own wife and children dealing law'" (Book X, 9, pp. 1864–5).

It is well known that Confucius did not place emphasis on law as a contributory factor in social harmony or ethical development. He remarks (Book XII, 13, p. 167) that "I could try a civil suit as well as anyone. But better still to bring it about that there were no civil suits!" Criminal law similarly is marginalized. "Govern the people by regulations, keep order among them by chastisements, and they will flee from you, and lose all self-respect" (Book II, 3, p. 88).

Crime and wrongdoing have to be seen as (by and large?) symptomatic of social evils such as poverty. Ordinary people who are daring and are suffering from great poverty will not long be law-abiding (Book VIII, 10, p. 134). The ruler who wishes to create a law-abiding polity in which the people trust their rulers has a first priority of seeing that the people have enough to eat (Book XII, 7, p. 164; see also Book XII, 9; Book XIII, 9).

None of this should be read as a rejection of law or, for that matter, of legal punishments. "Where gentlemen think only of punishments, the commoners think only of exemptions" (Book IV, 11, p. 104). This certainly suggests that Confucius believes in applying the full force of the law on some occasions. It may be linked to Confucius' scorn (Book XV, 16, pp. 196–7) for those who are capable of spending a whole day together without ever once discussing questions of right and wrong, who "content themselves with performing petty acts of clemency."

A plausible interpretation of Confucius' position is that law should be, both socially and ethically, a seldom-used tool of last resort, and that in any society frequent and heavy-handed legal compulsion is a sign that the ruling group is either ineffective or full of corrupt desires (cf. Book XII, 18) or both. An analogy might be with a teacher's use of discipline in a schoolroom full of young children. It can be a sign of inexperienced or poor teaching if discipline is constantly accentuated; conversely, a skilled teacher who is like a pole-star (see Book II, 1) to the class will normally (i.e., barring unusually difficult conditions surrounding the classroom) have little need for this.

Thus there is every reason to think that Confucius would have been incredulous at Aristotle's suggestion that law should have an important role in the education of young children. A more fundamental difference is this. Confucius clearly regards as very important the role of the ruler as an attractive model of what a person should be, like the polestar (Book II, 1, p. 88). When the ruler of Lu suggests that he could kill those who do not have the Way in order to encourage those who do, Confucius immediately counters by emphasizing the way in which a ruler's goodness can modify the nature of the people (like wind over grass): "If you desire what is good, the people will at once be good" (Book XII, 19, p. 168). "If the ruler himself is upright, all will go well even though he does not give orders" (Book XIII, 6, p. 173). Conversely, we see Confucius' harsh diagnosis of the ruler of Lu's trouble with thieves: "If only you were free from desire, they would not steal even if you paid them to" (Book XII, 18, p. 167). The negative moral force of the ruler's greedy desires are part of the problem. To put Confucius' message in a contemporary framework: conspicuous greed among the upper orders creates an atmosphere of greed that encourages crime among those below.

The general analogy between rulers and parents can be taken as informative in both directions. Good parents, like good rulers, influence their charges by their moral force as role models. Confucius presumably would have regarded punishment in both domains as an undesirable last resort.

It is important not to assume that the contrast here is clearer than it is nor to oversimplify. I am not suggesting that Confucius would totally reject Aristotle's line of thought about the rudders of pleasure and pain. One should bear in mind that pleasure and pain can be conveyed even to young children in a variety of ways: silent reproach from someone who is loved can lead to a train of painful thoughts, and enthusiastic smiles can be wonderfully pleasurable. Thus there is no reason to associate habituation linked to pleasure and pain with only the least subtle (and often most counterproductive) measures that might be employed. The chief difference between Aristotle's and Confucius' moral psychology, as it pertains to young children, is I think the latter's emphasis on the educational use of role-modeling. It is plausible to say that, in Confucius' view, the greatest contribution parents can make to the ethical education of young children would be to make them want to become people of an ethically developed sort. Adult goodness, in this view, typically owes a great deal to imitation, as well as to habituation that may be reinforced by management of pleasure and pain.

Implicit in the Confucian model is that tradition and community values enter the lives of young children primarily through their parents. Community values do not by themselves constitute goodness; think of the "honest villager." But Confucius would certainly have regarded these rudiments of everyday virtue as a major approach to goodness. An unwillingness to engage in deceit, dishonesty, and violent behavior is, to say the least, required for goodness. It is arguable also that effective agency requires relationships within a community (see Wong 1988, pp. 327 ff.). Community values provide categories that structure one's experience of human actions (see Kovesi 1967). A sometimes derided function of parents is to convey to children how their actions might seem to others in the community. This can be seen as basic education in the categories of social life.

Beyond this, the lessons of community values can be refined in the development of reflective culture. We can acquire a more subtle sense of the varieties of harm that we should not inflict on others, avoiding actions that might not strike the honest villager as wrong. There also can be a growing awareness of connecting elements in what appears to most people to be a hodgepodge of recommendations (cf. "the one thread" in *Analects* Book IV, 15, p. 105; Book XV, 2, p. 193).

The role of parents in introducing traditions to young children is more complicated and also is often less conscious. Perhaps the rudiments of a culture are conveyed in the songs and stories that children learn. Clearly there are lessons in how to live, exemplified in the behavior of heroes and heroines of these stories, in comments on everyday occurrences, and of course in the ways in which parents themselves behave. A complication is that the sum of these messages will inform the child not only about cultural norms but also about cultural antinorms. One learns about the available repertoire of ways of being a bad (or merely not-so-good) person. Thus the child who is developing a self learns early that there is a limited menu of major options. These will add up to a very large number of possibilities, all the same, partly because it is always possible to combine features taken from more than one model of life, and mainly because of the possibility of idiosyncratic variation on a basic orientation. Furthermore, there can be unusual cases in which someone, strongly driven by a sense of vocation that is almost impossible to formulate, creates a not entirely coherent self that in major respects does not approximate any existing models. Thus it was possible to become a lonely, emotionally troubled genius in the European Middle Ages. But it became much more possible in the nineteenth century.

It is arguable that people's personalities usually are largely determined by the time they pass from childhood to adolescence. Some philosophers have thought this, most notably Jean-Paul Sartre, who believed that a basic choice of self in childhood structures a person's choices throughout her or his life, rendering people largely predictable (see Sartre 1943, pp. 453 ff.). The freedom that many people associate with Sartre's philosophy involves either subtle variations on what is dictated by the basic choice in childhood, or (more importantly) the ever-present possibility that one could reconsider that choice and adopt different patterns of behavior (something however that, in his view, is very difficult and may require psychoanalytic help).

Even if people's personalities usually are largely determined by adolescence, it may be that their characters are not. We may know, that is, that so-and-so at the age of fourteen or fifteen is very likely always to be outgoing, fond of physical activity, and casually friendly to all sorts of people without knowing whether he or she is very likely to be a good person. A certain temperament and style of interacting with other people, along with a way of pursuing one's projects and goals, can be compatible with great goodness and also with moral depravity. If we adhere to psychoanalytic models, whether Freudian or existential, it is easy to regard the formation of self as largely complete by the onset of adolescence. If, on the other hand, we think of virtue or its lack as a crucial element of self, it becomes clear that much remains to be decided.

II. BECOMING REALLY GOOD

One suggestion that Confucius, like Aristotle, thought of education in real goodness – as something that takes place against the background of a partly formed self – is the exchange between Tzu-kung and Confucius reported in Book I, 15 (p. 87) of the *Analects*. Tzu-kung begins with "Poor without cadging, rich without swagger," to which Confucius counters "Poor, yet delighting in the Way; rich, yet a student of ritual." Tzu-kung then picks up the theme, quoting the *Songs*: "As thing cut, as thing filed, / As thing chiselled, as thing polished." Confucius is delighted by the acuity this displays.

A number of Confucian themes are captured in this small space, and they are worth noting. First of all, the extreme allusiveness of the dialogue answers to a basic Confucian conception of what constitutes effective teaching. It must present only, as it were, a corner of the subject, leaving the student to complete the rest (cf. Book V, 8, p. 109; Book VII, 8, p. 124). Confucius never engages in the "spoon-feeding" that is characteristic of so much American undergraduate teaching. If the goal is to develop really good people, his teaching strategy makes a great deal of sense, in that it engages the student and forces the student to be active rather than passive. We have already seen that passive absorption of an ethics does not guarantee reliable goodness, and it is plausible that only someone who comes of herself or himself to certain conclusions is likely to internalize them properly.

Second, there is a wealth of meaning in Confucius' initial reply to Tzu-kung. "Poor, yet delighting in the Way" may remind us of Confucius' view that it is unreasonable to expect the poor very generally to be law-abiding in times of great poverty, especially when they receive poor examples from above. This view is a generalization about human nature under pressure to which there are implicit exceptions. (There is some parallel to Plato's presentation of the Myth of Gyges in Book II of the *Republic*: there it is suggested to the reader that people who find a ring of invisibility, and realize that with it they could do anything with impunity, could not be trusted, but the reader is meant to think that this would not be true of Socrates.) A truly good person of course would be law-abiding and would continue to delight in the Way, even in poverty.

"Rich, yet a student of ritual" reminds us that ritual may seem more important to those in dependent positions than to those who are wealthy and powerful. (One might think of the ways in which rudeness has sometimes been taken, in some societies, as an aristocratic privilege.) Ritual is never completely and finally mastered, particularly in that it includes implicit attitudes and messages conveyed by posture of the body, facial expressions, and by the timing of one's movements. The way in which such nuances can be important is conveyed by Confucius' comment (Book II, 8, p. 89) that demeanor, above and beyond specific actions, is crucial in the treatment of parents. Therefore a good person will remain a student of ritual.

This is consonant with Confucius' repeated insistence that he himself had much (in general) to learn from others (cf. Book VII, 3, p. 123; Book VII, 21, p. 127; Book IX, 7, p. 140). Perfection is never presented as a realizable goal. It is a hallmark of a gentleman that he "grieves at his own incapacities" (Book XIV, 32, p. 188).

It is important that the central message of Book I, 15, is conveyed by a quotation from the *Book of Songs*. That collection might seem to most modern readers to have a folk song–like quality and to be without any significant philosophical or ethical content. (This quality is brought out nicely in the translation by Arthur Waley, and in some ways even more so in the translation by Ezra Pound.) Yet the masters of allusiveness found much of ethical importance in this source. A good student might be expected to know the *Songs*, as Tzu-kung did, and to be able (quite rapidly) to cite the right text in relation to a line of thought. This element of cultural tradition, in short, was seen as a wellspring of ethical insight.

Finally, we have to take seriously what Tzu-kung saw in the song he quoted. It refers, as did the earlier sayings, to the ethical ideal. The process of becoming the best kind of person involves something akin to cutting, filing, chiselling, and polishing. (We might speak of fine-tuning, but the point is essentially the same.) What is required, in short, is nothing like a conversion experience or a drastic realignment of character. Rather it is a slow and subtle process of refinement, which can be viewed as a number of kinds of adjustment (like cutting, filing, etc.) rather than a single unified change. Refinement will work, of course, only if what is refined is already near to true goodness: there must be the right kind of partly formed self at the outset of this stage. The *Songs* and ritual both play a part in the creation of this proto-self, but that does not mean that they cannot also have a role in its further refinement.

There may be a natural progression. At one point Confucius says, "Let a man be first incited by the *Songs*, then given a firm footing by the study of ritual, and finally perfected by music" (Book VIII, 8, p. 134). One of the uses of the *Songs*, apart from their implicit messages, is to incite emotions (Book XVII, 9, p. 212). Ritual, on the other hand, comes after groundwork (Book III, 8, pp. 95–6).

What music does is more subtle. Good music can be delightful. But the quality of music also is ethically and politically important. Confucius, like Plato, thought it to be important to insist on the right sorts of music. He wanted to do away with the licentious tunes of Cheng (Book XV, 10, pp. 195–6), which presumably were like the Lydian and Ionian harmonies that Plato (*Republic*, Book III) thought so little of. It is important when Lu reforms its music (Book IX, 14, pp. 141–2).

We know that Confucius himself played the zithern (Book XVII, 20, p. 214), and that he made evident his enthusiasm for good music (cf. VII, 13, p. 125; VIII, 15, p. 135). All the same, music means "more than bells and drums" (Book XVII, 11, p. 212). It may be that Confucius' view of the power of good music is like the view of aesthetic goodness developed by I. A. Richards (1925; see also Richards 1932). This is that the mark of aesthetic goodness is a work's function in rendering the psychological system (especially the attitudes) of one who appreciates it more balanced and nuanced. We know that a view in some respects like this was taken seriously in Confucius' circle. The disciple Tzu-yu, given command of a small walled town, teaches music and promotes musical performances (Book XVII, 4, pp. 209–10). Confucius teases him about it, comparing it to using an ox-cleaver to kill a chicken, but has to admit that there is some reasonable basis for Tzu-yu's policy.

The refinement of goodness plays a central role in the ethics of the *Analects*. It is clear that it is a long, gradual process, one that (if Confucius' remarks about himself are taken at face value) may never be finished. The process is not stressful, but it does require effort.

Why would someone devote himself or herself to this? Clearly there is no single answer that fits all cases, and perhaps there rarely or never is a simple answer that fits any case. Normally people have mixed motives. Let me suggest though that a common motive grows out of a sense of the value of some kinds of lives. I have argued elsewhere (Kupperman 1999) that there is emotional awareness of value that in some cases amounts to knowledge. Someone can have a sense of value linked to changes in his or her life. There always is the possibility also of a strong sense of the value of a certain kind of life as part of one's experience of a person who embodies it. This must have been a major factor for Confucius' students.

We can appreciate best the roles of tradition and community in the Confucian process of refining goodness if we contrast Confucius' view of the transition from conventional goodness to real goodness with that of the *Nicomachean Ethics*. The two views are often considered to be similar, in that neither Aristotle nor Confucius (despite his references to the "one thread") regard the best choices as algorithms derivable from fundamental principles or standards. Nor does either place emphasis (as many Western philosophers including Kant have) on a motivation to follow certain familiar general rules as a key element in personal goodness. Further, the Confucian Doctrine of the Mean is similar in many respects to Aristotle's account of the mean. Nevertheless, there are important and interesting differences in the two accounts of what is required for genuine goodness.

Aristotle, as is well known, emphasizes judgment of particulars (cf. Book VI, 11, pp. 1805–6). Experience and maturity help to develop this ability. "Therefore we ought to attend to the undemonstrated sayings and opinions of experienced and older people or of people of practical wisdom not less than to demonstrations...experience has given them an eye they see aright" (p. 1806). We need to become good judges not only of particular cases (in areas of life that are not simply rule-governed) but also of our own characteristic failings and distortions of judgment. Aristotle recommends that, in attempting to reach a mean between excess and defect, we adjust our aim slightly further (than we might) away from the extreme to which we are predisposed, as a way of compensating for personal bias (Book II, 9, p. 1751).

The image is of continuing education in problem-solving. One's basic orientation was provided by the early stage of ethical education, which besides establishing good habits would have made one hate what should be hated, admire what should be admired, and so on. Advanced ethical education is seen as primarily intellectual. Aristotle shares this with Plato, one difference being of course the greater role for Plato of mathematics in this intellectual development (whereas for Aristotle sensitivity to particulars and to the ways in which they are connected assumes paramount importance). Clearly both Plato and Aristotle believe that a genuinely good person internalizes goodness in ways in which a conventionally good person does not, but this emerges as a natural result of superior intellectual development supervening on a sound basic orientation.

One way of beginning to see the contrast between Confucius and Aristotle is to establish a model of the situation in which one must make a decision. For Aristotle, there will be a range of alternatives, along with one's ability to discriminate among them and to be aware of one's own characteristic weaknesses of judgment. Perhaps friends have advised one about some of these. The important thing is to judge well. It may be unrealistic to think of an optimal solution, but one must choose well enough. Aristotle seems to be a believer in what recently has been termed satisficing.

In Confucius' model, there is more than one person playing this game, and more than one possible point of view on the outcomes. A gentleman (Book II, 14, p. 91) "can see a question from all sides without bias. The small man is biased and can see a question only from one side." To appreciate more than one point of view is typically to realize that there are pros and cons. Confucius looks at these (Book IX, 7, p. 140). What this suggests is more of a view of superior ethical judgment as (at least sometimes) a form of negotiation within human relationships than Aristotle provides. Even rulers must win over the people. Among the three evils described in Book III, 26, is "high office filled by men of narrow views." (The alternative translations "not tolerant" or "intolerant" support the same point, if one bears in mind that to be tolerant is to take account of and to accommodate other views.)

Training in ritual and in music can be conducive to not having narrow views, especially in that ritual and music often (although not always) involve performance by more than one person, such that one must relate one's actions and demeanor to those of others. Training in ritual and music is important in other ways. Once we stop thinking of ethical deliberation as necessarily a search for single optimally correct solutions, the role of nuances – especially the style with which something is done – can seem important. The right kind of training in ritual and music is training in style. It can lead to a harmonization of subtle gestures and of the attitudes that they express. Harmony (Book I, 12) is crucial in the practice of ritual. Solutions to ethical problems typically are performed as well as thought, and some harmonization of style with others (along with responsiveness of ethical judgment) is part of reasonable accommodation.

This is consistent with a belief in the "one thread" of the *Analects*, which, like *li*, should *not* be thought of like an ethical principle that serves as an algorithm for (or a precise test of) ethical solutions. A better analogy is with a theme, which in various contexts can be expressed in more or less good ways.

We are now in a position to see more clearly the contrast between Confucius and Aristotle as regards the advanced stage of development of self, and also to see how Confucius' emphasis on tradition and community is implicated in this contrast. Confucius and Aristotle share an assumption that advanced ethical education, in order to be effective, must take place against the background of an already somewhat developed good character. Ornament and substance, Confucius says (Book VI, 16, p. 119), must be duly blended. I have suggested that Confucius and Aristotle also share the view that ethical judgment often looks for good, rather than perfect or optimal, solutions.

Within this shared framework, Aristotle gives us a picture of the search for good solutions that is literally timeless. The Aristotelian would-be good person of course does (or should) have experience of how various policies work out and situations develop. But she or he will act in a way that is not portrayed as dependent upon, or stylistically tinctured by, the ways in which others have acted before. Neither will cultural accomplishments of the past, comparable to the *Book of Songs* (see *Analects* Book II, 21) or the *Book of Documents*, play a part in readying someone to behave as a very good person.

Tradition is, in Confucius' presentation of the development of a good self, not only a source of inspiration and advice but also (more importantly) a source of modeling. The right kind of parent–child relation, in his view, has this character. One develops a self that of course is separate but is not entirely separate: there will be elements reminiscent of parents, who in turn had developed selves that included elements reminiscent of their parents, and so on. Rituals and music have an authority that derives in part from the ways in which they encapsulate styles of behavior and of feeling from the past. In listening to the music, or in performing the music or the rituals, one enters into (to some degree) these styles and makes them part of oneself.

Community also assumes a prominent role in the Confucian presentation of the development of a good self. In the foreground of the picture are the ways in which choice occurs within the context of a variety of points of view, which should be taken account of and often should be to some degree reconciled. Confucian development of the self also is very much in the context of what David Hume (*Treatise*, Book 2, Part 2, Section 5, p. 365) called mirroring fellow minds. Other people's opinions of us need to be taken seriously. Even if they fail to appreciate whatever virtues we have, they still may have noticed something in us that requires work; or it may be that we need to work on the ways in which we communicate to others. Finally, goodness can infect a community. Moral force, Confucius says (Book IV, 25, p. 106), "never dwells in solitude; it will always bring neighbours." This is one of the reasons why it is goodness "that gives to a neighbourhood its beauty" (Book IV, 1, p. 102).

The themes of the ethical importance of tradition and community have not been entirely absent from Western philosophy. Alasdair MacIntyre is an example of a contemporary philosopher who takes both seriously and has interesting things to say about them. David Wong's argument that effective agency requires relationships within the community also has been mentioned. Less recently, both Hume and Hegel come to mind as philosophers who assigned great importance to community. I want to suggest, though, that Confucius is uniquely good in his articulation of a moral psychology that explores the role of both tradition and community in the advanced stages of development of a very good self. He also offers a model in which tradition and community are not merely causal contributors but also constitutive of the self that develops.

In Confucius' view, the self that a person develops (assuming that things go reasonably well) will be based on a primitive layer of imitation of parents (who had imitated their parents, etc.), as well as of behavior that had been encouraged by parents. Are these things merely causes of the person one becomes? It is hard to deny that they become, generally speaking, constitutive. Often, that is, an adult will be acting, thinking, and talking much as her or his parents did, or in a manner retained and refined from childhood. It may be too much to speak of survival of some lives in other lives, or of children in adults. But much like quotations within a text, the adult self will include elements taken from outside or taken from earlier stages. Something like this is true also of the borrowings from tradition (e.g., *The Book of Songs*) and from the community-based interactions involved in ritual.

The distinction here between what is constitutive and what is merely causal is neither sharp nor precise. Certainly it would be rare for an element in someone's character or psychic life to be exactly the same as one in a parent or a traditional source. But there can be a degree of resemblance comparable to that between elements of different stages of the same person's life, and if the degree is fairly high, we would be inclined to speak of more than a merely causal relation.

Clearly, if there are such strong connections, the quality of the sources matters a great deal. The child of thugs has much to overcome; although interesting forms of departure, yielding good results, are possible. We are not condemned to be thoroughly like our parents, and what is present at a primitive layer of self can become inverted in subsequent development. Nevertheless, it is – from a Confucian, and indeed from almost any point of view – a great advantage in life to have good parents. Similarly, rituals of cruelty and absorption of soft and sentimental music can be (in the Confucian view, and in many others) major handicaps in the development of self. Even if we are not immediately aware in every case of their roles in the selves that develop, we can see that there is a case for regarding the qualities of ritual and of music as ethically important.

Elements of recognition of this can be found in many philosophies, including Plato's. The citations thus far should make clear, though, that Confucius is exceptional in the detail and persistence of his comment on these factors in the development of self. This, plus the complexity and subtlety of what he has to say, constitutes one of the excellences of his philosophy.

III. THE UNITY OF THE SELF, AND CREATIVITY

The remainder of this chapter will discuss some general issues concerning the self and also the creativity that can be at work in the development of self. It might be raised as an objection, either to Confucius (as I have portrayed him) or to my own view, that to regard a self as typically constituted in part by elements derived from outside sources is both to undermine (or deny) the unity of the self and also to slight the creativity involved in becoming "personally oneself." I want to suggest that such objections would reflect widespread misunderstandings, both of the self and of what creativity is. I also wish to defend from a recent attack (Harman 1998–9) the claim that a self can develop a distinctive character.

Let us begin with the formation of self and explore a view that seems to me very plausible; it cannot be attributed to Confucius, but it does seem at least to be consistent with what he says. Call it the self-as-collage. It holds that typically an adult's self can be viewed as layers that represent the absorption (or sometimes, rejection) of various influences at various stages of life, going back to early childhood. Different layers of the self will be evident under different circumstances. How this happens depends very much on the individual. Some people, for example, are much more prone than others to be childlike in moments of relaxation or distress.

This is not to suggest that any of the layers of a person's self can be regarded as *merely* a contribution from an outside source (e.g., a childhood environment). For one thing, the degree of acceptance or rejection can vary. Also, more importantly, different people will absorb influences in different ways. Rarely or never will a source of self be, so to speak, absorbed whole without at least some subtle modification. The selectivity of being influenced, along with the stylistic contributions, ensure that even what is very imitative will have some degree of individuality. It will be generally impossible to disentangle a personal (possibly genetic) contribution from what is owing to outside sources. And then, of course, much of the process of being influenced is not all that imitative. People frequently "take off from" what they admire. Further, the modification of sources and of layers of the self is ongoing and never ended.

In the end, whether an interpretative model such as the self-as-collage succeeds or fails depends very much on the light that it sheds (or does not shed) on particular lives. My sense is that it functions well in relation to the lives with which I am best acquainted, including my own. To speak for myself: increasingly I am aware at some moments of patterns of thought and reactive behavior that are uncannily and uncomfortably like one or the other of my parents. At other moments I find myself thinking and acting in ways that can be identified with middle-class groups in the place where I grew up, Chicago, and with that time. In the midst of more subtle personal interactions, there is sometimes a sense of spirit possession by a style that can be associated with the college where I was a graduate student, and (again) with that time. No doubt there are many other elements in the collage. To mention one: it is often observed that one of the results of long and reasonably successful marriages is increased similarity in responses, so that two people can come to have much the same outward look. This might be classified within demeanor, but there is much psychology that goes with it.

On the surface, this model may seem to destroy all thought of the unity of self, and also not to leave room for character. This would be a mistaken response, for a number of reasons. First, the unity of self should not be thought of as like a single tune that is endlessly repeated throughout a life. Nor does character require that someone be predictable on any given occasion. Indeed, I have suggested elsewhere (Kupperman 1991, p. 15), that it can be part of someone's character that under some circumstances a style of behavior becomes not altogether unlikely. An example is a person who is capable of great cruelty: this does not imply that we can predict cruel behavior on any given occasion, but it does mean that it sometimes is much more likely for that person than for most people.

For almost everyone, there will be multiple themes, various concerns, and styles of thought and behavior that can vary drastically with context. This last is brought out effectively in Erving Goffman's classic *The Presentation of Self in Everyday Life*. What is recognizably the same person can be very different in different settings.

The question then becomes how well these themes, concerns, and styles of thought and behavior are integrated in a life. A highly unified life will have recurrent themes, stable major concerns, and recognizable links among styles of thought and behavior in various contexts. Other lives may have rapidly changing themes, diffuse concerns, and real discontinuities among styles of thought and behavior. In addition, behavior in some contexts may serve to undermine the purposes of behavior in other contexts. The two great nineteenth-century philosophers who are often labeled as "existentialist," Kierkegaard and Nietzsche, can be read as emphasizing the importance of having a unified self organized around a relatively small number of major projects (Nietzsche) or one central religious project (Kierkegaard). It may be that what they emphasized was already beginning to be increasingly problematic. Certainly as modern industrial and consumer society develops, it can be taken less for granted that the influences of early childhood will be similar to later sources of self, and more diffusion of attention and interest becomes likely. Further along, increased mobility and patterns of distraction (nicely captured in Don DeLillo's novel, *White Noise*) help to create the self of postmodernism.

The unity of self, in short, is a matter of degree; and it may be that a high degree of unity is (for many people) much more difficult to achieve than once would have been the case. There is no reason, though, why someone whose self is a collage of quite various elements cannot achieve a reasonable degree of unity, forging connecting links and imposing some degree of consistency on the layers of self. This has to be understood against the background of the limits of what it is possible to achieve, through acts of will, in the management of a self. "Probably for most of us," Jonathan Glover has observed, "self-creation is a matter of a fairly disorganized cluster of smaller aims: more like building a medieval town than a planned garden city" (Glover 1988, 135; see also Glover 1983; Meyers 1989). Even limited goals, also, are normally not achieved instantly – or even quickly – by acts of will; results, if any, will be very gradual and usually require some management of the circumstances in which one places oneself, as well as one's routines.

The reasons for believing that entire unity of self is more an idealized abstraction than a reality are relevant to Gilbert Harman's attack on the concept of character. The attack centers on psychological evidence, principally that provided by the Milgram experiments, which shows that most people who might be presumed ordinarily to be decent can behave, in an unusual situation, in appalling ways. More generally, Harman appeals to the argument of the "situationist" school of social psychology that human behavior is heavily situation-dependent. From this Harman (1998–9, p. 316) concludes that it is highly doubtful that there are any "ordinary character traits of the sort people think there are." If there are no real character traits, this makes it doubtful also that Confucius' and

Aristotle's visions of the development of a self of high quality correspond to life in the real world.

There is room for confusion here, in that Harman's target sometimes seems to be the idea that anyone has what might normally be considered to be reliably *good* character. But the evidence he appeals to shows at most that there are fewer such people than might be commonly supposed, a conclusion with which Confucius (and also Plato and Aristotle) would concur. Situationist psychology also tells against any view of character that takes it to be something like a collection of constant pushes and pulls in life.

Does such a view fit the concept of character? It is true that, as David Wong observes, "we sometimes talk of character traits as if they were properties that 'stick' to us as we move from context to context. Yet," he goes on to say, "many of our traits must be described with implicit reference to situations that elicit or suppress the relevant behavior" (1988, p. 336). The last part of this characterizes a view that, it seems to me, is shared by most thoughtful people and is embedded in much of our discourse about character. It is far from clear that any of Harman's evidence counts against the claim that there are character traits (which, as Wong remarks, may be context-dependent) in this sense.

Indeed it is worth asking what *would* count as scientific evidence against the claim that people have character traits. One possibility is evidence that showed, for a representative range of situations, that by and large everyone behaves the same in the same situation. Even if one grants the situationist thesis that situations typically have a strong influence on behavior, the notion that everyone by and large behaves the same is on the face of it wildly implausible. Alternatively, the concept of character could be undermined by evidence that, for any A and B, if A and B behaved differently in situation X it was by and large the case that this difference would not be repeated in a significant number of situations like X. No doubt differences in behavior sometimes are not repeated: for one thing, people sometimes act out of character. But it again looks implausible to hold that the differences generally would not be repeated.

Hence nothing in Harman's attack poses any challenge to the concept of character, if this is understood properly. To have a character (or a strong character) does not imply that one is exactly the same at all moments of life. Arguably good character does imply that one is much the same when it really counts, and that one is reliable in important matters of the treatment of other people or the accomplishment of central projects. It is a separate issue whether good character requires a record of one hundred percent success in this. It may be that any plausible account of good character will set a standard less high than this, with much of course depending on the nature and severity of a person's lapses. The literature of moral learning and of repentance also suggests this. Milgram (1974) hoped that his experiment would lead to moral learning on the part of some of the participants.

Let us pursue the idea that good character (and, by implication, having a self that is of high quality) requires that one be much the same when it really counts. This amounts to an integration of self, at least in relation to important areas of choice. The account presented earlier in this essay suggests that at least two layers of self are especially involved in this. A relatively primitive early layer (or layers), which includes habits and attitudes toward others that are reasonably cooperative and "decent," along perhaps with habits of persevering toward personal goals, will play a role. But there will also be a more sophisticated layer, which includes the ability to make allowances for nuances and for unusual circumstances (especially in orienting onself toward a mean in making a difficult decision) as well as the ability to be skeptical of authority or of pressures to go along with others in order to be agreeable. These layers can be integrated in a style of life that is reasonably consistent where it counts. People who are not of the stature of Confucius or Socrates have been known to do it.

A self that is truly integrated in this way nowadays may seem like a creative achievement. Let us look at creativity, and at the insane (but alluring) idea that true creativity is *ex nihilo*. The only cure is to look at examples of people who actually are creative, and (even better) to listen to them. Igor Stravinsky has remarked that "The more art is controlled, limited, worked over, the more it is free." He insists that limits are required for creativity. "If everything is permissible to me, the best and the worst; if nothing offers me any resistance, then any effort is inconceivable, and I cannot use anything as a basis, and consequently every undertaking becomes futile" (Stravinsky 1970, p. 85).

This suggests that there is more than one way in which creative efforts, including those involved in self-creation, can use the surrounding culture and its traditions. These can be useful as starting points to draw upon and be inspired by (as Stravinsky used his Russian predecessors and selected early composers, such as Gesualdo and Pergolesi, whom he admired). But traditions can also be starting points against which one reacts, and which thus provide a kind of creative leverage. Tradition, in Stravinsky's view, is "entirely different from habit. . . . A real tradition is not the relic of a past that is irretrievably gone; it is a living force that animates and informs the present" (p. 75).

The point is not merely that creative things can be done with (and within) a tradition. It is also that it is impossible (or at least virtually impossible) to do creative things without a tradition. The creativity that is important in developing a self, to adapt Stravinsky's model, will always occur within a context (supplied by tradition and by the surrounding community), which will provide themes, the beginnings of elements of style, perhaps menus of options, and quite possibly loci of resistance. Despite the influences and all the other causal factors, there will be moments of (a degree of) self-creation, in which one accepts, shapes, modifies, or tries to reject elements of what one has begun to be.

The result will be to be "personally oneself." This is something that is often done in a haphazard and fairly thoughtless way, but it can be done intelligently and well. The central theme of this chapter is that Confucius offers an exceptionally rich moral psychology that offers guidelines on how to accomplish this.

Note

I wish to thank Kwong-loi Shun for some very helpful comments on a first version of this paper. A second version is included in my *Learning From Asian Philosophy* (Oxford: Oxford University Press, 1999), under the title "Tradition and Community in the Formation of Self." This version is expanded from that, principally in the final section, in order to take more account of general philosophical issues surrounding the development of self.

Bibliography

Aristotle, *Nicomachean Ethics* in *The Complete Works of Aristotle*, vol. 2, ed. Jonathan Barnes (Princeton, NJ: Princeton University Press, 4th C. B.C.E./ 1984).

Confucius, *The Analects*, trans. Arthur Waley (New York: Vintage Books, 6th C. B.C.E./ 1938).

Confucius, *Doctrine of the Mean (Chung-yung)* in *The Chinese Classics*, vol. 1, trans. James Legge (New York: Hurst, 3rd or 2nd C. B.C.E./1870).

Erikson, Erik, *Identity, Youth, and Crisis* (New York: Norton, 1968).

Glover, Jonathan, *Self-Creation. Proceedings of the British Academy* 59 (1983).

Glover, Jonathan, *I. The Philosophy and Psychology of Personal Identity.* (London: Allen Lane, 1988).

Goffman, Erving, *The Presentation of Self in Everyday Life* (New York: Doubleday Anchor, 1959).

Haney, Craig, Curtis Banks, and Philip Zimbardo, "Interpersonal Dynamics in a Simulated Prison," *International Journal of Criminology and Personology*, vol. I, (1973), pp. 69–97.

Harman, Gilbert, "Moral Psychology Meets Social Psychology," *Proceedings of the Aristotelian Society*, XCIX (1998–9), pp. 315–31.

Hume, David, *Treatise of Human Nature*, ed. L. A. Selby-Bigge, rev. P. H. Nidditch (Oxford: Clarendon Press, 1739/1978).

Keats, John, *Letters*, ed. Robert Gittings (London: Oxford University Press, 1970).

Kovesi, Julius, *Moral Notions* (London: Routledge and Kegan Paul, 1967).

Kupperman, Joel J., *Character* (New York: Oxford University Press, 1991).

Kupperman, Joel J., *Value. . . And What Follows* (New York: Oxford University Press, 1999).

Meyers, Diana T., *Self, Society, and Personal Choice* (New York: Columbia University Press, 1989).

Milgram, Stanley, *Obedience to Authority* (London, Tavistock, 1974).

Plato, *Republic*, in *Dialogues of Plato*, vol. 1, trans. B. Jowett (New York: Random House, 4th C. B.C.E./ 1937).

Richards, I. A., *Principles of Literary Criticism* (London: Kegan Paul, Trench, and Trubner, 1925).

Richards, I. A., *Mencius on the Mind* (London: Kegan Paul, Trench, and Trubner, 1932).

Sartre, Jean-Paul, *Being and Nothingness*, trans. Hazel Barnes (New York: Philosophical Library, 1943).

Stravinsky, Igor, *The Poetics of Music*, trans. A. Knodel and I. Dahl (Cambridge, MA: Harvard University Press, 1970).

Wong, David, "On Flourishing and Finding One's Identity in Community," *Midwest Studies in Philosophy*, vol. 13 (1988), pp. 324–41.

6

A Theory of Confucian Selfhood

Self-Cultivation and Free Will in Confucian Philosophy

Chung-ying Cheng

Confucius did not spell out the notion of self, inherent in his project of self-cultivation. This project is a self-motivated and self-oriented project of human personal moral development and moral amelioration. It is no doubt most important for the Confucian philosophy of society and state as well, because to Confucius and his followers a good society and a righteous government must start with and hence be founded on the moral perfection of the human person. Hence the question of how to conceive a human self for the purpose of meeting the needs of constructing a good society and a just government remains a core question for the Confucian enterprise. The purpose of this article is to introduce a theory of human self in which self-cultivation and moral self-development of the human person becomes not possible but necessary. In such a theory we are also able to meet the challenge of clarifying what constitutes a free will against the background of the Confucian–Mencian notion of human nature.

We shall start with our empirical observations on the two aspects of the human self, which we shall show correspond to the implicit two dimensions of meaning of the concept of the human self in common Chinese discourse. It is to be shown that this common Chinese notion of human self is embodied in the Confucian statements on cultivation of moral virtues of the human self. Specifically I wish to relate this notion of self to the underlying notions of human mind and human nature in the Confucian reference to human self. On this basis, we can see how self-cultivation is both possible and necessary and how a free will to good is essential for the moral development of the human person.

I. FROM TWO ASPECTS OF SELF TO HUMAN MIND
AND HUMAN NATURE

Self-cultivation (*xiuji* or *xiushen*)[1] in Confucianism implies a self-reflective understanding of the self. Whether self is or is not substance or essence having an independence of its own, it is always the center and source of doing things, moving one's own body, or making a choice in view of a goal or a vision. Not only this, the self has the ever reflective self-conscious capacity of rational thinking, which articulates itself in logical and moral reasoning and develops itself in terms of its interaction with world, culture, history, learning and knowledge. Given this developmental and interactive process, the human self could also be conceived to grow in regard to its capabilities and philosophical visions or value orientations. This dynamical and creative side of the notion of self must be recognized as reflecting the fact that the self is always engaged in time and world. We may call this side of the self the active side of the self or simply the active self. As the active self is engaged in activities in time and in consciousness of time, we may also call it the temporal self or time-engaged self.

But there is also another aspect of the self, namely the aspect of the self that gives the self the identical consciousness or consciousness of self-identity among all changes of the active self and thus can reflect on things in the world and its own temporal interactive engagements with the world from a seemingly time-transcendent point of view which is hidden and evasive and as if above the time. This is the self, which is often referred to as the subject-self: in this regard, the reflective self need not be considered as if above the world or above the time. For one could still think and reflect in time even though what one thinks and reflects upon need not be governed by a temporal sequence.[2] We call this self transcendent because it transcends the active self and its activities in order to reflect on itself. Its transcendence depends on what it transcends and would not have an independent content apart from what is objectively given in the transcended. I say this because it is possible for what is transcended to function as the "transcendental condition" for the transcendent; therefore, we need not to posit or reify the transcendent aspect of the self as an independent entity.[3] In a similar way, we need not to posit a super-time or eternity out of time in order to think of time. We can still reflect on the super-time in time. Thus we could think that the transcendent self is still within a time structure that gives rise to both the self (as a dynamic process and structure of engagement and reflection) and the subject of the reflective self by reflection which is time-oriented.[4]

Here I wish to stress that there are two sides of the self, the temporal and the transcendent, the engaged and the reflective, but not two selves, because there is no reason why the transcendent aspect of the self must be objectified into an entity by itself. There is no positing of externality and consequent external transcendence. The intimate experience of reflection and reflection of reflection makes it apparent that the transcendent side of the self is as much an integral part of the self as the temporal one and thus forms two aspects of the same self.

Interestingly, these two aspects of the human self are reflected in the Chinese notion of self as *ziji*. It is also interesting to note that the Chinese notion of self as *ziji* is composed of the two characters *zi* (from) and *ji* (self) each of which respectively stands for a different aspect of self. But what is the difference between these two aspects as indicated by these two words? Based on common use and an etymological analysis,[5] it seems clear that the use of *zi* suggests that it stands for the active and initiating aspect of self or the self that can take action upon oneself, whereas the use of *ji* suggests that it stands for the reflective aspect of self or the self that is the result of the reflective action on the self. But one must point out that even though *zi* indicates source and origin of action, it at the same time embodies the ability to reflect or go back to itself. Hence there is also an aspect of reflection in *zi*. In the case of *ji*, apart from indicating the result of reflection, it can be seen as the subject of reflection and hence the reflective aspect of self. With this observation, it is clear that the meanings of the words *zi* and *ji* overlap insofar as self-reflection is concerned.[6] Here we may represent this composite notion of self as *zi-ji* as composed of this structure: origin → reflection / reflection → achievement or target *zi ji*.

This notion of self as *ziji* is precisely the underlying view of self that Confucian notion of self-cultivation (*xiuji*) implies and demands. In such a notion of self-cultivation, the self is that which engages itself with people and things in the world but which is also reflected upon for improvement and transformation from a reflective point of view that arises from the active self. Upon reflection, the self acquires an identity as well as a power for self-transformation. In such context, Confucius calls the self which is to be cultivated or self-cultivated in light of its own act of reflection the *ji*.

Apart from speaking of *ji* as both the object of cultivation and the subject of self-reflection, Confucius also speaks of *ji* as both an object and a subject of universal or general self-reference as we can see from such statements as "Don't make a friend of one who is not as worthy as oneself (ji)" or "If one (ji) wants to establish oneself, it should establish others; if one (ji) wants to perfect oneself, it should perfect others."[7] In such use of universal self-reference, there is no confining of the self to the immediate subject-self of the speaker because the self could creatively grow and change in accord with time by way of self-reflection. Now we may raise the question as to which aspect of the self is to actually carry out the acts of cultivation, befriending, establishing and perfecting. The subject of the creative or active self gives rise to the reflective act of ji: namely, in the functioning of ji, the active aspect of the self, which is indicated by the use of the word "zi", occurs.

Zi is the active aspect of the self that arises from and is accentuated by the self-reflection of the self, which makes possible the ji, the object of self-reflection. In this regard, we may see ji as the reflective object of the self, whereas zi becomes the reflective subject of the self, being at the same time the active source of change and transformation. Zi and ji are thus interdependently related and mutually defined. The engagement of self with things in the world is carried on by the active-reflective aspect (zi) of the self, whereas the identity of self would arise from this process of action and reflection of self, which is marked by the use of the term ji.

Thus when Confucius says: "Seeing unworthy people, one (zi) should reflect on internally (meaning reflect on the internal self (ji))" or "I have not yet seen one (zi) who, being capable of seeing one's errors, would criticize oneself (ji) internally",[8] the self that is capable of reflecting on oneself and criticizing oneself is the reflective self, which is the subject of self-reflection and self-criticism. Because its receding back as a subject can be regarded as transcending, the ji becomes the transcendent self. But this transcendent self is not posited as an independent object or entity by itself, as even indicated in the syncategorematic use of the term "zi": zi is simply a common indicator of direction and source as in the opening Confucian statement of the *Analects* "There are friends from (zi) far, is it a pleasure?" Hence we see no reason why the subject of the self must be posited an independent object apart from the substance of the self, namely the activities of the self as reflected in the temporal ji.[9]

The interesting thing to note about these two aspects of the self in the Confucian context and in the larger Chinese philosophical context is that the self is finally conceived to be composed of the two levels of zi and ji and hence called "$ziji$" as is commonly used in modern Chinese. The human self is hence a union and unity of the reflective-substantive ji and the initiative-reflective zi, hence the resulting notion of $ziji$.

That there is such a union and unity of the subject and the object of self, the transcendent and the temporal, is also a matter of philosophical understanding of the self, not only found in the *Analects* of Confucius but in the Confucian discourse of Mencius and Xunzi.

In the *Mencius*, we see the talk of *zifan* (self-reflection), *zide* (self-attainment), *zibao* (self-violation) and *ziqi* (self-abandonment), all referring to the self-reflective action of a given subject-self of a person whether first person, second person or third person. But when speaking of *zhengji* (straightening oneself) or *fan-qiu zhu-ji* (reverse to seek in oneself), Mencius apparently sees *ji* as an object of mental action. But in other uses of *ji*, there is no denial that *ji* is used as the subject of the first person such as in *ru ji tui er neizhi gou zhong* (as if I have pushed them into the trench). In the *Xunzi*, the same distinction of *zi* and *ji* also holds. *Zi* suggests an active role of the self in self-controlling (*zhizhi*) and self-enabling (*zhishi*), whereas *ji* suggests the achieved result of a self that is capable of being reflected on, acted on apart from being capable of acting as the subject of a first person. In sum, the *ji* is the substantive self in a state of self-awareness.

We may then suggest that the self as the union of *zi* and *ji*, the active and reflective, and for that matter, the self as the resultant formation of the continuous interaction between an active power of self and the receptive power of self, represents at least a relationship of the mind and the nature of a person insofar as we can identify the active power of thinking and willing of human mind with *zi*-self and the reflective-receptive power of human nature with the *ji*-self. Then we can see that the unity and union of self can be expressed on these two levels: the heart–mind (*xin*) and the nature (*xing*). The heart–mind reflects, thinks and feels and in this sense is the subject of the self, as subject of the self the heart–mind can make correct judgments of right and wrong and choose to pursue the good, but it is equally capable of committing mistakes and being overwhelmed by desires and passions and obscured by prejudices. When the heart–mind chooses good, it is guided by something it sees and feels. When the heart–mind pursues good in action, it does so by engaging the human self with people and things in the world, and it will become reflective and receptive in light of the receptive potentiality and sustaining power of the *ji*. In a process of interaction between action and reflection of the human self, which are functions of mind, we come to realize the nature of a human person. In this initial self-reflection and action of the human mind or human self, it may be said that the human self discovers its ability to initiate action as well as its capacity to reflect on itself and to learn from others.

Now with the composite notion of the self as *ziji*, we should not see *ziji* as representing a dichotomy or bifurcation of the self. Instead, we should see how the self dynamically transforms itself in terms of the mutual conditioning and transformation of *zi* and *ji*. This interaction of *ziji* leads a person to act out correctly and respond correctly in terms of knowledge and values. The human self is capable of taking lessons and improving or developing and growing toward self-fulfillment because it is active in pursuing the good and receptive in terms of absorbing experience for change. It is therefore self-transformative with internal power for initiative judgment and action in light of its incessant self-reflection. In this sense, the active *zi* and the reflective *ji* coalesce to form and become a new self or a new *ziji*.

That the *ziji* is capable of doing this is suggested by the Confucian notions of human mind (*xin*) and human nature (*xing*) as knowable and realizable in a person. Without going into the details of the rise of the notion of *xin* and *xing* in the Confucian classics, I wish to maintain that *xin* is a concept that connotes the open self, which can play double roles of creativity and receptivity and can change and transform into the subject and substance of self so that it can fulfill its potentiality as suggested by the concept of *xing*, consists in being the deepest unity and harmony with heaven.[10]

Confucius does not speak of nature as such nor does he speak very much of mind as such. But his speaking of *ji* as an object of cultivation indicates that he has hinted at a potential or virtual notion of nature, and his speaking of *zi* indicates that he has developed a cognitive awareness of mind or heart–mind and a conscientious awareness of its valuative creativity, for the terms "self-introspection" (*zisheng*) and "self-criticism" (*zisong*) or "self-insulting" (*ziru*) and "severe self-remanding" (*zihou*) in the *Analects* are not just a matter of thinking or reflection but a matter of feeling. On this foundation of a theory of self, we could then speak of the self-cultivation as a characteristic view of the Confucian enterprise, and the Confucian insight into self-cultivation is then an insight into mind and nature of the human person, without which no one could properly and really understand the Confucian view of self-cultivation and the consequent development of this theory in Mencius in terms of his reflections of nature and mind and his doctrine of the dialectical deepening of "fulfillment of heart–mind" (*jingxin*) into "knowing the moral nature" (*zhixing*) and then of the latter into "knowing the heaven" (*zhitian*).

As to the nature of the unity and union of the *zi* and *ji*, as would be disclosed or revealed in our understanding of *xin* and *xing*, I wish to underscore the internal link between the two aspects that makes them not only inseparable but also mutually dependent and mutually defining just as in the case of *xin* and *xing*. In the first place, the *ji* is manifested in the body (*shen*) of a person at the most basic level. The body of a person is the part of the person that presents the appearance of a person and carries out the action of a person. It is the immediate presentation of a person to other persons and a medium for direct interaction with other people. In a broad sense, it is furthermore the physical symbol of a person to which intention, responsibility and other meanings can be attributed. Like the linguistic symbols that generate meanings in contexts of discourses, the body as a physical symbol of the person can generate meanings in terms of its activities and actions. Therefore how one moves one's body or expresses oneself via one's body is an important matter commanding serious attention because it has import for aesthetics, morality and politics and thus forms the essence of the formation of the *li* (social rituals). Thus in this sense, the human body is the whole of human person or the human self and therefore the self-cultivation as *xiuji* is also spoken as *xiushen* (cultivation of the body). In the *Analects*, even the term *xiushen* is not used, the talk of "reflection on my *shen*", "rectifying one's *shen*", "not insulting one's *shen*", and so on, provides a sufficient context for understanding the broad significance of the *shen* and what cultivation of one's *shen* could mean, which forms an important part of the self-cultivation of a person. "To reflect on my *shen* three times a day" is not to reflect on my body as such but to reflect on the person with regard to its intentions and actual behaviors. In this sense of the body, body is not only the basic manifestation of the person but also the full and ultimate expression of the moral fulfillment of the person. It is in this sense that Confucius puts great stress on moral action (*xing*) and even considers *xing* as one of his essential teachings: letters (*wen*), moral action (*xing*), loyalty (*zhong*) and integrity (*xin*).[11]

Apart from the level of body, there are two more important levels of the manifestation of the human self in the Confucian thinking, namely the aforesaid mind and the nature of the human person. The idea of the Confucian mind or rather the idea of the Chinese mind is different from what is conjured in the Western Cartesian-oriented philosophical literature, for the Confucian mind is not simply a cognitive and rational entity or a state of consciousness or awareness of the subjectivity. It is all the purposeful activities of feeling, valuation, will and conscientious efforts directed toward a goal or value. In fact, the very core of cultivation of self or of the virtue in the self is a matter of efforts of the mind. Insofar as mind has all the functions of will, feeling and effort, it is heart–mind as I have used the term years ago. In terms of the two layers of the self as subject and the substance, it is the subject for the substance of the body. Relative to the body as the temporal aspect of the self, heart–mind is the transcendent aspect of the self and therefore plays an active and creative role in determining and directing the activities and actions of a person. In this sense, Confucius even speaks of "*congxin suoyu, erbu yuju*" (follow my heart–mind's wishes and yet not transgress against any moral standards),[12] implying clearly that the heart–mind is volitional and appetitional. But just as the active and reflective aspects of the self are intimately interlinked, so also mind and body are inseparable, interpenetrating and mutually defining.[13] They collectively refer to the selfhood of a person, and emerge as something to be experienced as the nature of a human person. Confucius did not speak of human nature (*xing*) as such, but when he mentions that all human persons have natures closely similar and says that the human person is born to be straight, he has made an observation regarding the natural source of the human self and revealed his own moral conviction on the nature of such natural source of human self.[14]

II. FROM HUMAN NATURE TO HUMAN WILL: FREE WILL MADE FREE BY NATURE

For Mencius, human nature (*xing*) has at least two layers or two levels of existence on the side of the temporal self: the bodily or physical nature and the nature of heart–mind in terms of feelings. But there is a sense of nature that Mencius identifies as the ability to recognize, to develop, that nature in the sense of insisting on doing the right thing. Here it is clear that Mencius has come to recognize something of the human self that has been briefly mentioned by Confucius: it is the will of the self called the *zhi*, that is a choice and decision the self makes in view or in recognition of an ideal value or a potential reality that can be achieved through one's efforts. Apart from meaning the actual choice made, "*zhi*" as the verb is the power of making choice and decision. Thus Confucius said that he has decided (*zhi*) to engage in learning at fifteen. When Confucius asked his disciples to describe their different pursuits (*zhi*), he also spoke of one's devoting himself (*zhi*) to the *dao*. He praised Peiyi and Xuqi as "capable of not yielding their wills (*zhi*), nor insulting their persons".[15] Zixia speaks of "learning widely and commit (*zhi*) yourself to a goal whole-heartedly".[16] From all these uses of the term, one can see how *zhi* is to be understood as an independent decision and choice or commitment one could make in one's mind (the word for *zhi* has a mind radical), which one may hold and persevere in spite of adverse circumstances. *Zhi* is furthermore a vision or a goal that can be projected into the future and pursued and actualized in time by one's efforts.

As a future goal or vision, *zhi* is a choice of value and a choice of a form of life that one comes to embrace and identify with as one's innermost own. In this sense, *zhi* is the self-conscious active power of decision making and choice making based on recognition of a goal and thus more than a common will but a will to value. Yet the meaning of *zhi* does imply and presuppose the notion of common will, for *zhi* is first and foremost an independent decision-making power that is absolutely free. Why so? Because it is conceivable that Confucius would not choose to devote himself to learning and instead make a different pursuit. Besides, there is nothing in the learning that would compel the choice of learning as the objective of pursuit. Similarly, it is not necessary that one must dedicate oneself to the *dao*, and there is nothing in the *dao* to compel the choice of *dao* as a goal of pursuit. In other words, one can devote (*zhi*) oneself to totally different matters, even contrary to inclinations of one's nature. This is not necessarily the result of what Aristotle calls the weakness of will (*akrasia*), rather it occurs because one could choose one's goal on a lower level of one's self such as physical desires without considering or reflecting on one's total self or a deeper/higher self.

If we look into the structure of the *xing*, it is also clear that one does not necessarily need to set one's mind on self-cultivation and that there is nothing in nature that would compel one's choice of following nature. However what makes nature nature is that *zhi* is part of nature for it is natural for one to make a choice of lifelong values or to make a commitment regarding one's pursuit. Insofar as there is nothing external to prejudice and to force a choice, it is natural to see *zhi* arising from nature even though *zhi* may not choose what nature represents.

Thus *zhi* is not a physical human desire, nor a mental wish, nor simply a recognition of a truth. It is nothing more and nothing less than an independent power of free choice that could choose a goal based on considerations, which could lead to the successful creation of a life-world. In this sense, *zhi* is the creative power of the nature directed to the possibilities of a future based on one's reflection or understanding of the self and directed toword the self in interaction and transactions with the world. In this explanation, we may even regard *zhi* as a rational will or will functionally as practical reason or the Aristotelian phronesis. It is not the pure will of Kantianism, which disallows incentives and abstracts rational will from concrete contexts of deliberations and processes of reflections except reflection on itself. But it is still a moral will if it chooses what *xing* inclines one to choose, and it certainly has the ability to make such a choice among other alternatives. For Mencius, *zhi* has acquired an even more outstanding position than in Confucius. This means that the structure of heart–mind and consequently the structure of nature has become more differentiated in the consciousness of the selfhood. As a decision-making power *zhi* becomes the center of one's personality in the following sense: *zhi* is not just one's conscious choice of a goal but a conscious choice in terms of which one comes to define oneself. Because one has a nature of morality (*ren* and *yi*), Mencius thinks that one should respect and follow a will (*shangzi*),[17] which no doubt is a will itself. But what action does Mencius intend for this will to take? Mencius replies: "It is (to respect and follow) *ren* and *yi*."[18] This is no doubt to make *zhi* a matter of conscious choice of morality or moral nature by the nature of morality or moral nature in a human person. This is to make *zhi* a matter of "will to the nature". However, does this imply that the nature will prejudice the *zhi* as will to follow the nature because it is part of the heart–mind, which is again part of the nature? The reply is: not necessarily. For the whole point of self-cultivation is to make the nature influential and will-like, namely to make the will naturally choose the nature. For without the force of self-cultivation, it is not necessary that the will must choose according to *xing* and morality.

This is specially the case in light of what Mencius has to say regarding the natural effect of "falling and drowning (*xianni*) of one's heart–mind". He says: "In the time of rich harvest, more young people are prone to laziness; in the time of poor harvest, more young people are prone to violence. It is not that heaven has given different talents to people, it is because people's minds are fallen and drowned thereby."[19] Mencius even mentioned the difference of trees due to difference in the soil. Hence it is not necessary that one's *zhi* will follow the *xing* nor will it follow the times. In neither of the times or one's *xing* will the will find an absolute choice. Just as times and *xing* do not wield absolute influence on the will, will does not have absolute influence on either times or nature. However, for Mencius, it is precisely because of the independence of the will that he thinks that one's *zhi* can withstand all trials and tribulations or hardships in order to shoulder more responsibility or to command more influence. Thus Mencius says:

> If heaven is to endow a large responsibility on a person, he would first make his heart–mind and his will (*zhi*) suffer, belabor his muscles and bones, impoverish his body and skin, weaken his whole person, cause events to create disorder on his activities. This is to move his heart–mind and make his nature patient (*dongxin renxing*), ever to increase what he is incapable of.[20]

This is said in a subjunctive mood by Mencius. The whole point of this passage is that one should regard all hardships and difficulties one encounters in pursuit of one's goal as purposeful trials of heaven so that one will see that the meaningfulness of one's *zhi* will increase rather than decrease because of these trials. This is particularly significant in light of the fact that for Mencius negative forces of circumstances could make a negative influence on the heart–mind and will of people. The more a person is able to withstand difficulties and hardships, the more one is able to prove the strength and independence of his will, and consequently the more he is proven to be worthy of large responsibility. This implies that independence and freedom of will is to be earned with effort, and the possibility of earning this is in the inherent power of freedom of the will to nature: for the will (*zhi*) has to make a decision at each moment or at each crisis of pressure whether from outside or from inside to uphold his vision and conviction, to reject temptation and diversions. He has to stand on his own will or the conviction that his will embodies. He could give a purposeful interpretation of the events so that he can view them as purposeful trials, but he need not to make such an interpretation.

In this regard, a worthy person facing his trials is like Job facing trials given to him by God according to the Old Testament of Christianity. Even though Job has initial faith in God, the misfortune that falls on him could provide an occasion or give him a reason to give up his faith in God. Yet he chooses to believe in God despite the severity of the bad things falling on him. He stood alone and could lose everything, but he would not lose his faith, which may be called a "will to faith". Similarly, in the case of the worthy man in *Mencius*, this worthy man could suffer a great deal and yet he would not change his original will and commitment because he has faith in the goodness of nature, and whether he succeeds or fails he will keep his faith in his nature. He could even interpret his will as rooted in a transcendent source that is none other than this own nature simply because he can choose to believe this or interpret this to retain his will.

He is thus set free from the world, and the strength of his will has made him free. This also means that the initial freedom of will to nature has created this will to freedom. Freedom is hence a force inherent in the nature of a person. It is the will to nature and the will to goodness (as nature embodies goodness).

In considering the trials of a worthy person, we cannot but also feel that the freedom and genuineness of a will is not unlike the truth of a scientific hypothesis put to testing: the more it can resist falsification, the more is it proven to be true. Needless to say, truth according to the Popperian principle of falsification is again a matter of earned independence like the freedom of will of a person.

With this freedom of will, it is clear that a person can make creditable choices. For Mencius, a worthy man of will of freedom is one who therefore cannot be bent by force, corrupted by wealth and position. It is a person who can choose death over life if life is found unworthy of living or if a value worthy of being preserved is in conflict with life and is found larger than life. This implies that there is a transcendent self who would see, judge and decide or choose.[21]

It is often thought that insofar as there is no transcendent belief in a transcendent God in Confucianism, the Confucianist could not have a self that exists independent of the empirical self, which is capable of only suffering social shame but is incapable of admitting guilt before a supreme law governing his empirical self. The Christian self can have guilt because he can face God and accept God's judgment. Besides, he can be moral because he can develop or rather have a surrogate transcendent self (called the rational soul or the rational will), as if made in the image of God, that would legislate universal and necessary law for his action to conform to if he is to be his true self. This is precisely the view of Kant, which is apparently formed in light of Christian theology and Newtonian physics.

In this view, the transcendent self is given by God, and its legislation of the universal law of action is an expression of the transcendent self's absolute freedom of will for the legislator has no higher will than the will that can legislate for universal law. For the self, which is regarded as the same self that legislates, to follow this law is an expression of freedom in necessity and the reason that gives rise to the law embodied in the will that carries out the order in action: the reason becomes thereby an instrument of will and at the same time the will becomes an instrument of reason, just as freedom becomes an instrument of necessity at the same time that the necessity becomes an instrument of freedom.

Does the Mencian or Confucian view of self and will fail to achieve freedom in this sense? No, it does not fail to achieve this Kantian sense of freedom because what it has achieved included this Kantian freedom and yet included something more than this Kantian freedom.

In the first place, even though a person is not conceived to be created by God in his image because there is no such God in Confucian metaphysics,[22] a person has nature (*xing*), which on reflection achieves self-consciousness of heart–mind, which rises upon the empirical self by reflection and becomes what is called a transcendent self, which is nevertheless not separable from the empirical self and, in fact, becomes the nature of the self that combines the immanence of the temporal and the transcendence of the transcendent. It is in the nature of *xing* that such a transcendence is possible. With this transcendence, we can see how independent judgment, evaluation, valuation, choice and decision can be made. Once made, it is immediately rooted in the nature of the human person and becomes a basis for action. The transcendent does not legislate like the reason or rational soul in Kant, but it does reveal and disclose what is deep in nature and make the nature the law because the law is already contained in nature (as we see what the *Doctrine of the Mean* has said). In fact, the transcendent self that arises from the nature can go back to nature as well, thus making practice of morality a matter of following the nature.

Because nature has the empirical side that engages life and because nature also gives rise to the life-world and is related to many tasks and relationships in life, the moral not only has a sanction owing to its transcendent freedom but also has a concrete relevance that is missing in the Kantian morality: the moral nature rather than the moral law contains its own conditions of applicability as a result of the preexisting unity of the transcendent and the empirical or temporal in the whole selfhood, which is none other than the nature of self. Lacking the concrete conditions of applications, Kant calls the performance of the moral law a matter of duty and for him all moral virtues must achieve quality of morality by becoming duties; hence, he uses the term "duties of virtues". On the other hand, the Confucian and Mencian virtues are derivations from human nature by reflection and independent understanding and decision making in the process of self-cultivation, which is none other than a process of free and independent choices of doing the right thing toward a goal consistent with one's nature. They are not simply duties, but they contain duties as necessary components, for virtues are self-enriching and self-fulfilling, and they transform the person from an imperfect state to a more perfect state (no such transformation is conceived in the Kant case).

Furthermore, life is more open to make virtue more applicable and more efficacious. In this sense, virtues are more germane to the nature of man and are more creative than duties; therefore, duties as parts of virtues are therefore to be regarded as "virtues of duties" so that they become more applicable and more meaningful as vehicles for the transformation of the state of human existence toward an ideal state. Hence we conclude that the Confucian theory of nature is different from the Kantian approach, even though in theory and in practice it comprises the spirit of the Kantian approach. Lawrence Kohlberg's theory of linear development of morality using Kant as an ideal form[23] is mistaken; it not only has not paid attention to the Confucian philosophy in totality or in detail and fails in understanding the spirit of Confucian morality but also fails in understanding the nature of morality in terms of its immanent and transcendent demands. His linear approach is too rigid, too narrow and too single-tracked to do justice to the Confucian tradition of moral philosophy.[24]

Specifically, Mencius has developed a theory of the human self in terms of the *qi* (vital force) and the human will in terms of its being the leader (*shuai*) of the *qi*. In addressing Gaozi's motto – "If one has not gained (something) from the speech, do not seek it from the mind; if one has not gained (something) from mind, do not seek it from the *qi*" – Mencius says: "If one has not gained (something) from mind, it is fine that one does not seek it from the *qi*. But if one has not gained (something) from mind, it is wrong that one does not seek it from one's mind. *Zhi* is the leader of *qi*. *Qi* is the filling of the body. It is the *zhi* which is supreme and *qi* which is secondary. Therefore it is said that 'Hold the *zhi* and do not give up the *qi*.'" On being questioned on why one should hold the *zhi* and not give up the *qi*, Mencius's reply is: "If *zhi* is one then it moves the *qi*, whereas if *qi* is one then it will move the *zi*. For example, if someone in the course of walking falls down, this is a matter of *qi*, but it will affect the mind in a reverse direction."[25]

What Mencius argues here has to be understood in light of the rooting of the *zhi* in the heart–mind and nature. It is in light of this rooting that *zhi* is stronger than *qi* and is hence regarded as the leader of the *qi*. The difference between what is called *qi* here and what is called *zhi* here is not that *zhi* cannot be a matter of *qi* (in fact, ontologically speaking, *zhi* is a matter of *qi* as far as the theory of universal *qi* is concerned), but that *qi* here pertains to the body alone whereas *zhi* pertains to mind and nature.

Mencius comes to his distinction in his reflection on the virtue of *bu dongxin* (nonmoving of heart–mind). Mencius reflects on his having this virtue in contrast with Gaozi's having this virtue. He uses the difference of two types of courage to illustrate this difference. There is the courage of sheer bravery, which he interprets or describes as a matter of keeping *qi* alone, and there is also the courage that reflects on one's own abilities. There is also a third type of courage, which is derived from faith on one's being on the right and which therefore depends on reflection on one's mind: this is a matter of keeping a principle of conviction (*souyue*) as exemplified in Zhengzi. In this case, one's courage reflects on one's determination of will.

In light of this difference, Mencius regards *zhi* as a matter of keeping a principle of conviction and explains this in reference to his contrast between the courage of *qi* and the courage of *zhi*. The *zhi* is stronger because it is derived from reflection on heart–mind and nature and in another sense can be said to arise from heart–mind and nature and as such does not pertain to the physical *qi*. One sees clearly a distinction being drawn between the transcendent self and the temporal self, the former being the heart–mind and nature in reflection and the later a matter of *qi*.

It is nevertheless stated by Mencius that *zhi* and *qi* are reciprocally influential, which suggests a unity existing between them. It is clear then that the *zhi* has the power of will of leading and directing the *qi*, although the *qi* in its unity and intensity could affect and even possibly change the *zhi*. The importance of strengthening the *zhi* becomes ever manifest in Mencius. His theory of nourishing the "great flood of *qi*" (*haoran zhiqi*) which is derived from between heaven and earth and which gives rise to righteousness in response to the righteousness of the heart–mind is not only significant as a cosmological theory but very critically meaningful for his understanding of the effort of self-cultivation as a way of achieving freedom of will and will of freedom, which wills nature and brings out the morality of nature.

Once we see heart–mind as an active subject, then in speaking of "fulfilling heart–mind" (*jingxin*), Mencius addresses the need of exercising all the functions of the heart-mind and thus assuming different roles of heart–mind as a subject. It is only when heart-mind can assume a role of supreme subject, which rises above different functions of heart-mind, that one can speak of actively realizing the different functions of the heart–mind: the *jing* involves evaluation and decision and the best employment of mental activities to the best purposes and thus also presupposes the full freedom of the will in making this evaluation and decision. At this point, *xing* provides both resources and standards by comparison for such evaluation and decision. Hence in fulfilling the functions of the mind, the subject comes to see the nature as an object and a ground for heart–mind: it is an object because the heart–mind can read and understand what it offers and presents in terms of the activities and possibilities that heart–mind engages with in dealing with the world. It is also a ground because the very energy and the justification of judgment and decision would come from the nature. Hence in fulfilling the subjectivity of mind, mind comes to recognize its own source as an object of understanding.

On the other hand, when one fulfills the nature and takes nature as the field of activities of the understanding and evaluation, then one would come to encounter the ultimate source of energy and meaning, and this no doubt should be the ontological grounding of heaven. Hence Mencius says that in knowing the nature (*zhixing*) one would come to know heaven (*zhitian*). Here we see a trilevel structure: the heart–mind to be preserved for active and independent decision making and choice making, the nature to be nourished for reference and resources exploration and the heaven as an ideal state of emulation and regard. Then the whole project of self-cultivation becomes a project of preserving the heart–mind, nourishing one's nature and emulating and understanding heaven so that one can deal with all possibilities of life and overcome any issue time and future may bring about. Thus Mencius says: "To live long or short is equally an exclusive thing, so one would cultivate oneself to encounter it in either way. This is the way of establishing one's destiny (*liming*)."[26] The whole project of self-cultivation then consists of preserving one's mind, nourishing one's nature, serving heaven and establishing destiny, all on the ground of the active role of heart–mind as a supreme subject that is not separable from the self as a structured process realized on the levels of body, heart–mind, nature, destiny and heaven.

III. UNITY OF HUMAN NATURE AND FREE WILL: SELF-DETERMINISM

In regard to the function of mind as the subject of the self, the will first appears as intention (*yi*), as we have seen. The idea of *yi* has received emphatic consideration in the works of the *Great Learning* and the *Doctrine of the Mean*. The basic proposition regarding *yi* is "to make *yi* sincere (*chengyi*)" in the *Great Learning*. For the *Doctrine of the Mean*, the central consideration is "*chengshen*" (to make oneself [*shen*] sincere), and from there to participate in the creative activities of heaven and earth. It is clear that there could exist a highly important thread of unity between the *Great Learning* and the *Doctrine of the Mean* apart from the obvious concern with the Confucian project of self-cultivation, namely the sincerity of will as the ultimate and originative source and ultimate ground in a person for achieving progressive levels of fulfillment of the human self, humanity and ontocosmological creativity. In this light, not only does *cheng* become a crucial creative act of the heart–mind and the person, but *yi* also becomes the free conscious presentation of the heart–mind on which *cheng* could reflect and substantiate into the basis for self-cultivational development and the making of a life-world. In this sense, we could see how *chengyi* is the basis for formation of *zhi* and how it also represents a grounding of the freedom of will in *zhi* in the ontocosmological sense. *Zhi* is not only the goal and direction one chooses but also the very choice or choosing of the goal and direction.

The *Great Learning* describes *chengyi* as "Don't deceive oneself." But what is "not deceiving oneself"? It is only when the self is able to verify and confirm its own intentions and wishes that we can say that the self does not deceive itself. Thus if one hates bad smell and likes good sight, he must be able to see that he does hate bad smell and does like good sight and that the smell he hates is bad and that the sight he likes is good. There should be no gap between the commanding self (the transcendent self) and the engaging self. If the engaging self is doing something that the transcendent self cannot confirm or verify, then there is self-deception. In this once again, we should remember that there is no requirement that this transcendent self is ontologically separable from the engaging self (perhaps we could speak here of a transcending self to stress its independence and autonomy), or that the two selves must be dichotomized as two. In fact, as I have made clear previously, there is the underlying nature that assures not only the dialectical unity of the two but also the dialectical relatedness of the two in the unity.

Perhaps, the best way to indicate this sameness of unity and relatedness and consequent difference is that nature can assume both roles so that it is both the freedom and the law, both the necessity and the transcendence beyond the necessary, both the autonomy and the heteronomy, both the verifier and the verified. In this sense, we may call the transcendent (transcending) self the inner self and the engaging self the outer self. Therefore, the authenticity of a person (or self) consists in the unity and unification of the inner and the outer selves, which are not ontologically separable in the first place because they are rooted in the nature (*xing*).

The *Doctrine of the Mean* states that "To accomplish oneself is a matter of *ren*; to accomplish things is a matter of *zhi*. (Both are) the inherent quality/virtue(s) of the nature. It is the way of unifying the outer and the inner. It is therefore the appropriateness of meeting/fitting the time." The engaging self can be conceived as the accomplishing of the self and therefore a matter of *ren*, whereas the transcending self can be conceived as the accomplishing of things when the engaging self is projected as a verifiable object, and therefore a matter of *zhi*.

To achieve authenticity of self, one has to achieve the well-directedness of *ren* in *zhi* and the well-situatedness of *zhi* in *ren*, and hence their mutual accord and substantiation. This is the way of "sincere-fy" or "authenticate", which "*cheng*" suggests is an act of the self in unity (the autonomy of heart–mind). In this way, self is achieved as a whole self but is not given as the mere self, and freedom of will in the self is achieved as freedom of self because the self, the will, and the freedom of the self and will are not given as such: what is given is nature of a person. It is through the self-making act of the nature that self could become self and will could become will and freedom of will could become freedom of will. We may say that *cheng* is self-individuation and self-creation by which the nature is created and individuated into the self, which is always capable of transcending and examining its engagements.[27] Thus the *Doctrine of the Mean* says:

> *Cheng* is self-accomplishment (or self-completion/*zicheng*). And *dao* is self-direction (and self-presentation or self-saying/*zidao*). In *cheng* (hence in self-accomplishment and self-presentation) there is the beginning and the end of things. If there is no *cheng*, there are no things. Hence the morally superior one considers it important to reach or fulfil the *cheng* (*chengzhi* or to fulfil the *dao*). In *cheng* it is not a matter of just accomplishing oneself, but to accomplish things thereby.[28]

If we interpret *cheng* as a self-creative and self-individuative principle, it seems clear that the beginning of things or self is the engaging self and the end of the self is the transcending self and that together they form the whole self, which is accomplished by the self-accomplishment of self in nature. On the whole, it is also clear that *cheng* is presentation and authentication of presentation of reality: it is the ultimate principle of self-creation of reality, which seeks self-consistency and completion. This refers to the whole ontocosmological philosophy of the *Zhong Yong* in which one can see that the key word is "fulfillment of nature" (*jinxing*). It is again from the nature as the source and motive of creativity that self and will and freedom of will are possible, and when the term "*cheng*" is to be applied, it can be applied on different levels: to *chengyi*, to *chengshen*, to *chengxin*, and so on, all of which can be regarded as ways and stages or levels of *jinxing*, which is the inner activation of the human creativity in accordance with and in continuation of the creativity of heaven and earth, the ontocosmological reality. This is why the Great Appendix of the *Yi Jing* says: "To accomplish is the nature (of things and thus the way), to continue to do so is goodness."

It is known that the first Jesuit to China Mateo Ricci has raised the question concerning the incompatibility of *xing* and free will in his criticism of neo-Confucian philosophy.[29] This is a serious issue not to be let by lightly. In answering this question, we must make the following observation.

In the first place, we must note that there is a difference between random action and free action: random action can be caused by any cause that is not known or not knowable by the given state of knowledge, but free action is caused by choice of a human person. But does choice imply freedom already, for choice must be free choice and not forced choice or choice dictated by a known cause? We can however formulate criteria of free choice so that we can use them to make a distinction between a free choice and forced choice. But this amounts to a free determination and definition of freedom which could be subject to the same or similar questioning of presupposition. This also means that one cannot offer an acceptable and tenable set of free-choice criteria without knowing what we intuitively know to be a free action and without offering in the first place a theory of integrating all such cases of free choice.

An operative requirement of free choice is that one would recognize the alternatives for the decision to be made, one would make a genuine decision as to what choice is to be made among those alternatives, one thus would recognize the reason for the choice as one's own and one would be responsible for what he has chosen. This also means that the self is the ultimate concept and that "to recognize as one's own" is the ultimate base for the realization of freedom. In the ultimate analysis, the concept of freedom is eventually identified with what is ultimately real, which is recognized and identified as the source and the subject of action. It is also in this sense that free will must be the source of creativity or creative power that one may or must call one's own. Apart from the source component of freedom, there is also the intelligence component of freedom; namely, free will or freedom involves a consideration of which alternative to choose among all alternatives. This is possible because we normally recognize that one sort of cause gives rise to many sorts of results, and that one sort of effects could be originated from many sorts of causes.

Besides, we also recognize that there could be distinctions between primary causes and secondary or even tertiary causes, and that there are conditions under which primary causes could become secondary causes and vice versa. With these considerations, a free will choice (free will/free choice) would involve an intelligent plan for adopting a certain recognition of a choice of alternatives to achieve an intended goal. In other words, a free choice presupposes perception of a goal and a relevant decision on a course of action for achieving or attaining the goal that may actually be attained or may not be thus attained.

In light of the argument made here, it is clear that there is no incompatibility between *xing* as the source of free will and also as a determining force that would be regarded as good and that however would still allow one's deviation from it. This is because the will of the heart–mind could see alternatives and could make choices. The most important thing is that *xing* as given by heaven is the ultimate reality to which one needs to be awakened to for one's own identity. This can be called "seek one's lost heart–mind". Does this make Mencius' theory of *xing* a kind of "soft determinism" that allows us to say that we make free choice in the absence of compulsion and ignorance, even though this choice may still be described by causation from beliefs and desires? But the soft determinist lacks the recognition of self-recognition or self-acknowledgment of one's own identity and the efforts to integrate oneself in a self-conscious and self-conscientious process of self-cultivation as we have shown in Confucianism.

In other words, soft determinism does not presuppose or lead to/require a theory of transformative selfhood. In this sense, the free will or free action could be as superficial as the notion of the self is superficial. In this sense, one can also avoid the problem of having artificially created willingness and desire for choosing things we normally would not choose. An intoxicated or drugged person could be said to do certain thing according to his choice, but he would know that he is not free and he would distinguish his intoxicated self from his real self. Similarly, to affirm one's true identity is a necessary although often implicit ground for one's freedom, and this is precisely the high point or benchmark of the free will in the Confucian theory of cultivation, which is therefore different from soft determinism.

It is in this sense of free will that an action can be said to be morally good and morally bad because it leads to a choice between what is morally good and what is morally bad. Because morality requires and presupposes such a free choice so that one can be morally responsible for one's choice, one must conclude that free will, which is nature consciously entertained, is the very foundation of morality in the Confucian theory of selfhood. In this sense, we may call the Confucian view on free will the "self-determinism of free will" in distinction from the "non–self determination of free will", which characterized the "soft determinism" as generally understood.

Notes

1. The term "*xiuji*" was used in the *Analects,* when Confucius says: "Cultivate oneself for/with reverence, cultivate oneself for/with bringing peace to others, cultivate oneself for/with bringing peace to the people" (*Analects* [or *Lunyu*], 14–42). Here one must beware of the ambiguity of the particle "*yi*". "*Yi*" (by means of, in virtue of, therewith) is instrumental as well as teleological. Hence we should interpret and understand this Confucian statement carefully. D. C. Lao's translation that "He cultivates himself and thereby achieves reverence. He cultivates himself and thereby brings peace and security to his fellow men. He cultivates himself and thereby brings peace and security to the people", though correct with regard to the sense of teleology of "*yi*", is deficient with regard to the sense of instrumentality of the "*yi*". Do we have independent content of the self-cultivation? If the independent content of self-cultivation is a fixed process, then we need not consider the instrumental aspect of cultivation in this quotation. The instrumental use of "*yi*" in the *Lunyu* is amply exemplified in such sentences as "*daozhi yi zheng, qizhi yi xing*", "*daozhi yi de, qizhi yi li*", which are respectively translated by D. C. Lau as "Guide them by edicts, and keep them in line with punishments", "Guide them by virtue and keep them in line with rituals." In this essay, all my quotations from *Analects* (*Lunyu*), *Mencius* (*Mengzi*), the *Doctrine of the Mean* (*Zhong Yong*) and the *Great Learning* (*Da Xue*) are from the Index Editions of the Confucian texts of the Harvard-Yenching Institute. But I have done the actual English translations from the Confucian texts.
2. For example, one could think in time on mathematical structures or logical analytical reasoning. In reflection, one could reorder different elements from a subject matter drawn from life and world. This is how theoretical and scientific thinking is possible.
3. With regard to Kant, we could think of experience as the transcendental condition for the rise of categories or as the source from which categories emerge by reflection. Since there is no absolute necessity that one set of categories must be uniquely relevant and explanatory, there could be many and alternative sets of categories for epistemological or scientific explanation. In fact, development of modern science has shown that discovery of new phenomenon and enlargement of experience, whether controlled experimentally or not, gives rise to new theoretical constructs or even revolutionary theoretical revolutions. Thomas Kuhn's discussion of logic of discovery and structures of scientific revolutions in paradigm shifts illustrates at length that there are no transcendental categories fixed for all in a transcendental

ego but instead that our empirical inquiry into reality and our reflection on our findings determine or give rise to laws and theories: laws and theories emerge from reflections on inquiries. As empirical inquiry is an open process so is the process of reflection. In this connection, I want to show that similar arguments can be given against Kant's model of moral reasoning. It seems clear that Kant reaches his notion of moral agent as a lawgiver and moral law as a categorical imperative as a result of modeling his transcendental ego as defining and dictating the categorical forms for the formation of knowledge. Similarly the formation of morality (or moral action) must be defined and determined in accordance with the moral law of the transcendental moral ego. But then if we could substitute an *Emergence Model* for the *Transcendence Model* of knowledge, we could analogically substitute an *Emergence Model* for the *Transcendence Model* of morality so that we could conceive morality as resulting from emergence of a right principle in our concrete grasp of a moral situation in light of all relevant facts of world and history. This is precisely how we could understand the Confucian philosophy of morality, and this is the point Mou Tsungshan wishes to convey in his construction of a moral metaphysics, which unfortunately he has failed to do.

4. Augustine says: "I know well enough what time is, provided nobody asks me to explain. But if I am asked what it is and try to explain, I am baffled." (See his *Confessions*, Book XI.) But in trying to identify time, Augustine comes to the conclusion that "Time is insofar as it tends not to be." The essence of time is its ability to absent itself. Similarly we could say that the subject of self consists in its ability to absent itself and is found only in reflection of the subject as object, and the reflective activity of the subject is a presentation or emergence based on the object as subject. The reflection defines the subject and gives it transcendence, but there is nothing else to be posited for the subject or its content.

5. In common use, *zi* means "from" whereas *ji* simply means oneself being referred to by whoever is speaking. Together *ziji* means "from oneself". When we know whichever person is identified as the speaker or subject of a sentence by a noun or a pronoun, *ziji* refers back to that person so identified. Hence we can speak of "myself" (*wo ziji*), "himself" (*ta ziji*), or "Wang himself" (*Wang ziji*). Hence *ziji* as a whole performs a reflective or self-reflexive function. But between *zi*, and *ji*, *zi* represents an action originating from the self as a source, whereas *ji* represents the source from which an action originates. Etymologically, in light of a careful inquiry into the oracle bone inscriptions, we can see that *zi* originates from the script symbolizing "nose". We also know that, according to early Chinese understanding, a human embryo shapes into a human form by first growing a nose. Hence the term *zi* embodies not only the meaning of the human self but the meaning of a natural development of a human being. On the other hand, *ji* has a more complicated etymological background in oracle bone inscriptions. It originates from the system of qualities for seasons and directions (so-called heavenly stems) in which *ji* (together with *wu*) stands for the earth as the center of a system of five powers. In this way, *ji* refers to the self as an inner and central position as opposed to an outer and peripheral position. It is obvious that one gains this metaphorical

insight because one can compare the inner with the outer, the central with the peripheral, from consideration or reflection on a whole system of locations. Even more important is the fact that one has to reflect on oneself as something located in the center of the world, hence comparable to the *ji* or *wu-ji* position in the five powers. To assign a reflective function to *ji* is no doubt warranted. As to the use of the composite term *ziji* to refer to self, it is obviously a modern term that does not appear in the Confucian classics and other classics. For the etymological explanations of *zi* and *ji*, please confer with Duan Yucai's *Shouwn Jiezi Shou* (Taipei: Culture Books Company, 1979), pp. 142, 769–70.

6. But for *zi*, the reflection on self is a matter of either originating or having source from self, whereas for *ji* the reflection on self is a matter of relating to a target, namely to what the self wishes to achieve.

7. See the *Analects*, 1–8, 6–30.

8. See *Analects*, 4–17, 5–27.

9. In *Lunyu*, we have a total count of nine cases of the use of *zi* as subject of self and a total count of twelve cases of the use of *zi* as source or direction. In both accounts, *zi* is used as a syncategoretic term that signifies no positing of an independent entity.

10. My purpose here is to show that the Confucian notion of the human self can be explained in relation to the notions of mind and nature of the human person on the one hand, and that the notions of mind and nature of the human person can be illuminated by the active and reflective powers of the human self as the term *zi-ji* connotes under a philosophical interpretation of *zi* and *ji* on the other hand.

11. See *Analects*, 7–25.

12. See ibid., 2–4.

13. As we shall see, the basis and the medium for the unity and mutual transformability of the mind and body is the nature understanding the person or the self.

14. See *Analects*, 7–12, 6–19. In this connection we can identify the active or empirical self as the "heart–mind–body" (*xin-shen*) of the person, and we can identify the transcendent or reflective self as the "heart–mind–nature" (*xin-xing*) of the person.

15. See *Analects*, 18–8.

16. Ibid., 19–6.

17. See *Mencius*, 7a–23.

18. Ibid.

19. See *Mencius*, 6a–7.

20. See *Mencius*, 6b–15.

21. For this one needs to read *Mencius*, 6a–10, on his discussion on the choice between fish and bear palm and the analogical choice between life and righteousness (*yi*). That a person could choose righteousness over life is because his will can desire and has desired righteousness more than life. Therefore, it chooses the latter over the former.

22. There are nevertheless the notion of Lord on High (*shangdi*) and the notion of the Heaven (*tian*) in the *Shangshu* (*Book of History*) and *Shijing* (*Book of*

Odes), which have been suggested to reflect a notion of God. But we must be aware that the Hebrew notion of Jehovah has transformed into the later and modern Christian notion of God, and that the pre-Confucian notions of *shangdi* and *tian* have also transformed into the Confucian notion of *ren* and the Mencian notion of *xing* or for that matter the Daoist notion of the *dao*.

23. See Lawrence Kohlberg, *Essays on Moral Development* (New York: Harper and Row, 1981). Carol Gilligan (in her *In a Different Voice: Psychological Theory and Women's Development* [Cambridge, MA: Harvard University Press, 1982]) and Nel Noddings (in her *Caring: A Feminine Approach to Ethics and Moral Education* [Berkeley: University of California Press, 1984]) have attempted to describe a different route of moral development, which is centered on caring rather on rational law. This approach is close to the Confucian doctrine of *ren* but lacks the metaphysical considerations and thus the metaphysical basis of moral virtues from the understanding of the human person.

24. In recent feminist literature, "care ethics" and "trust ethics" have been proposed as alternative models for moral development and moral understanding other than the rational ethics of Kant and the Kohlbergian development of the rational morality. Confer with Carol Gilligan's book *In a Different Voice* op. cit.

25. See *Mencius*, 2a–2.

26. See ibid., 7a–1.

27. In fact, one may consider that this creative individuation of the self is presented as first the creative individuation of nature into heart–mind and then second as the creative individuation of heart–mind into intention and will in the heart–mind, and finally we can see the freedom of will (hence that of mind and self) as a matter of creative individuation of will into freedom or individuative creation of freedom from the will.

28. See the *Doctrine of the Mean* (*Zhong Yong*), Section 25.

29. See his book *Tianzhu Shiyi* (*The Substantial Meanings of the Catholic Religion*) (English-Chinese version: St. Louis: St. Louis University Press, 1985), pp. 352–4.

7

The Virtue of Righteousness in Mencius

Bryan W. Van Norden

In not isolating a privileged conception of moral guilt, and in placing under a broader conception of shame the social and psychological structures that were near to what we call "guilt," the Greeks, once again, displayed realism, and truthfulness, and a beneficent neglect.

– Bernard Williams
Shame and Necessity

The shamefulness of being without a sense of shame is shameless indeed.

– Mencius

Of the four cardinal virtues of the Platonic and Thomistic traditions (wisdom, justice, courage, and moderation), only one corresponds, even approximately, to any of the four cardinal Mencian virtues (benevolence, righteousness, propriety, and wisdom).[1] Consequently, philosophers who study virtue should find Mencius a rich resource. Unfortunately, there are not many detailed published studies of the Mencian virtues. In this paper, I want to examine in some depth Mencius' understanding of the virtue of *yi*, conventionally translated as "righteousness." In Section I, I lay the background for my discussion of righteousness by outlining the Mencian view of self-cultivation and the virtues as a whole. In Section II, I examine how the virtue of righteousness is related to the key Mencian notion of "extension." In Section III, I discuss the relationship between righteousness and shame. Finally, in Section IV, I briefly discuss some of the philosophical problems raised by Mencian righteousness.

I. OUTLINE OF MENCIAN VIRTUES AND SELF-CULTIVATION

In *After Virtue*, Alasdair MacIntyre describes the pre-Enlightenment West-ern ethical scheme as one in which "there is a fundamental contrast between man-as-he-happens-to-be and man-as-he-could-be-if-he-realized-his-essential-nature.... The precepts which enjoin the various virtues and prohibit the vices which are their counterparts instruct us how to move from potentiality to act, how to realize our true nature and to reach our true end."[2] The language here is distinctively Aristotelian. Fur-thermore, there are immense differences in how an Aristotelian and a Mencian would fill out the details of this scheme.[3] However, the basic picture of there being a human potentiality that is expressed in and re-alized through following a certain way of life corresponds closely to the Mencian view.

As a Confucian, Mencius thinks that every human has the potential to become virtuous.[4] He also thinks, however, that most of us have not real-ized or actualized this potential. He uses several agricultural metaphors to describe this potential, one of the most striking of which is the metaphor of the four "sprouts."[5] The sprouts are incipient tendencies to act, feel, de-sire, perceive, and think in virtuous ways. Each sprout corresponds to one of Mencius' four cardinal virtues: *ren* (benevolence), *yi* (righteousness), *li* (propriety), and *zhi* (wisdom). Even in the uncultivated person, these sprouts are active. They manifest themselves, from time to time, in virtu-ous reactions to certain situations.[6] In one of the most famous passages in the *Mengzi*, our philosopher offers the following thought-experiment to illustrate the workings of the sprouts. "Suppose," Mencius says,

someone suddenly saw a child about to fall into a well: everyone in such a situation would have a feeling of alarm and compassion – not because one sought to get in good with the child's parents, not because one wanted fame among their neighbors and friends, and not because one would dislike the sound of the child's cries. (2A6)

This is a manifestation of the sprout of *ren*. It is apparently this same sprout that manifests itself in one's compassion for a suffering animal (1A7), one's service to (4A27) and love of (7A15) one's parents, and the disinterested concern of virtuous rulers for their subjects (1A7, 2A6, and passim). The translation of *ren* as "benevolence," though standard, is somewhat misleading, since we frequently think of benevolence as a virtue that, when fully developed, extends equally to each human being, while Mencius thinks that a fully virtuous person will have more concern for, and special ethical obligations to, those tied to her by kinship, friendship and certain social roles (3A5, 4B24, 7A45).

Mencius thinks the presence of the sprouts of benevolence, righteousness, wisdom, and propriety guarantees our capacity to become virtuous (6A6). He does *not* think, however, that humans are born with fully developed virtues. As Mencius' carefully chosen sprout metaphor suggests, humans innately have only incipient tendencies toward virtue. These incipient virtues frequently fail to manifest themselves in situations where they should. So we feel sorry for the stray puppy we see out in the rain, but ignore the humans searching for scraps in our dumpsters.[7] We do no tolerate a minor slight from the checkout clerk at the supermarket, but we eagerly kowtow to employers who buy our integrity from us.[8] Consequently, Mencius says that we must "extend" the manifestations of our sprouts, our innate but incipient virtuous reactions, from the paradigmatic cases where we already have them to relevantly similar cases where we should, but do not yet, have the reactions. As he goes on to say in 2A6:

> In general, having these four sprouts within oneself, if one knows to fill them all out, it will be like a fire starting up, a spring breaking through! If one can merely fill them out, they will be sufficient to care for all within the Four Seas. If one merely fails to fill them out, they will be insufficient to serve one's parents.

Mencian extension can be thought of as having two aspects, which we might label "cognitive extension" and "affective extension." Cognitive extension is coming to see the relevant similarity between situations in which one currently has appropriate ethical reactions. Affective extension is actually coming to have, and act on, the appropriate ethical desires, attitudes, and emotions. Extension raises many issues, some of which I discuss here in Section IV.C.[9]

II. RIGHTEOUSNESS AND EXTENSION

What is righteousness and how does it fit into this general framework? One early text gives a definition of *yi* that would probably be accepted by all Chinese thinkers: "*Yi* is what is appropriate (*yi*[b])" (*Zhongyong*, 20.5).[10] But this is only a "thin definition." Philosophers differ over what *is* appropriate, and how to determine it. Thus, the Mohists, defending a form of universalistic consequentialism, argued that what is righteous is what benefits everyone as a whole.[11] Mencius, in contrast, argues against using benefit or utility as a metric for choosing appropriate action (1A1, 6B4).

Just as 2A6 is especially illuminating of the sprout of benevolence, so I think that 6A10 offers special insight into the sprout of righteousness:

A basket of food and a bowl of soup – if one gets them then one will live; if one doesn't get them then one will die. But if they're given with contempt, then even a homeless person will not accept them. If they are trampled upon, then even a beggar won't take them. However, when it comes to a salary of ten thousand bushels of grain, then one doesn't notice propriety and righteousness and accepts them. What do ten thousand bushels add to me? Do I accept them for the sake of a beautiful mansion? . . . In the previous case, for the sake of one's own life one did not accept what was offered. In the current case, for the sake of a beautiful mansion one does it. . . . Is this indeed something that one can't stop doing? This is what is called losing one's fundamental heart.

Although the term "sprout" does not occur in this passage, it seems to be read most naturally as an illustration of the sprout of righteousness. Mencius makes the psychological claim that no human would allow himself to be disgraced, even if that were necessary for survival. If this is true, then it follows that all humans have the sprout of righteousness, since the disposition that drives us to avoid disgrace, even at the cost of our lives, is precisely this sprout. However, the psychological claim Mencius makes is implausible. We all know of cases of individuals who have humiliated themselves in all sorts of ways in order to survive. However, in order to demonstrate the existence of the sprout of righteousness, Mencius does not need to make such a strong claim. For the purposes of demonstrating that there is a sprout of righteousness, Mencius only needs one claim to be true: for every human there are some things that she avoids doing because she believes they are shameful.[12]

Mencius also wants to convince us in 6A10 of a further claim: there are things we do not currently regard as unrighteous, that we should regard as unrighteous, because they are similar in ethically relevant respects to things we do recognize as unrighteous. For example, we should be just as unwilling to sacrifice our dignity for a huge salary as we are for a handout.

That Mencius thinks we must extend our reaction in this sort of way is especially clear from 7B31:

People all have things that they will not bear. To extend this reaction to that which they will bear is benevolence. People all have things that they will not do. To extend this reaction to that which they will do is righteousness. If people can fill out the heart that does not desire to harm others, their benevolence will be inexhaustible. If people can fill out the heart that will not trespass,[13] their righteousness will be inexhaustible. If people can fill out the core reaction[14] of not accepting being addressed disrespectfully, there will be nowhere they go where they do not do what is righteous. If a scholar may not speak and speaks, this is flattering by speaking. If one should speak but does not speak, this is flattering by not speaking.[15] These are both in the category (*lei*) of trespassing.

Here Mencius clearly states that all humans have a disposition to avoid certain actions and resist certain kinds of treatment.[16] In addition, Mencius states that we become fully righteous by extending these reactions to other situations of the same kind (*lei*) where we do not yet have them. He illustrates this with a scenario that would be familiar to his audience in ancient China: should a scholar who is employed as a government official join with courtiers in flattering the ruler, or remain silent? Should he voice his objections to imprudent policies, or not? When extension is achieved, Mencius says, we will regard doing what is wrong in these cases the same as we now regard trespassing or accepting demeaning treatment.

III. RIGHTEOUSNESS AND SHAME

A. Shame

Mencius also connects each of the sprouts with an emotion or attitude that is characteristic of it (2A6, 6A6). Thus, benevolence is characterized by compassion, wisdom by approval and disapproval, propriety by either respect (6A6) or deference (2A6), and righteousness by *xiu wu*. This binome is rendered "shame and dislike" (by Legge), "shame and repugnance" (by Giles), "shame and disgrace" (by Dobson), simply "shame" (by Lau), and (surprisingly) "conscience" (by Hinton).[17] Obviously, one issue we will have to decide is whether *xiu wu* refers to one reaction or two. In addition, while each of these translations connects the sprout with "shame," no one has yet presented a detailed textual argument that *xiu wu* (or any other classical Chinese terms) correspond to the Western "shame vocabulary." I shall argue that none of the preceding translations are really accurate; however, the first four are correct in seeing some connection between *xiu wu* and shame. In order to show this, I shall first review some of the major Western discussions of shame. Then I shall examine how "*xiu*," "*wu*," and related terms are used by Mencius and some other early Chinese thinkers. We have reason to believe that we have successfully identified the ancient Chinese "shame vocabulary" to the extent that the use of the Chinese terms corresponds to the use of Western shame terms. For example, do Chinese writers use *xiu* (and related terms) to describe attitudes or reactions that we would expect (given our knowledge of the cultural context and our best use of "sympathetic imagination") to be attitudes and reactions connected with shame as we understand it?

Before turning to this task, it will be useful to make some preliminary observations and terminological distinctions. Let "shame" refer to an emotion of a certain sort. Now, there is an immense literature in recent philosophy on the nature of emotions, which I cannot summarize here.[18] Consequently, I shall assume the following without argument. Emotional reactions can be either "rational" or "irrational" (or "warranted"/"unwarranted," or "justified"/"unjustified"), in at least two ways. For example, my fear of flying in airplanes is irrational (unwarranted, unjustified) in two ways: both because I *believe* that flying is not particularly dangerous, and because my belief on this topic is itself *warranted*. On the other hand, if a teenager believes that it is shameful that he was not chosen for an athletic team, then we should say (I submit) that his feeling of shame is not *objectively* warranted because he is mistaken in thinking that such a thing is shameful. However, his feeling of shame is *subjectively* warranted because (unlike my fear of flying in airplanes) he holds beliefs that would warrant his feelings (if those beliefs were themselves justified). Furthermore, I assume that, because of these interesting connections between emotions and the beliefs that warrant them, the best methodology in trying to understand particular emotions is to begin with cases in which emotions are warranted (at least subjectively).

Mencius' discussion of "extension" shows that he thinks emotions can be, in some sense, warranted even in cases in which a particular person does not feel those emotions. We shall see (Section IV.C) that Mencius also thinks some emotions that a person *does* feel can be unwarranted. We shall also discover that Confucius and the later Confucian Xunzi agree with both these judgments.

Continuing with matters of terminology, let "shamefulness" or "disgracefulness" refer to the property of an action or a situation such that a properly perceptive person who performed that action or was in that situation would feel shame, and let "a sense of shame" refer to a disposition of a certain sort. Let us further distinguish between a "sense of shame" in a narrower and broader sense. In a narrower sense, "a sense of shame" is a disposition to feel shame in situations that one recognizes are shameful for oneself or for those with whom one identifies.[19] In a broader sense, "a sense of shame" is a disposition to recognize when actions or situations are shameful (whether for oneself or for others, and whether past, present, future, or hypothetical), and to have appropriate emotional and behavioral reaction to this recognition.

Finally, it is common, in recent Western discussions, to understand shame contrastively with guilt. There are various ways of cashing out this distinction. One of the most helpful, in my view, is to distinguish the emotions in terms of their focuses. As Bernard Williams puts it:

> *What I have done* points in one direction towards what has happened to others, in another direction to what I am. Guilt looks primarily in the first direction.... Shame looks to what I am.[20]

Furthermore, the two emotions are distinguished by what reactions they anticipate in others:

> What arouses guilt in an agent is an act or omission of a sort that typically elicits from other people anger, resentment, or indignation.... What arouses shame, on the other hand, is something that typically elicits from others contempt or derision or avoidance.[21]

This paper focuses on shame, for the simple reason that (as I hope to show) Confucian accounts focus on it. It is an interesting question, to which we shall return in Section IV.B, what ethical significance this emphasis has and to what extent it is illuminating to think of ancient China as a "shame culture."

B. Western Discussions of Shame

In his most detailed discussion of shame in the *Nicomachean Ethics* (Book 4, Chapter 9), Aristotle seems uncharacteristically confused, conflating the emotion of shame with a sense of shame, and failing to distinguish between shame in the narrower and broader senses.[22] (Indeed, I submit that Mencius and other early Confucians are actually much clearer about the nature and significance of shame and related concepts than are Aristotle and many other Western philosophers.) Aristotle begins by stating that "Shame is not properly regarded as a virtue, since it would seem to be more like a feeling than like a state [of character]."[23] He adds that "we think it right for young people to be prone to shame, since they ... often go astray, but are restrained by shame.... No one, by contrast, would praise an older person for readiness to feel disgrace, since we think it wrong for him to do any action that causes a feeling of disgrace."[24] Aristotle is correct to point out that it is simply a category mistake to identify the *emotion* of shame as a virtue. In addition, he is correct to claim that it is not, in general, a good thing to feel shame, since it implies that one has done (or at least *believes* that one has done) something disgraceful. (The exception to this claim is children, who frequently do what is wrong, but learn from their shame.) But what about a sense of shame?

This is a disposition, so it *is* the right category of thing to be a virtue. Furthermore, Aristotle's remarks elsewhere in the *Nicomachean Ethics* suggest that he recognizes an important role for a sense of shame in a flourishing life. Specifically he condemns "shamelessness" (1115a14) and connects recognizing and avoiding the shameful with virtue (1179b11–13). Surprisingly, however, Aristotle goes on to deny that a sense of shame is a virtue:

> Further, if someone is in a state that would make him feel disgrace if he were to do a disgraceful action, and because of this thinks he is decent, that is absurd. For shame is concerned with what is voluntary, and the decent person will never willingly do base actions. Shame might, however, be decent on an assumption; for if [the decent person] were to do [these disgraceful actions], he would feel disgrace; but this does not apply to the virtues.[25]

This is not altogether clear. However, I suspect Aristotle's point is the following. It is true that the virtuous person has a disposition, such that, were she to do something disgraceful, she would feel shame. However, there are conceptual problems with identifying this disposition as a virtue. First, the virtuous person, qua virtuous person, will not do what is shameful, and so will have no occasion for exercising this disposition. Second, the exercise of virtues is constitutive of human flourishing, but the exercise of a disposition to feel shame is decidedly not constitutive of human flourishing. Hence, it seems that this disposition cannot be a virtue. Aristotle's points are well taken, but we should add the following qualifications. While it is true that virtuous people do not, qua virtuous people, do what is shameful, no real humans are perfect. Real humans will have opportunities to exercise the disposition to feel shame. Furthermore, Aristotle seems to have restricted his discussion in this passage to a sense of shame in a narrow sense. As some of the passages I referred to earlier suggest, Aristotle's view in the *Nicomachean Ethics* as a whole seems to require that he recognize a sense of shame in a broad sense as a virtue.

Patricia Greenspan has made some remarks that might help to explain why Aristotle seems to deemphasize shame in comparison with Mencius:

> Aristotle's dismissal of shame in virtuous adults underlines the uncompromising quality of his conception of virtue. The list of virtues derived from Aristotle is not really well-designed, one might say, to advise an agent *in media res*, as opposed to an educator or someone else who is in a position to plan lives from the outset or to judge them as a whole.[26]

In contrast, in the *Mengzi*, we find our philosopher typically advising far-from-perfect adults *in media res*.

Aristotle also presents a detailed account of what we might call "the phenomenology of shame" in the *Rhetoric* (Book II, Chapter 6). He says there that "we feel shame at such bad things as we think are disgraceful to ourselves or to those we care for. These evils are, in the first place, those due to moral badness."[27] As examples of moral badness, Aristotle lists cowardice, licentiousness, greed, meanness, flattery, and boastfulness. Of special interest to us for our comparison to Mencius is the fact that Aristotle puts particular stress on examples of obtaining profit via shameful means:

... making profit in petty or disgraceful ways, or out of helpless persons, e.g. the poor, or the dead ...

... borrowing when it will seem like begging; begging when it will seem like asking the return of a favor; asking such a return when it will seem like begging; praising a man *in order that* it may seem like begging; and going on begging in spite of failure....[28]

Aristotle's examples here are very similar to the examples of shameful begging in *Mengzi* – 6A10 (discussed in Section II) and 4B33 (in which a wife and concubine cry in shame about their husband, whom they discover has been begging for meat and wine – considered luxury items – at funerals).

In addition to ethical badness, Aristotle notes that we feel shame at "lacking a share in the honourable things shared by every one else, or by all or nearly all who are like ourselves." Finally, we are "ashamed of having done to us ... acts that involve us in dishonour and reproach ..., e.g. when we submit to outrage."[29]

Aristotle also raises a thorny issue that continues to dog discussion of shame, although his own view on this topic is unclear. Specifically, does one feel shame only about what others observe and regard as shameful? Or can we also feel shame about what is done in private, or what others do not regard as shameful? Aristotle stresses the social context of shame, noting that "the people before whom we feel shame are those whose opinion of us matters to us,"[30] and that "no one feels shame before small children or animals." However, he also makes in passing a distinction between being ashamed of "genuine faults," as opposed to being ashamed of "conventional ones."[31]

Perhaps the most influential recent account of shame is John Rawls's discussion in *A Theory of Justice* (§67). Rawls characterizes "shame as the feeling that someone has when he experiences an injury to his self-respect or suffers a blow to his self-esteem."[32] One has self-respect to the extent to which two conditions are met: (1) one has a "secure conviction that his conception of his good, his plan of life, is worth carrying out," and (2) one has "confidence in one's ability, so far as it is within one's power, to fulfill one's intentions." Furthermore, Rawls makes what are apparently empirical psychological claims about "the circumstances that support . . . the sense of our own worth." First, humans tend to find value in activities when they have a rational plan of life, and in particular one that satisfies the "Aristotelian Principle."[33] Rawls gives a detailed and subtle discussion of what it is to have a rational plan of life. Briefly, a rational plan of life is a plan, amongst those consistent with certain principles of rational choice, that the agent would choose "with full deliberative rationality, that is, with full awareness of the relevant facts and after a careful consideration of the consequences."[34] As for "the Aristotelian Principle," Rawls explains that

> The intuitive idea here is that human beings take more pleasure in doing something as they become more proficient at it, and of two activities they do equally well, they prefer the one calling on a larger repertoire of more intricate and subtle discriminations.[35]

Second, "unless our endeavors are appreciated by our associates it is impossible for us to maintain the conviction that they are worthwhile."[36]

Rawls's account of shame has been critiqued from a variety of perspectives. Martha Nussbaum has objected to the subjectivism of Rawls's account. Consider, Nussbaum says, an assembly-line worker for General Motors:

> All day long he performs a single repetitive task. The things he helps to make are not under his control. And yet he feels good. He is proud to be part of the bustling capitalist economy; he may even be convinced that the capability to perform simple repetitive tasks is the only capability he possesses, that he could not handle a larger demand. Does his inner sense of worth count as genuine self-respect?[37]

It is important to stress that what is shameful about the life of such a worker is not that it involves physical (as opposed to intellectual) labor. A good foreman will exercise political virtues, a good carpenter will be creative, a small-business owner must be prudent, and so on. However, Nussbaum suggests that, while the worker she describes meets the Rawlsian criteria for self-respect, his way of life is shamefully narrow – not because it requires physical labor, but because it is limited to labor that is uncreative, unchallenging, and not subject to his control. Such a worker may not feel shame, but he ought to.

Now, as Nussbaum recognizes, Rawls's theory *does* have the resources to say something about this case. Rawls says that, owing to the Aristotelian Principle, humans will not tend to find worthwhile simple, rote, monotonous activities. But it is not at all clear that the Aristotelian Principle is true for all, or even most, humans. Rawls "may seriously underrate our capacity for low contentment."[38] What should we say about the self-respect of people of whom the Aristotelian Principle is not true? Rawls himself gives us a suitable example and makes clear that he accepts the consequences of his subjectivism about plans of life:

imagine someone whose only pleasure is to count blades of grass in various geometrically shaped areas such as park squares and well-trimmed lawns. He is otherwise intelligent and actually possesses unusual skills, since he manages to survive by solving difficult mathematical problems for a fee. The definition of the good forces us to admit that the good for this man is indeed counting blades of grass.[39]

Once again, many would object that Rawls's grass-counter's life is shameful and lacks self-respect, whatever his subjective judgment of his own life.

Interestingly, Mencius might disagree with both Rawls and Nussbaum here. As we have seen, Mencius' account of shame is not subjectivistic; hence, it is closer to Nussbaum's in this respect. However, Nussbaum is in the Aristotelian tradition, which has tended to minimize the importance of the family and to emphasize the exercise of virtues in theoretical and political contexts. In contrast, Confucians place great emphasis on the importance and value of participation in the family. For example, Mencius relates the story (5A1) of future Sage King Shun, who, although he was offered riches, beautiful wives, and power by the current monarch, was still unhappy – because his parents did not love him. Thus, Mencius might suggest that the worker Nussbaum describes need not feel shame so long as he is a good husband, father, son, and whatever other familial roles he occupies.

For all her disagreements with Rawls, Nussbaum nonetheless agrees with him in linking shame and self-respect.[40] John Deigh, in contrast, challenges Rawls on this point. He adduces examples to suggest that one can suffer an injury to one's Rawlsian self-respect without feeling shame, and (conversely) can feel shame without suffering injury to one's Rawlsian self-respect. As an example of the former, Deigh asks us to consider a high school tennis star who comes to believe (on the basis of the best evidence then available to him) that he has the potential to become a successful professional player and adopts this as one of his goals in life. However,

> when this young player enters his first state tournament, he quickly discovers that his skills are below those of the top seeded players. His first defeat need not be humiliating, just convincing. And though he will surely lose some self-esteem, we need not suppose that he feels any shame.[41]

Though such stable and well-adjusted teenagers may be rare, finding them is not impossible. However, one wonders if such a teenager could avoid shame without having other sources of self-esteem in his life (e.g., his belief that, whether he was a star tennis player or not, he was a good son, or a loyal friend, or a pious Muslim, etc.).

Perhaps more telling against Rawls are Deigh's scenarios in which humans might feel shame, even though their self-respect (as characterized by Rawls) had not been injured. For example, we often feel shame over a gaucherie, faux pas, or anything that makes us appear ridiculous to others.[42] These examples suggest that

> shame is often more, when it is not exclusively, a response to the evident deprecatory opinion others have of one than an emotion aroused upon judgement that one's aims are shoddy or that one is deficient in talent or ability necessary to achieve them.[43]

As an alternative to the Rawlsian analysis, Deigh suggests that "we should conceive shame, not as a reaction to a loss, but as a reaction to a threat, specifically, the threat of demeaning treatment one would invite in giving the appearance of someone of lesser worth."[44] This characterization is equally problematic, however, for (as Mencius recognizes) one can (and often should) feel shame about things that others do not regard as shameful. But if others do not regard something as shameful, then there is no "threat of demeaning treatment" to which one can react. Consequently, I find Deigh's characterization of shame, like Rawls's, too subjectivistic, for Deigh does not distinguish between seeming shameful and being shameful.

This distinction is central to the treatment of shame offered by Arnold Isenberg. Although Isenberg acknowledges that we "feel ourselves disgraced by those qualities which evoke the contempt and aversion of others," nonetheless "we must allow for the existence of an autonomous conscience, for the fact that a man may feel himself disgraced by something that is unworthy in his own eyes and apart from any judgement but his own."[45] Isenberg also resurrects the issue (first brought to life by Aristotle) of "whether shame can serve any useful purpose." On the one hand, Isenberg admits that "to brood over our infirmities . . . is morbidity. Despondency is *weakness*; it reduces the power to act; it confirms us only in despondency, in loathing of self; it indicates no direction in which effort may move."[46] On the other hand,

we cannot reflect upon errors without exposing ourselves to the attack of shame. . . . Shame, then, is seen as a *price* we may have to pay for our weaknesses and the attempt to cope with them; and morbidity, or the tendency to linger in self-reproach, is the evidence of the failure of that attempt, of the inability to act.[47]

Despite the many virtues of his account, I submit that Isenberg's definition of shame is too broad, for he writes that shame "is the feeling that comes with consciousness of faults, weaknesses, disadvantages – that is, of qualities deemed undesirable."[48] But surely I need not be ashamed of every undesirable trait or disadvantage I have (e.g., a physical handicap)?[49]

The difficulties in adequately defining shame might lead us to agree with John Kekes that shame

is not amenable to a precise definition. It shades into embarrassment, humiliation, chagrin, guilt, dishonor, regret, remorse, prudishness, disgrace, etc. To attempt to list necessary and sufficient conditions for shame is arbitrarily to simplify a naturally complex experience.[50]

While eschewing a general definition of shame, Kekes gives an analysis of a particular type of shame that he thinks has a particular relevance to moral progress. This type of shame

is a self-conscious detached comparison yielding the conclusion that we are in some way deficient, because we have fallen short of some standard we regard as important; and . . . we feel the importance of the standard we violated, because our conception of a good life requires that we should have lived up to it.[51]

Kekes suggests that this type of shame can be subdivided, depending upon the nature of the standards that have been violated to occasion the shame. For example, "if all standards are or ought to be internalized public ones," then we have "honor-shame."[52] In contrast, "worth-shame" is connected with the violation of standards that are "private" or "personal," in the sense that they may differ from public standards.[53] Finally, Kekes makes two evaluative claims. First, he says that the "movement of individuals from liability . . . to honor-shame, to worth-shame is one kind of moral progress."[54] More controversially, Kekes suggests that it would also be indicative of moral progress if individuals and cultures were to move "away from all forms of shame toward other responses to moral failure."[55] Kekes begins by pointing out that

shame is not the only possible reaction to our violation of moral commitments. Anger at ourselves, resolution to improve, the desire to make amends, a quest for understanding why we did what we regarded as wrong are some others.[56]

Furthermore, shame itself "weakens moral agents and it leaves a residue which adds a burden to the deficiency with which they already have to contend."[57]

What do we make of Kekes's denigration of shame? Our first reaction might be to suggest that it is psychologically impossible for humans to not feel shame in response to their failure to live up to personal ideals they regard as essential components of a good life. Surprisingly, Kekes admits this very point: "If we have self-respect and know that we have failed morally, shame will come to us." But while the feeling of shame may be inevitable in certain circumstances, "we can refuse to concentrate on the feeling, relegate it into the background, and deliberately hold some other object in the focus of our attention." Specifically, this alternative object of our attention "should be our conception of a good life."[58] At this point, it is difficult to know what is at issue. If Kekes's point is that an excessive and debilitating concern with one's own failings is vicious, it is hard to image who would disagree with him. Isenberg, for example, explicitly criticizes "morbidity." Furthermore, given the immense human capacity for self-deception, one wonders whether a determined effort to ignore feelings of shame will not often lead to ignorance of the reasons for the shame as well. As the Jim Bakkers of the world demonstrate, one can easily focus one's attention on a conception of the good life, and ignore the extent to which one fails to live up to that ideal, with disastrous consequences. Consequently, it seems that, as long as we have ideals of character that we hope to live up to, we will have a capacity to feel shame.[59] And, as long as we do not lapse into morbidity, this capacity will serve a crucial ethical function.

What have we learned from this brief survey of the Western literature on shame? Despite all their disagreements, I submit that there are really only two paradigmatic kinds of shame. The various views only differ regarding which paradigm they stress, and how they flesh out some of the details of the paradigm. I shall adopt the terms "conventional shame" and "ethical shame" to distinguish the two paradigms.[60] At one extreme, conventional shame is a sort of unpleasant feeling we have when we believe those whose views matter to us look down on us (or on those with whom we identify), on the basis of a standard of appearance we share. Let us examine some of the consequences of this definition. First, "those whose views matter to us" is not limited to people we like or admire. We can be ashamed, in this sense, before our "enemies." Notice also that this kind of shame is dependent upon what our standards of appearance are. Belching in public may be cause for shame in one culture but not in another. You may think less of me because my clothes are inexpensive, but this will not cause me shame if I do not share your standards of appearance.[61] Feelings of conventional shame may be criticized as inappropriate or unwarranted in several ways: others do not look down on us, the opinions of those who look down on us do not matter, we should not identify with those others who look down on us, we should not share the standard of appearance that makes others look down on us. For example, in trying to relieve our friend's shame, we say things like, "Nobody cares about your accent except you," "Who cares what he thinks? He's a jerk," "It's your husband who made a fool of himself at the party, not you," "I don't care whether they thought it was tacky. I think it's very tasteful."

Ethical shame, in contrast, is a sort of unpleasant feeling we have when we believe that we (or those with whom we identify) have significant character flaws. It seems that we can also have ethical shame about our actions (or the actions of those with whom we identify). This is true, but I submit that we are ashamed of our actions because of what we think they reveal about our character. Feelings of ethical shame, like feelings of conventional shame, can be criticized as inappropriate or unwarranted because we are identifying with someone with whom we ought not to identify: "It was your brother who got arrested for shoplifting, not you." However, it is *not* relevant to ethical shame whether others are aware of our character flaws, or whether they look down on us because of them, or whether their opinions matter to us.[62] It *is* relevant to ethical shame whether our character is really flawed. Thus, we may tell our friends, "You shouldn't be ashamed for something that happened twenty years ago. You're a different person now," or "Don't be so Victorian! There's nothing wrong with those kinds of feelings."

Deigh's is the closest to an account of pure conventional shame. Nussbaum's is the closest to pure ethical shame. Aristotle, Rawls, and Isenberg offer hybrid accounts with elements of both conventional and ethical shame. Kekes's distinction between honor-shame and worth-shame is the closest to my own. Using the distinctions I drew in

Section III.A, we can further distinguish between conventional *shameful-ness* and ethical *shamefulness*, and between a conventional and an ethical *sense of shame*.

Let's look at some concrete example. (1) Susan is angry at herself for being cross with her husband in the morning. But, Susan reasons, she was rushed and irritable about all the papers she had to grade. Her momentary irascibility doesn't reflect any stable character flaw. She resolves to apologize when she gets home and put the matter behind her. In this case, Susan feels no shame, and justly so. (2) On her way to work, Susan's hair is blown up by the wind, so that it is sticking straight up when she gives her morning lecture. When Susan sees herself in the mirror after the lecture, she experiences conventional shame. (3) Susan has an extra-marital affair. She and her husband have a happy, successful marriage, they do not have an open relationship, and Susan would be hurt and resentful if she found out her husband had had an affair. Now, what would it reveal about Susan's character if (regardless of whether the affair was discovered) she did *not* have feelings of ethical shame about what she had done? Is it even *intelligible* to suggest that she recognizes a serious discrepancy between the kind of person she thinks she should be and the kind of person she has discovered she is, yet she feels no shame?

Is it just homonymy that we call both conventional and ethical shame "shame"? I think there is a deep connection between the two emotions. The connection exists because, as Aristotle and Mencius long ago emphasized, humans are social animals. Humans are social, not only because humans enjoy interacting with other humans but also because interacting with other humans is necessary to help us correctly exercise our theoretical and practical reason. Part of being a good theoretician (be it economist, physicist, or professor of English) is being responsive to the opinions of one's colleagues. A researcher who is completely indifferent to the praise and criticisms of her colleagues is, ipso facto, a bad researcher. Likewise, part of being a good practical reasoner is being responsive to the opinions of the members of one's ethical community. One who is completely indifferent to the ethical opinions of others is a dangerous fanatic.[63]

I realize that not everyone will share this conception of theoretical and practical reason. In his *Discourse on Method*, Descartes presents a vivid and influential picture of the theoretical reasoner, "shut up alone in a stove-heated room," tracing out his thoughts without the distraction of other people.[64] This has its ethical counterpart in the hero of much modern literature, following his pure conscience in the face of the mob.[65] And certainly there are cases in which people ought to stick to their theoretical and practical commitments in the face of even extreme criticism and opposition. But just as an inability to innovate or challenge others shows an unhealthy lack of pride, so does unresponsiveness to the opinions of others show the vice of hubris.

So ethical shame and conventional shame are closely related because caring about how one appears to others is required by the virtue of humility. I am not denying that it is conceptually possible for there to be creatures subject to ethical shame but not conventional shame. But I do not think humans are that kind of creature. I submit that it is not psychologically possible for humans to have the kind of humility that allows us to learn from others, yet not be liable to conventional shame.

C. Xiu, Wu, *and Related Terms*

I noted in Section III.A that Mencius describes *xiu wu* as the mental state characteristic of the virtue of *yi*. Attributing particular emotions to individuals far removed from us culturally and historically is always an uncertain matter. However, when we look at how *xiu*, *wu*, and related terms are used by Mencius and some other early Chinese philosophers, we shall find that they are used to describe attitudes toward situations in which we would judge that conventional or ethical shame would be appropriate. This provides good prima facie evidence that these terms are related to the Western conceptions of shame. Based on this identification, I shall argue that the sprout of *yi* is an ethical sense of shame in a broad sense. Let us now look at the usage of what I claim are the Chinese shame terms.

Zhu Xi is perhaps the first commentator to address the issue of the precise meaning of the binome *xiu wu*. He suggests that "*Xiu* is to be ashamed about (*chi*) what is not good in oneself. *Wu* is to hate what is not good in others."[66] However, as Kwong-loi Shun has pointed out, this cannot be correct, because Mencius sometimes uses *wu* to describe one's attitude toward one's own unethical actions (e.g., 6A10, 6B6).[67] Donald Munro argues that "'dislike' [*wu*] suggests an innate sense of repugnance at some acts, and 'shame' [*xiu*] suggests the feelings (considered to be universal) that follow transgressions."[68] However, it seems to me that any effort to make a precise distinction between *xiu* and *wu* is doomed to failure because Mencius sometimes uses the terms interchangeably. Thus, in 2A9 and again in 5B1, we are told that Liuxia Hui did not *xiu* serving a corrupt lord, while in 6B6 we are told that he did not *wu* serving a corrupt lord.

The term *xiu* is not very common in the *Mengzi*.[69] In addition to the example involving Liuxia Hui, Mencius described a chariot driver who is *xiu* regarding helping an archer cheat in a ritual hunt (3B1), and a wife and concubine who are *xiu* regarding their husband's begging to gain luxuries (4B33).[70] However, *xiu* is closely related to two other shame terms in classical Chinese: *chi* and *ru*. Indeed, the three terms are frequently defined in terms of one another.[71] Consequently, I shall assume that the use of the latter two terms sheds light on the meaning of *xiu*.

From the *Analects* of Confucius, we learn that, although people sometimes are *chi* about wearing poor clothes, eating poor food (4:9), asking questions of social inferiors (5:15), and being poorly dressed in the presence of those who are well dressed (9:27), they should not be *chi* about these things. We also learn that, whether they are or not, people *should* be *chi* about being poor and lowly in a well-ordered state, or being wealthy and esteemed in an ill-ordered state (8:13), not living up to one's words (4:22), and toadying and feigning friendship (5:25).

From *Mengzi*, we learn that a ruler can be *chi* about military defeats his state has suffered (1A5.1), about the outrageous behavior of another ruler (1B3.7), about accepting the orders of another state (4A8.3–4), or about allowing a worthy person to starve for want of employment in his state (6B14.4). In general, one can be *chi* about being the servant of another (2A7.3), about one's reputation exceeding one's merits (4B18.3), about taking an official position and not succeeding in having a positive ethical effect (5B5.5), and about not being as good as others (7A7.3).

Both Confucius and Mencius stress the importance of a sense of shame for being a good person. For example, when asked what is necessary in order to be a true scholar, Confucius responds (13:20), "Conducting himself with a sense of shame (*chi*), and not doing dishonor to (*ru*) his ruler's mandate when sent abroad as a diplomat – such a person could be called a scholar." In a similar vein, Mencius says that, "A person may not be without a sense of shame (*chi*). The shamefulness of being without a sense of shame is shameless indeed" (7A6).[72] He also asks the rhetorical question, "If one is not ashamed of not being as good as others, how will one ever be as good as others?" (7A7). However, there does seem to be more stress in the *Analects* on the importance of *not* feeling shame when it is inappropriate to do so (e.g., a scholar should not be ashamed of honest poverty).

Xunzi (the last major Confucian of the classical period) presents a philosophically sophisticated discussion of *ru* (shamefulness, disgrace) in response to some claims that had been advanced by the earlier philosopher Songzi. Songzi argues that (1) to suffer an insult is not a disgrace, (2) the belief that suffering an insult *is* a disgrace leads to violence, and (3) the realization that to suffer an insult is not a disgrace will eliminate (or, at least, lessen) violence. Xunzi raises two objections to Songzi's position. First, he notes that regarding behavior as disgraceful to oneself is neither a necessary nor a sufficient condition for violence. Humans often are violent in response to behavior that they dislike (*wu*), even if they do not regard it as disgraceful.[73] For example, one who assaults a robber need not do so because he regards the robber's behavior as humiliating.[74] Likewise, humans sometimes do not resort to violence, even if they do regard behavior as demeaning to them. For example, jesters accept humiliating insults, and may not even dislike them.

Xunzi's second objection is especially interesting for our purposes, for he makes a distinction between "righteous" (*yi*) honor and disgrace, as opposed to "conventional" (*shi*) honor and disgrace:

Cultivated intentions, many virtuous actions, insightful thinking – this is the honor that comes from within. It is this that is called righteous honor. Respected titles, great emoluments, superior power: at the highest being emperor or feudal lord, or at the lowest being viceroy, prime minister, functionary, or grand official – this is the honor that arrives from without. It is this that is called conventional honor. Licentiousness, baseness, overstepping boundaries, bringing chaos to order, being arrogant, destructive, and greedy – that is the disgrace that come from within. It is this that is called righteous disgrace. Being reviled, insulted, grabbed, hit, flogged, mutilated, beheaded, drawn and quartered, led in chains – this is the disgrace that arrives from without. It is this that is called conventional disgrace. These are the two kinds of honor and disgrace.

Hence, a noble can have conventional disgrace, but cannot have righteous disgrace. A petty person can have conventional honor, but cannot have righteous honor.[75]

Note that the distinction that Xunzi draws between different kinds of disgrace seems to be very similar to the distinction I identified in the Western tradition between what is "conventionally shameful" and what would be "ethically shameful." In general, I submit that if we review the examples from all three of the preceding Confucians, we find that what might be considered *ru*, or what is considered a possible object of *xiu* or *chi*, corresponds very closely to paradigmatic examples of what is regarded as either conventionally or ethically shameful in the Western tradition.[76]

Wu is quite common in early Chinese texts and has several distinct meanings. I shall limit my discussion here to occurrences that I think are particularly illuminating of the connection of *wu* with righteousness.

Often, *wu* seems to mean simply "dislike," as when Mencius talks about disliking dampness (2A4) and death (4A3, 6A10) and having an injured finger (6A12), or when he advises rulers not to do to their subjects what they dislike (4A9). In other passages, however, *wu* seems closer to *xiu*, in that it involved regarding something as ethically condemnable, and not just as undesirable. Thus, Mencius talks about "disdaining disgrace" (2A4, *wu ru*), "disdaining the violation of ritual" (3B7), "disdaining drunkenness" (4A3), "disdaining [to serve] a base ruler" (6B6), "disdaining one's ethical sense (*xin*) not being as good as others'" (6A12), "disdaining what is specious" (7B37), "disdaining to associate with unseemly individuals" (2A9), and "disdaining to accept humiliating treatment" (6A10).[77]

Given that *wu* has such a broad range of meanings (some of which have nothing to do with the sort of ethical disdain characteristic of *xiu*), why does Mencius use the binome *xiu wu* for the attitude that corresponds to the virtue of righteousness? Here I think a suggestion of Kwong-loi Shun's is helpful. He argues that the attitude of *wu* "can be directed at any object of dislike," while *xiu* and *chi* can only be "directed at things that one regards as reflecting adversely on oneself" or those with whom one stands in some "special relation."[78] This seems correct to me. Consequently, if Mencius had only used *xiu* to describe the attitude characteristic of righteousness, or had invented the binome *xiu chi*, he would seem to be limiting the sprout of righteousness to a sense of shame in a narrow sense (see Section III.A). But Mencius clearly wants to suggest that the virtue of righteousness is a sense of shame in a broad sense.

Shun makes the additional suggestion that there is a difference between *wu* and *xiu* even when each is directed toward "one's own actions or things that happen to oneself." Namely, "the attitude involved in *wu* when so directed is like the attitude that one has toward what one dislikes in others." This may be correct.[79] But recall Liuxia Hui. As I noted previously, Mencius says in 2A9 and again in 5B1 that he did not *xiu* serving a corrupt lord, while in 6B6 we are told that he did not *wu* serving a corrupt lord. We know that serving a corrupt lord was something Liuxia Hui actually did, so it is in the class of actions that involve himself. On Shun's interpretation, Mengzi must wish to attribute to Liuxia Hui slightly different attitudes toward his serving a corrupt lord in 2A9/5B1 and in 6B6. In order to be convinced of Shun's second suggestion, I would like to have an explanation of why Mencius wishes to attribute different attitudes to Liuxia Hui in these passages.[80]

There seems to be good reason to believe, then, that *xiu* and *wu* are Chinese shame terms. Specifically, in the sense in which Mencius uses them, to *xiu* X is to regard X as shameful, and depending on the context to *wu* X can be to regard X as shameful. Depending upon the relationship between X and oneself, to *xiu* X or *wu* X may or may not involve feeling the emotion of shame. So *xiu* and *wu* refer to the attitudes related to, but not identical with, the emotion of shame. We might, therefore, refer to them as "emotional attitudes" and translate them as "disdain and dislike" in passages such as *Mengzi*, 2A6 and 6A6.

The capacity to have these emotional attitudes (what Mencius calls "the sprout of righteousness") is precisely a sense of shame in a broad sense. It is, furthermore, an ethical sense of shame, since (as the preceding examples show) Mencius almost always uses his shame vocabulary in connection with failures of character, as opposed to standards of appearance. In general, the examples we have considered suggest that early Confucians are at pains to minimize the significance of conventional shame and to emphasize the importance of ethical shame.

IV. PROBLEMS AND PROSPECTS

In the last section of this essay, I want to discuss briefly three philosophic issues raised by Mencius' account of righteousness. One is whether Mencius' position can be modified so as to be consistent with a nonteleological worldview. The second issue is whether ancient China is best understood as a "shame culture." The final issue involves the connection between righteousness and practical reasoning.

A. Mencius Naturalized

Mencius' ethics is grounded in a sort of metaphysical biology. The cosmos (including human beings) is structured teleologically by a quasi-theistic entity, *tian* (usually translated "Heaven").[81] *Tian* endows humans with dispositions toward virtue (3A5.3, 6A6.8, 6A7.1, 6A15, 7A1; cf. *Zhongyong*, 1). For many intellectuals today, this kind of metaphysical biology seems implausible. However, our earlier conclusions about shame give us other reasons for believing that all humans have the sprout of righteousness. Specifically, we have seen that anyone who has some ideal conception of her character (no matter how inchoate or confused it may be prior to extension) will have a sense of shame (or, as Mencius would put it, a sprout of righteousness). Now, if it is true that anyone capable of leading a recognizably *human* life would need to have an ideal conception of character, it follows that anyone capable of leading a recognizably human life would have the sprout of righteousness. And it does seem that living a recognizably human life requires having such an ideal. A "human" who lacked the sprout of righteousness would be indifferent to any and all changes in her own character and would set no limits on the satisfaction of even the most fleeting desires. I submit that no one capable of living in a distinctly human way could view her own desires and character in this way.

An example might help if one is unconvinced of this claim. Recall the gut-wrenching scene in the movie *Midnight Express* in which Billy is visited in prison by his fiancée. His animalistic behavior seems almost subhuman and shows that, owing to the cruel treatment that he has received, Billy's sprout of righteousness has been (almost?) destroyed.

Interestingly, not everyone in the early Chinese tradition would agree with me about the importance of a sense of shame. *Chi* and *xiu* never occur in the Inner Chapters of the "Daoist" work the *Zhuangzi*, nor do they ever occur in the Mohist writings. Why not? As we have seen, a sense of shame is related to one's ideal conception of ethical character. However, both the Mohists and Zhuangzi, for different reasons, are not interested in ethical character cultivation. In the case of the Mohists, this is connected with their belief that, owing to the extreme malleability of human nature, ethical self-cultivation is largely superfluous.[82] They believe that human desires and dispositions can so easily be altered that, among converts to their cause, significant failures to live up to their consequentialist ideal are unlikely. Hence, there will be no need for, or occasion to exercise, a sense of shame. Regarding Zhuangzi, I have argued elsewhere that he thinks the highest sage overcomes ordinary human desires and ethical commitments.[83] Consequently, Zhuangzi holds that shame is to be transcended.

In short, the Mohists ignore shame because they are uninterested in ethical cultivation per se, and Zhuangzi ignores shame because he does not emphasize the importance of living a distinctively human life.

B. Shame Culture or Guilt Culture?

Bernard William has provided a philosophically revealing discussion of shame in connection with classical Greek thought in his *Shame and Necessity*.[84] Much of what Williams says in this book should be of interest to students of early Chinese thought as well, but here I shall focus on one point: his discussion of the oft-heard claim that ancient Greece had a "shame culture" as opposed to our own contemporary "guilt culture."

As Williams illustrates, this claim can be very misleading if we assume a crude caricature of what shame is.[85] Furthermore, the Greeks sometimes used their shame vocabulary to describe emotions that can focus on the victim (rather than the agent) of wrong action, and they think that disgraceful actions can properly precipitate feelings of righteous indignation from others (as opposed to feelings of contempt). But, as we saw earlier (Section III.A), these are among the distinguishing characteristics of guilt. These points place significant limits on the usefulness of thinking of Greece as a shame culture.[86]

My sense is that, when people describe Greece or China as a "shame culture," they often have in mind conventional shame, to the exclusion of ethical shame. However, we saw that the early Confucian tradition emphasizes ethical shame over conventional shame. So long as we keep this qualification in mind, I think that we may fairly say that ancient Chinese culture was more thoroughly a shame culture than was ancient Greece. In all examples I have discovered, Chinese shame always focuses on the subject of the emotion, rather than those whom the subject affects (if any). I am ashamed of what *I* do, or of what *I* am subjected to, but not of what happens to *you* because of what I do. Is there, then, no room in Chinese ethics for the perspective of the victim? There is, but it is provided in a different way. Virtues such as benevolence (*ren*) and kindness (*en*) and their associated emotions (such as compassion) focus on victims. For example, consider *Mengzi*, 1A7, in which a ruler is asked to show compassion toward his subjects (whose suffering is caused, in great part, by the ruler's neglect and abuse).[87]

What about the righteous rage associated with Greek shame? The Confucian attitude toward righteous rage is complicated. For example, it seems to have been a conventional view among Confucians during Mencius' era that one should not succumb to bitterness (*yuan*), even if the cause of the rancor is bad treatment by others (2B13, 5A1.2, 5B1.3, 6B3.1).[88] Mencius sometimes seems to share this view (2A9.2, 5A3.2, 5B1.3) but elsewhere seems to be at pains to justify the bitterness or anger (*nu*) of the virtuous (1B3, 2B13, 5A1.2, 6B3.2–4). Thus, he commends Sage King Shun because he did not "store up anger, or dwell in bitterness" toward his brother, despite the fact that his brother attempted fratricide (5A3.2)! On the other hand, Mencius also refers approvingly to Sage King Wu, who, being "ashamed" that there were people in the world "behaving obstinately," "brought peace to the people of the world with one burst of anger" (1B3.7). However, note that King Wu is ashamed *that others are behaving in an obstinate way*. Their behavior is an affront to

Heaven (see Section IV.A in this chapter), with whose "will" Wu identifies. It would seem odd to say in this context that the King felt "guilty" that others were behaving obstinately. Furthermore, another passage (5A6.5) says of someone who undergoes a moral transformation that he "regretted his errors, was *angry with himself,* and reformed himself" (5A6.5). These examples suggest several conclusions: (1) the early Confucian attitude toward righteous rage was ambivalent; (2) Confucian shame is *not* like guilt in anticipating the righteous anger of others; insofar as righteous rage is connected with shame, it is anger toward oneself, or toward others who subject oneself to shame; and (3) as we noted previously, Confucian shame focuses on the subject of the emotion, rather than the victims (if any) of shameful actions.

These differences between one of the "founding traditions" of China and one of the founding traditions of the West may help to explain other differences. For example, it has been suggested that the Chinese tradition has no indigenous conception of "human rights."[89] This is perhaps too extreme a claim. The notion of a "right" can be conceptualized in so many different ways that it is hard to imagine there are no corresponding concepts of any kind in the Chinese tradition.[90] For example, in some broad sense, we might say that Confucians think that the people have a "right" to benevolent treatment by their rulers. But it does seem that ancient Greece placed more emphasis on something like guilt than did ancient China, and rights are more closely associated with guilt: when we consider a violation of a person's rights, the focus is typically on the victim, whose righteous rage we anticipate. Consequently, despite all the ways in which the culture of Homer is alien to us, the average Westerner who is intent on seeing her rights observed has more in common in this respect with "the best of the Achaians" than with Sage King Shun.

C. Cognitive Extension

A third problem raised by the Mencian conception of righteousness is that of determining how to recognize which acts and situations are of the same category (*lei*) as paradigmatically shameful ones. There are two ways in which such cognitive extension can fail, and Mencius recognizes both of them. As our earlier examples suggest, he focuses on our failures to recognize that genuinely shameful acts are shameful. But Mencius is also aware that we may fail cognitively by regarding as shameful things that are not shameful. Thus, in 2A9, he condemns as "narrow" Bo Yi, who "extended his sense of disdain for badness, [to the point that] if he contemplated standing with a villager whose cap was not on straight, he would leave him in a haughty manner, as if he was about to be defiled by him."[91]

Usually, Mencius picks examples in which it is fairly clear why actions are (or are not) of the same moral type. Few of us will be in doubt, for example, that humiliating yourself for a large amount of wealth is just as shameful as humiliating yourself for a small amount of wealth (6A10), or that a violation of etiquette is appropriate when the alternative is allowing an innocent person to die (4A17.1). Mencius focuses on such obvious cases, in part, because he thinks that our minimal ethical obligations are fairly easy to recognize, and that the world would be much better off if people merely lived up to these minimal requirements: "The Way lies in what is near, but people seek it in what is distant; one's task lies in what is easy, but people seek it in what is difficult. If everyone would treat their kin as kin, and their elders as elders, the world would be at peace" (4A11). This does not seem, to me at least, to be an absurd conviction.

Nonetheless, one does not need to be a sophist to think there are some genuine "quandary cases," and we would like our ethics to provide us with some guidance in these cases. However, there are different ways of providing ethical guidance, and we should not assume without further argument that one of them is privileged. Specifically, we might be tempted to assume that our ethics (if it is to provide us with practical guidance in quandary cases) must specify a general decision procedure for determining which actions we should perform in particular contexts. Certain versions of Kantianism and utilitarianism promise to do just this, as does Mohism. Thus Mozi said, "When one advances claims, one must first establish a standard of assessment. To make claims in the absence of such a standard is like trying to establish where the sun will rise and set on the surface of a spinning potter's wheel. Without a fixed standard, one cannot clearly ascertain what is right and wrong and what is beneficial and harmful."[92] If judged by its success in meeting the demand for a general decision procedure, Mencian ethics fares quite badly, for Mencius proposes no such algorithm. However, this demand has been criticized as pseudo-rational by a variety of contemporary ethicians. The literature on this topic is already immense,[93] and this is not an appropriate place to rehearse the arguments on each side. I would like to say something, however, about what Mencius offers in lieu of an ethical decision procedure.

Mencius stresses the context-sensitivity of virtuous actions. Different virtuous individuals do different things in different contexts. (See especially *Mengzi*, 2A2.22–4, 4A1, 5B1, and 6B1.) Nonetheless, there are (in particular contexts) objectively right and wrong reactions. Thus, Mencius insists that if virtuous individuals "exchanged places, they all would have done as the others."[94] In a similar vein, he says (4B1) of the Sage Kings Shun and Wen that, although born a thousand years apart, at opposite ends of the known world, "when they obtained their goals, and put them into effect in the Middle Kingdom, it was like uniting two halves of a tally. The former sage and the later sage – their judgements were one." Finally, he notes that, although some worthy sovereigns resigned their thrones to their ministers, while others passed them on to their sons, "their righteousness was *one*" (5A6).[95]

Mencius also seems to recognize at least some inviolable (but extremely general) moral rules. After describing how various wise individuals acted differently in different situations, Mencius was asked, "In that case, were there any similarities?" Mencius says that there were: "if any could obtain all under Heaven by performing one unrighteous deed, or killing one innocent person, he would not do it" (2A2.24).

The model Mencius prefers for acquiring practical wisdom is acquiring the skill of a craftsperson (5B1.7), rather than memorizing and applying a set of instructions. A craftsperson must acquire the techniques and wisdom accumulated by earlier practitioners. Thus, Mencius compares learning the techniques of the Sage Kings to a music master using a pitch pipe, or a carpenter using a compass and T-square (4A1). But the skill of a craftsperson goes beyond anything "in the book." Thus, Mencius notes that "A carpenter or a wheelwright can give another his compass or T-square, but he cannot make another skillful" (7B5).[96]

Thinking of practical wisdom as being like a very context-sensitive skill does not commit Mencius to ethical antirationalism. Rationality requires that we treat relevantly similar cases similarly. It is not a requirement of *rationality*, however, that the relevant similarities be captured by highly general rules, or that good practical reasoners appeal to highly general rules in arriving at their conclusions. Furthermore, Mencius acknowledges that we can intelligently discuss what the ethically salient characteristics are in particular contexts. Indeed, much of Book 5 of the *Mengzi* shows our philosopher teaching by means of concrete case studies drawn from history and literature. For example, in 5A2.1, Mencius is asked why Sage King Shun got married in violation of the ritual rule that one must inform one's parent before marrying. As is clear from 5A2.3, Shun's parents and brother were deeply abusive of him. Presumably, they would have opposed his marriage had they found out about it. Consequently, Mencius explains:

If he had informed them he would have been unable to take a wife. For a man and a woman to dwell together in one home is the greatest of human relations. If he had informed them, he would be abandoning the greatest of human relations, which would have caused resentment toward his parents. Because of this he did not inform them.

Notice that Mencius does not say that it is always acceptable for a person to marry without informing his parents. He also does not say that it is always acceptable for someone who has abusive parents to marry without informing them. Nor, it seems to me, is he required by rationality to state, or even have in mind, a perfectly general rule, with complete defeasibility conditions, that explains when it is acceptable not to inform one's parents that one is getting married. Nonetheless, his context-sensitive comments do provide us with information and can help us to acquire the skill for spotting what is ethically salient in other contexts.

V. CONCLUSION

I explained in Section I that Mencius holds that each human is capable of becoming virtuous owing to the presence of innate but incipient tendencies toward virtue (which he calls sprouts). To become fully virtuous, we must cultivate these sprouts so that our virtuous reactions *extend* to more and more appropriate situations. In Section II, I explained how this applies to the virtue of righteousness. Then in Section III.A, I noted that characteristic of each sprout is a particular set of emotions or attitudes. Thus, righteousness is characterized by *xiu wu*. I went on to investigate the relationship between *xiu wu* and Western notions of shame. In Section III.B, I surveyed several major Western conceptions of shame, and in Section III.C, I examined the use of "*xiu*," "*wu*," and related terms by some early Confucians. This investigation substantiates the thesis that the sprout of *xiu wu* corresponds to what I defined as an ethical sense of shame in a broad sense. The comparison of Western and Chinese discussions of shame also (I hope) sheds light on the philosophic problems surrounding shame in general. Thus, I have argued that shame can be divided into two kinds – conventional shame and ethical shame. These two kinds of shame are related because our understanding of what is shameful is, and ought to be, informed by the views of others about what is shameful. In Section IV, I discussed three issues raised by the Mencian understanding of shame and righteousness. First, Mencius' claim that the sprouts are universal is based on a sort of metaphysical biology that many of us today find untenable. However, our discussion of shame suggested that liability to shame is inescapable, so long as we are committed to any ideal conceptions of character. This consideration might be thought of as a way to "naturalize" belief in the sprout of righteousness. However, reflection on the Mohists and Zhuangzi helped to make clear that a sense of shame is important only if one thinks that achieving and maintaining an ideal character is difficult, and only if one is interested in living a distinctively human life. Second, Mencius' treatment of shame raises the question of whether ancient China can be understood as a shame culture. I argued that, in fact, China was more of a shame culture than ancient Greece, and that this fact has ramifications for the later development of the Chinese and Western traditions. The final problem I discussed was Mencius' antinomian conception of practical reasoning. I suggested that Mencius' view is not irrationalist and (at the least) is consistent with certain important trends in contemporary Western ethics.

I hope it is clear from this essay that the Mencian conception of the virtue of *yi* or righteousness is intrinsically philosophically interesting. Furthermore, I hope to have given an example of how the study of Chinese philosophy can productively inform, and be informed by, Western philosophy. Finally, while I recognize there are still many issues that need to be addressed, I hope my account suggests that a sort of neo-Mencianism is of more than antiquarian interest and shows promise as a viable philosophic position.[97]

Notes

I am indebted to Taylor Carman, Margaret Holland, Eric Hutton, Philip J. Ivanhoe, Kwong-loi Shun, Robert Solomon, David Wong, and two anonymous referees for helpful feedback on this chapter.

1. Mencius is the Latinization of the Chinese name "Mengzi." Mengzi was a fourth-century B.C.E. Confucian philosopher. He is known today largely through a book known simply as the *Mengzi*. Although courage (*yong*) is not a cardinal virtue for Mencius, he does offer an intriguing discussion of it. See Bryan W. Van Norden, "Mencius on Courage" in Peter A. French et al. eds., *Midwest Studies in Philosophy: Volume 21: The Philosophy of Religion* (Notre Dame, IN: University of Notre Dame Press, 1997), pp. 237–56.

2. MacIntyre, *After Virtue*, 2nd ed. (Notre Dame, IN: University of Notre Dame Press, 1984), p. 52.

3. Cf. n. 6 in this chapter and my discussion of Nussbaum in Section III.B.

4. Donald Munro stresses that this commitment is characteristic of Confucianism in his seminal *The Concept of Man in Early China* (Stanford, CA: Stanford University Press, 1969).

5. On the translation of *duan* as "sprout," see D. C. Lau, "Theories of Human Nature in *Mencius* and *Shyuntzyy*," *Bulletin of the School of Oriental and African*

Studies, vol. 15, no. 3 (1953), p. 547, n. 1; A. C. Graham, *Two Chinese Philosophers*,
reprint (Chicago: Open Court Press, 1992; original printing 1958), pp. 53–4;
and Sarah Allan, *The Way of Water and Sprouts of Virtue* (Albany: SUNY Press,
1997), pp. 113–14. Like Plato, Mencius does not usually stick to a narrow technical vocabulary. He uses several terms meaning "sprout," including *"duan"*
(2A6), *"miao"* (2A2.16), *"nie"* (6A8), and *"meng"* (6A8, 6A9). Likewise, his
terms for "extension" (see later in this section) include *"tui,"* *"ji"* (1A7.12),
"da" (7A15, 7B31), and *"kuo er chong"* (2A6). Citations of passages from
the *Mengzi* follow the sectioning and "verses" in James Legge's translation
(*The Works of Mencius* [New York: Dover Publications, 1970; original printing
1895]). For a review of various translations of the *Mengzi*, see David S. Nivison,
"On Translating Mencius" in *The Ways of Confucianism* (Chicago: Open Court
Press, 1996), pp. 175–201. References to other early Chinese texts are to the
sectioning in the *Harvard-Yenching Institute Sinological Index Series*. All translations from the Chinese are from Philip J. Ivanhoe and Bryan W. Van Norden
eds., *Readings in Classical Chinese Philosophy* (New York: Seven Bridges Press,
2000), unless otherwise noted.

6. Here there seems to be an interesting difference between the Aristotelian
   and Mencian conceptions of the virtues. According to Aristotle, in order to
   act virtuously, one must act out of a "firm and unchanging state" (Aristotle,
   Nicomachean Ethics, Terence Irwin, trans. [Indianapolis: Hackett Publishing,
   1985], Book ii, Chapter 4, p. 40). Mencius's use of a "sprout" metaphor
   makes clear that our innate reactions are not fully developed virtues. However,
   he seems to allow that these reactions are already virtuous and not merely
   "virtuous." (For example, in what is apparently a reference to our innate
   but incipient reactions in 6A6, he identifies a "feeling of compassion" with
   benevolence.) For a further contrast, see Nivison, op. cit., pp. 116–18. For
   a general discussion of the intriguing similarities and differences between
   Mencian and Aristotelian ethics, see Lee H. Yearley, *Mencius and Aquinas:
   Theories of Virtue and Conceptions of Courage* (Albany: SUNY Press, 1990).

7. Compare King Xuan in *Mengzi*, 1A7.

8. Compare Mencius' examples in 7B31 and 6A10, discussed in Section II in
   this chapter.

9. The understanding of Mencian ethics outlined here is derived from the work
   of David S. Nivison. See especially his "Two Roots or One?" pp. 133–48, and
   "Motivation and Moral Action in Mencius," pp. 91–120, both in *The Ways of
   Confucianism*, op. cit. Other important studies of Mencian extension include
   Kwong-loi Shun, "Moral Reasons in Confucian Ethics," *Journal of Chinese
   Philosophy*, vol. 16, no. 3/4 (September/December 1989), pp. 317–43; Bryan
   W. Van Norden, "Kwong-loi Shun on Moral Reasons in Mencius," *Journal of
   Chinese Philosophy*, vol. 18, no. 4 (December 1991), pp. 353–70; David Wong,
   "Is There a Distinction between Reason and Emotion in Mencius?" *Philosophy
   East and West*, vol. 41, no. 1 (January 1991), pp. 31–44; and Philip J. Ivanhoe,
   "Confucian Self-Cultivation and Mengzai's Notion of Extension," in *Essays
   on the Moral Philosophy of Mengai*, Philip J. Ivanhoe and Xiusheng Liu, eds.
   (Indianapolis: Hackett, 2002), pp.221–41. In my judgment, many interpre-
   tations of Mencius, even today, are overly influenced by the metaphysical

assumptions of the neo-Confucian commentarial tradition. For an example of how Mencius was misread by one of his leading neo-Confucian exponents, see Philip J. Ivanhoe, *Ethics in the Confucian Tradition: The Thought of Mencius and Wang Yang-ming* (Atlanta: Scholars Press, 1990).

10. Translation mine; not in *Readings in Classical Chinese Philosophy*, op. cit.

11. See A. C. Graham, *Disputers of the Tao* (Chicago: Open Court Press, 1989); idem, *Later Mohist Logic, Ethics and Science* (London: School of Oriental and African Studies, 1978), pp. 44–52; and Philip J. Ivanhoe, "Mohist Philosophy" in *The Routledge Encyclopedia of Philosophy*, vol. 6 (London: Routledge Press, 1998), pp. 451–5.

12. I argue later (Sections III.B and IV.A) that there is some reason for believing that this is true.

13. Literally: "If people can fill out the heart that will not bore through or jump over [a wall, in order to steal from someone else]" (cf. *Mengzi*, 3B3).

14. The use of "*shi*" here and in *Mengzi*, 4A27, suggests that it is a technical terms for Mencius, referring to the paradigmatic reactions of the sprouts. Hence, I render it, "core reaction."

15. Compare *Analects*, 15:8. Normally, *bu keyi* has the sense of "should not," and *keyi* has the sense of "can" or "may." So one might translate this sentence, "If one may speak, but does not speak." However, sometimes (as here) *keyi* seems to require the stronger sense of "should" or "ought to." (Cf. the use in *Xunzi*, 85/22/60.)

16. The comment of the Song Dynasty philosopher Zhu Xi (C.E. 1130–1200) on this passage seems quite correct: "Humans all have the hearts of compassion and *xui wu*. Hence, no one does not have things that he will not bear and will not do. These are the sprouts of benevolence and righteousness" (*Sishu jizhu*, 7B31.1). On *xiu wu* as the emotional attitudes characteristic of righteousness, see Section III.A.

17. Legge, op. cit.; Lionel Giles, trans., *The Book of Mencius* (Rutland, VT: Charles E. Tuttle Company, 1993; o.p. 1942), W. A. C. H. Dobson, *Mencius* (Toronto: University of Toronto Press, 1963), p. 132; D. C. Lau, *Mencius* (New York: Penguin Books, 1970); David Hinton, *Mencius* (Washington, DC: Counterpoint Press, 1998).

18. See, for example, Jean-Paul Sartre, *The Emotions: Outline of a Theory* (original printing 1948) in Wade Baskin ed., *Essays in Existentialism* (New York: Citadel Press, 1993); Robert Solomon, *The Passions: Emotions and the Meaning of Life* (Indianapolis: Hackett Publishing, 1993), revised edition of *The Passions: The Myth and Nature of Human Emotions* (1976); and Ronald de Sousa, *The Rationality of Emotion* (Cambridge, MA: MIT Press, 1987).

19. As I am using the term, one cannot *recognize* that X is Y unless X really is Y.

20. Bernard Williams, *Shame and Necessity* (Berkeley: University of California Press, 1993), pp. 92–3 (emphasis in original).

21. Ibid., pp. 89–90. On both this and the previous way of distinguishing guilt and shame, compare John Rawls, *A Theory of Justice* (Cambridge, MA: Harvard University Press, 1971), p. 445, and Allan Gibbard, *Wise Choices, Apt Feelings* (Cambridge, MA: Harvard University Press, 1990), p. 139.

22. Classical Greek has a variety of terms related to shame, including *aidōs*, *aischunē*, and *aischros*. Unfortunately, these terms are not used consistently to distinguish between "shame," "shamefulness," and "a sense of shame."

23. Irwin, op. cit., p. 114. The bracketed phrase is supplied by Irwin.

24. Ibid., p. 115.

25. Ibid., p. 115. The bracketed phrases are supplied by Irwin.

26. Patricia Greenspan, "Guilt and Virtue," *The Journal of Philosophy*, vol. 91, no. 2 (February 1994), p. 62.

27. Richard McKeon ed., *The Basic Works of Aristotle* (New York: Random House, 1941), p. 1392.

28. Ibid., p. 1392. (Emphasis in original.)

29. Ibid., p. 1393. Cf. *Mengzi*, 7B31, discussed here in Section II.

30. Ibid., p. 1393.

31. Ibid., p. 1394.

32. Rawls, op. cit., p. 442. Rawls uses the terms "self-respect" and "self-esteem" interchangeably (p. 440). The two are distinguished by Gabriele Taylor (see her *Pride, Shame, and Guilt* [New York: Oxford University Press, 1985], pp. 77–9). Taylor also attempts to distinguish shame from embarrassment and humiliation. For more on Taylor, see n. 84 in this chapter.

33. Rawls, op. cit., p. 440. The phrase "Aristotelian Principle" is misleading. Nussbaum's account of shame (see n. 37 in this chapter) is much more Aristotelian than Rawls's.

34. Ibid., §63, p. 408. For more on the principle of rational choice, see §63. For more on deliberative rationality, see §64.

35. Ibid., §65, p. 426.

36. Ibid., §67, p. 441.

37. Martha Nussbaum, "Shame, Separateness, and Political Unity: Aristotle's Criticism of Plato," in A. O. Rorty ed., *Essays on Aristotle's Ethics* (Berkeley: University of California Press, 1980), pp. 398–9. Nussbaum advises me (in correspondence) that the view of shame in this article has been superseded by the detailed account of shame in her *Upheavals of Thought: The Intelligence of Emotions* (New York: Cambridge University Press, 2001), Chapters 4 and 9–16.

38. Nussbaum, "Shame," op. cit., p. 401.

39. Rawls, op. cit., §65, p. 432. Rawls does not raise this example in connection with the issue of shame and self-respect, but I take it that the application of it to that issue is unproblematic.

40. Nussbaum, "Shame," op. cit., p. 428, n. 2. Nussbaum does not follow Rawls in giving "self-respect" a narrow technical definition, though (p. 403).

41. John Deigh, "Shame and Self-Esteem: A Critque," in John Deigh ed., *Ethics and Personality* (Chicago: University of Chicago Press, 1992), p. 139.

42. For this and other examples, see ibid., pp. 139–44.

43. Ibid., p. 141.

44. Ibid., p. 150.

45. Arnold Isenberg, "Natural Pride and Natural Shame" (original printing 1949), reprinted in A. O. Rorty ed., *Explaining Emotions* (Berkeley: University

of California Press, 1980), p. 366. I find it interesting that Isenberg's account of shame, which is one of the best I have seen, was originally written over 50 years ago.

46. Ibid., p. 374. Emphasis in original.
47. Ibid., p. 375. Emphasis in original.
48. Ibid., p. 365.
49. Isenberg makes an effort to address this objection (ibid., p. 370), but I find his solution obscure.
50. John Kekes, "Shame and Moral Progress," in Peter French et al. eds., *Midwest Studies in Philosophy, Volume XIII: Ethical Theory, Character and Virtue* (Notre Dame, IN: University of Notre Dame Press, 1988), p. 283.
51. Ibid., p. 286.
52. Ibid., p. 288.
53. Ibid., p. 290. Kekes also identifies "propriety-shame," in which the standards are simply ones of appearance (regardless of whether the appearances reflect anything about what one is really like as a person). Nonetheless, Kekes also draws a distinction between honor-shame and worth-shame in terms of whether appearances are relevant. I worry that this leads Kekes to conflate the following distinctions: (1) shame that does, and shame that does not, focus on how one appears to others, and (2) shame that does not, and shame that does, distinguish one's own standard of shame from the public standard. For example, one could have purely individual standards that deem one's appearances to others crucial to shame, or there could be public standards that regard appearances as irrelevant to shame.
54. Ibid., p. 290.
55. Ibid., p. 291.
56. Ibid., p. 292.
57. Ibid., p. 291.
58. Ibid., p. 294.
59. This is a conclusion to which I appeal again in Section IV.A.
60. I was influenced here by the discussion of moral shame in Kwong-loi Shun's "Virtue, Mind and Morality: A Study in Mencian Ethics" (Ph.D. dissertation, Stanford University, 1986), §2.1.
61. There is an exception to this. If others persistently look down upon me on the basis of some standard that I do not share (say, because of my ethnic heritage), I may come to feel shame nonetheless. This is one of the reasons racism is so insidious.
62. As we shall see later in this section, it is really more precise to say that the opinions of others are not as *directly* relevant to ethical shame as they are to conventional shame.
63. That Mencius sees a connection between conventional standards and ethical shame is suggested by the intimate relationship he sees between the virtue of righteousness and the virtue of propriety. On this point, see Bryan W. Van Norden, "Yearley on Mencius," *Journal of Religious Ethics*, vol. 21, no. 2 (Fall 1993), pp. 369–76.
64. *Descartes: Selected Philosophical Writings*, Cottingham, Murdoch, and Stoothoff, trans. (New York: Cambridge University Press, 1988), p. 25.

65. Indeed, Williams criticizes what he calls "ethical Cartesianism" (Williams, op. cit., p. 99), and my position here is, I think, very close to his own.
66. *Sishu jizhu*, 2A6.4.
67. Kwong-loi Shun, *Mencius and Early Chinese Thought* (Stanford, CA: Stanford University Press, 1997), p. 60.
68. Munro, op. cit., p. 75.
69. "*Xiu*" occurs once in the *Analects* (13:22).
70. Notice, incidentally, that this passage shows that Mencius believed women have the sprout of righteousness as well as men.
71. For examples, see the entries for "*chi*" (4-10585), "*ru*" (10-38686), and "*xiu*" (9-28471) in Morohashi Tetsuji, *Daikanwajiten*, rev. ed. (Tokyo: Taishukan shoten, 1984). There are some grammatical differences among the three terms. *Wu xiu zhi* and *Wu chi zhi* could both mean either "I am ashamed of it" or "I bring shame upon it." *Wu ru zhi*, however, could only mean "I bring shame upon it." *Chi* is, I think, the only one of the three that can refer to a sense of shame. (Note that in 2A6 and 6A6 Mencius is using "*xiu*" not to refer to the sense of shame, but to the attitude characteristic of that sense.)
72. Translation mine; not in Ivanhoe and Von Norden, *Readings in Classical Chinese Philosophy*, op. cit.
73. This use of "*wu*" shows that sometimes the term is used to describe an attitude distinct from that of regarding something as shameful. See also the discussion later in this subsection.
74. Presumably, Songzi thought that regarding suffering an insult as a disgrace was *one* source of violence, not the only one. However, Xunzi uncharitably took Songzi to be making the stronger claim.
75. Translation mine; see Xunzi, *Zheng lun*, 69/18/105–9.
76. Shun concludes that *xiu* and *chi* are attitudes of disdain toward things that fall below certain standards, and that these standards can be either "social standards" (Shun, *Mencius and Early Chinese Thought*, op. cit., p. 60) or "ethical standards" (ibid., p. 62). This seems in line with my own conclusion.
77. Note that the last three citations are paraphrases, and not direct quotations. None of the quoted passages are in Ivanhoe and Van Norden, *Readings in Classical Chinese Philosophy*, op. cit., except for 7B37, which I translate slightly differently here.
78. Shun, *Mencius and Early Chinese Thought*, op. cit., p. 60.
79. Ibid., p. 60.
80. Beyond this minor disagreement, the analyses of *xiu*, *wu*, and related terms that Shun and I present share many similarities. However, in his *Mencius and Early Chinese Thought*, Shun does not link these terms specifically to Western accounts of shame in the way that I do. I originally did the work presented in this essay prior to the publication of Shun's book. However, I had read, and benefited greatly from, Shun's doctoral dissertation, "Virtue, Mind and Morality," op. cit., which does make passing reference to Western accounts of shame.

81. See, for example, 2B13, and Philip J. Ivanhoe, "A Question of Faith: A New Interpretation of *Mencius* 2B.13," *Early China*, vol. 13 (1988), pp. 153–65.

82. On this point, see Nivison, "Philosophical Voluntarism in Fourth-Century China," *The Ways of Confucianism*, op. cit., p. 130, and *Mozi*, "Chapter Sixteen: Impartial Caring" in *Readings in Classical Chinese Philosophy*, op. cit.

83. Bryan W. Van Norden, "Competing Interpretations of the Inner Chapters," *Philosophy East and West*, vol. 46, no. 2 (April 1996), pp. 247–68.

84. Williams, op. cit. In addition to advancing a number of original theses, Williams develops some of Gabriele Taylor's ideas (op. cit.) in ways that, I think, make them considerably more perspicuous. Consequently, I have not included a separate discussion of Taylor's work.

85. Williams argues against the claim that being motivated by shame is, in any simple way, superficial, heteronomous, or egoistic (ibid., chapter 4, passim).

86. Nonetheless, Williams thinks there is some point to the distinction: their emotional reactions "were not simply guilt if they were not separately recognised as such; just as shame is not the same when it does not have guilt as a contrast" (ibid., p. 91).

87. Note also that, in contrast, benevolence is not mentioned as a virtue by either Plato or Aristotle.

88. *Mengzi*, 2B13, raises interesting and complicated issues on this point. For a discussion, see Ivanhoe, "A Question of Faith," op. cit. The remaining translations in this section are mine; they are not in Ivanhoe and Van Norden, *Readings in Classical Chinese Philosophy*, op. cit.

89. See, for example, Henry Rosemont, Jr., *A Chinese Mirror* (La Salle, IL: Open Court, 1991), Chapter III.

90. On this point, see the review of *A Chinese Mirror* by Melissa Macauley, *Journal of Asian Studies*, vol. 53, no. 1 (February 1994), pp. 175–7.

91. Translation mine; not in Ivanhoe and Van Norden, *Readings in Classical Chinese Philosophy*, op. cit.

92. *Mozi*, "Chapter Thirty-five: A Condemnation of Fatalism" in Ivanhoe and Van Norden, *Readings in Classical Chinese Philosophy*, op. cit. See *Mozi, Fei ming* 56/35/6-7.

93. See, for example, Martha C. Nussbaum, "The Discernment of Perception: An Aristotelian Conception of Private and Public Rationality," in her *Love's Knowledge* (New York: Oxford University Press, 1990), pp. 54–105; David Wiggins, "Deliberation and Practical Reason" in A. O. Rorty ed., *Essays on Aristotle's Ethics* (Berkeley: University of California Press, 1980), pp. 221–40; and Charles Taylor, "The Diversity of Goods" in S. G. Clarke and E. Simpson eds., *Anti-Theory in Ethics and Moral Conservatism* (Albany: SUNY Press, 1989), pp. 223–40.

94. *Mengzi*, 4B29.5, 4B31.3.

95. The last two translations are mine; they are not in Ivanhoe and Van Norden, *Readings in Classical Chinese Philosophy*, op. cit.

96. Cf. MacIntyre's comments on virtues as what sustains "practices," and on the need for a background of previous practice and wisdom in order for there to be genuine innovation (*After Virtue*, op. cit., pp. 181–203).

97. Other stimulating recent efforts to show the contemporary philosophical relevance of Confucianism include Philip J. Ivanhoe, "Confucianism and Contemporary Western Ethics" in Lee Hyun-jae ed., *The Universal and Particular Natures of Confucianism* (Seoul: Yong Jin-sa, 1994), pp. 165–83, and Joel J. Kupperman, *Learning from Asian Philosophy* (New York: Oxford University Press, 1999).

8

Conception of the Person in Early Confucian Thought

Kwong-loi Shun

I. INTRODUCTION

In recent discussions of comparative ethics, various claims have been made about the inapplicability of certain Western notions to the Confucian conception of the person. For example, some have observed that Confucians do not have a notion of self and do not draw a distinction between mind and body.[1] Others, while working with the notion of self, have argued that the Confucian conception of self is constituted primarily by the social roles one occupies and that the notions of autonomy and rights are inapplicable to Confucian thought.[2] The inapplicability of these notions is seen as reflecting distinctive features of Confucian thought, features that have an important bearing on our understanding of the ethical values of Asian societies influenced by the Confucian tradition and the potential inapplicability of certain Western political ideas to such societies.

While these claims about the inapplicability of certain Western notions are suggestive, the exact content and significance of such claims remain to be explored. On the one hand, if we build substantive Western philosophical presuppositions into the notions under consideration, claims about their inapplicability become uncontroversial and of dubitable significance. For example, the claim that Confucian thinkers do not subscribe to a Cartesian distinction between mind and body or a Kantian notion of autonomy is not one that many would dispute. On the other hand, if we construe the notions under consideration in a very general manner, claims about their inapplicability appear clearly false. For example, if we construe the notion of self in such a way that it is always presupposed in

the use of reflexive pronouns to talk about oneself, it seems uncontroversial that Confucian thinkers do work with such a notion. So, questions
about the applicability of these Western notions to Confucian thought
is to some extent a terminological issue since whether we answer such
questions affirmatively or negatively depends in part on how we construe
the notions under consideration.[3]

Still, the interest in these questions reflects an interest in more substantive questions about how the person is viewed in Confucian thought
and how this view differs from those of Western traditions. In this chapter,
I will adopt a methodological approach to these questions that sidesteps
the terminological issues. The use of the Western notions under consideration is associated with a range of phenomena, some of which are
more and some less heavily emphasized in their use. My discussion will
focus on various features of the Confucian conception of the person that
bears some relation to this range of phenomena. By highlighting these
features, I try to show the extent to which such phenomena are, or are
not, instantiated in Confucian thought, without directly addressing the
issue of the applicability of these notions.

My discussion will draw on the thinking of Confucius (sixth to fifth
century B.C.E.), Mencius (fifth century B.C.E.) and Xunzi (fourth century
B.C.E.), as recorded in the *Analects*, the *Mencius* and the *Xunzi*, respectively, and will also refer to two other early Confucian texts, the *Zhongyong*
and the *Daxue*.[4] While these texts differ in their emphases and diverge
on certain issues, I will focus primarily on ideas that are common to these
texts. I will begin by considering the terms used in these texts to talk
about the various features of a person and then discuss those aspects of
the Confucian conception of a person that relate to the range of phenomena associated with the notions of self, of a mind–body distinction, and of
autonomy and rights. To avoid issues pertaining to the interpretation of
Western traditions, I will not draw explicit comparisons between Confucian thought and Western traditions, though I will focus on those aspects
of Confucian thought that bear on issues raised in recent comparative
discussions.

II. CHINESE VIEW OF THE PERSON

Chinese thinkers use the term "*ti*", often translated as "body", to talk
about one's body, and they also have terms for referring to parts of the
body, such as the four limbs (to which "*ti*" also refers) and the senses.
These parts of the body are not regarded as inert; not only do they have

certain capacities, such as the eye's capacity of sight, but they also exhibit certain characteristic tendencies. For example, the four limbs are drawn toward rest, while the senses are drawn toward such ideal objects as beautiful colors or pleasurable objects of taste. Such tendencies are referred to as "*yu*", a term often translated as "desires" and paired with the opposite term "*wu*", often translated as "aversion". These terms have, respectively, the connotations of being drawn toward and being repelled by certain things. The terms can be used not just for parts of the body but also for the person as a whole to describe how the person is drawn toward things like life and honor and repelled by things like death and disgrace.

That human beings have such tendencies as part of their basic constitution is regarded as a fact about them that is pervasive and difficult to alter. Facts of this kind are referred to as the *qing* of human beings, where "*qing*" has the general meaning of facts and, in this context, the connotation of certain facts about human beings that reveal what they are genuinely like. Later, "*qing*" comes to refer to what we would describe as emotions, including such things as joy, sorrow and anger, these also being regarded as part of the basic constitution of a person.

There is another feature of the Chinese view of the person for which it is difficult to find a Western equivalent. The body of a person is supposed to be filled with *qi*, a kind of energy or force that flows freely in and gives life to the person. *Qi* is responsible for the operation of the senses; for example, it is supposed to make possible speech in the mouth and sight in the eyes. Conversely, it can be affected by what happens to the senses; for example, *qi* can grow when the mouth takes in tastes and the ear takes in sounds. Also, *qi* is linked to the emotions, and what we would describe as a person's physical and psychological well-being is regarded as dependent on a proper balance of *qi*. For example, both illness and such emotional responses as fear are explained in terms of the condition of *qi*.

Among the different parts of the person, special significance is attached to *xin*, the organ of the heart, which is viewed as the site of what we would describe as cognitive and affective activities. "*Xin*", a term often translated as "heart" or "mind", can have desires (*yu*) and emotions (*qing*) and can take pleasure in or feel displeasure at certain things. It can also deliberate (*lu*) about a situation, direct attention to and ponder about (*si*) certain things and keep certain things in mind (*nian*). One capacity of the heart/mind (*xin*) that is particularly important for Confucian thinkers is its ability to set directions that guide one's life and shape one's

person as a whole. Such directions of the heart/mind are referred to as
"*zhi*", a term sometimes translated as "will". "*Zhi*" can refer to specific intentions such as the intention to stay in or leave a certain place, or general
goals in life such as the goal of learning to be a sage. It is something that
can be set up, nourished and attained; it can also be altered by oneself or
swayed under others' influence and lost through insufficient persistence
or through preoccupation with other things. Early texts sometimes compare setting one's *zhi* in certain directions to aiming at a target in archery,
and "*zhi*" is sometimes used interchangeably with another character that
means recording something or bearing something in mind. Probably, *zhi*
has to do with the heart/mind's focusing itself on and constantly keeping in sight certain courses of action or goals in life, in such a way that
zhi will guide one's action or one's life unless it is changed by oneself or
under others' influence, or unless one is led to deviate from it by other
distractions.

Zhi (directions of the heart/mind) differs from *yu* (desires, being
drawn toward certain things) in that, while *zhi* pertains specifically to
the heart/mind, *yu* can pertain to the heart/mind or to parts of the body
such as the senses or the four limbs. Furthermore, while *zhi* involves focusing the heart/mind in a way that guides one's actions or one's life in
general, *yu* involves tendencies that one may choose to resist rather than
act on. There is another term, "*yi*", sometimes translated as "thought" or
"will", which refers to tendencies that differ from both *zhi* and *yu*. The
term can refer to one's thought or opinion, or the meaning of what one
says. It can also refer to one's inclinations, involving one's wanting to see
certain things happen, or one's thinking of bringing about certain things.
Unlike *yu*, which can involve tendencies (such as the senses being drawn
toward certain sensory objects) that just happen to obtain without one's
having a reflective awareness of one's wanting certain things, *yi* is more
reflective in that the object of one's *yi* is something one is aware of as part
of one's thoughts, which pertain to the heart/mind. On the other hand,
yi is in a less focused or directed state than *zhi* in that, while *yi* can be just
a thought in favor of something without one's actually having decided to
act in that direction, *zhi* involves one's actually forming the intention or
aim to so act.

III. SELF IN EARLY CONFUCIAN THOUGHT

With this survey of the different aspects of the Chinese view of the person as background, let us return to some of the questions that we started

with. First, let us consider whether the notion of self has any application to Confucian thought. Now, besides the use of first-person pronouns, the Chinese language has two characters with the meaning of "oneself". "*Zi*" is used in reflexive binomials referring to one's doing something connected with oneself, such as one's examining oneself or bringing disgrace upon oneself. "*Ji*" is used to talk about not just one's doing something connected with oneself but also others doing something connected with oneself (such as others appreciating oneself), oneself doing something connected with others (such as oneself causing harm to others) or one's desiring or having something (such as having a certain character) in oneself. The two characters differ in that the former emphasizes one's relation to oneself, while the latter emphasizes oneself as contrasted with others. In addition, the character "*shen*", which is used to refer sometimes to the body and sometimes to the person as a whole, can also be used to refer to oneself or one's own person when prefixed with the appropriate possessive pronoun.

These linguistic observations show that the Chinese have a conception of the way one relates to oneself. Furthermore, in Confucian texts, the characters just mentioned are often used to talk about one's examining oneself and cultivating oneself on the basis of such self-examination. This shows that Confucian thinkers also work with a conception of one's being related to oneself in a self-reflective manner, with the capacity to reflect on, examine, and bring about changes in oneself. So, they have a conception of self in the sense of a conception of how one relates to oneself in this self-reflective manner.

Confucian thinkers ascribe this capacity for self-reflection to the heart/mind (*xin*), to which they also ascribe a guiding role. They emphasize the importance of self-cultivation – that is, the process of constantly reflecting on and examining oneself, setting one's heart/mind in the proper direction, and bringing about ethical improvements in oneself under the guidance of the heart/mind. There has been extensive disagreement within the Confucian tradition about how the heart/mind can set itself in the proper direction. For example, Mencius and Xunzi disagree about whether a certain ethical direction is already built into the heart/mind and whether one should derive the proper direction by reflecting on the heart/mind or by learning. Despite such disagreement, they agree that the heart/mind plays a guiding role in the process of self-cultivation. The capacity of the heart/mind at self-reflection and its guiding role in self-cultivation is highlighted in Chapter 6 in this volume by Chung-ying Cheng.

Furthermore, Confucian thinkers regard the heart/mind as independent of external control in that it has the capacity to hold on to the directions it sets without being swayed by external forces, a point that Cheng puts in terms of the idea of "freedom". For example, both the *Analects* and the *Mencius* emphasize its guiding role, comparing the directions (*zhi*) of the heart/mind to the commander of an army.[5] In addition, the *Analects* notes one point of dissimilarity – while an army can be deprived of its commander, even a common person cannot be deprived of the directions set by the heart/mind. Such directions can, of course, be influenced by outside factors, but the point is that the heart/mind has the capacity to resist such influences, and, for the Confucian thinkers, one should ideally cultivate oneself to attain such a steadfastness of purpose after having set the heart/mind in the proper directions. This independence of the heart/mind from external control is also emphasized by Xunzi, who compares the heart/mind to the position of the ruler and the senses to the offices of government; like the ruler, the heart/mind issues orders but does not take orders from anything.[6]

Not only is the heart/mind independent of external control, but it also has the capacity to constantly step back to reflect on and improve on its own operations. In three early Confucian texts, the *Xunzi*, the *Zhongyong* and the *Daxue*, we find the idea that the heart/mind should cautiously watch over its own activities to ensure that all of its activities, however minute or subtle, are completely oriented in an ethical direction.[7] This idea is presented in terms of watching over *du*, where "*du*" refers to the minute and subtle workings of the heart/mind that are not yet manifested outwardly and to which one alone has access. In the *Daxue*, this idea is related to the idea of making one's *yi* (thoughts and inclinations) fully oriented in the ethical direction, an idea viewed as an important part of the self-cultivation process. This aspect of Confucian thought shows that the Confucians ascribe to the heart/mind a reflexiveness; for any of its own activities, however minute and subtle, it has the capacity to reflect on and reshape such activities to ensure their orientation in an ethical direction. This reflexiveness is related to the independence of the heart/mind from external control; even though its activities can be influenced by external circumstances, the heart/mind has the capacity to constantly step back and reshape its own activities under the conception of what is proper that it forms on the basis of its own reflections.

Given their emphasis on the distinctive role of the heart/mind, does this mean that Confucian thinkers do emphasize some kind of mind–body distinction? In a sense, they do emphasize a distinction between the heart/mind and other aspects of the person. The heart/mind has the distinctive capacity to reflect on these other aspects as well as on its own activities, to form a conception of what is proper and to regulate and shape other aspects of the person and its own activities under such a conception. On the other hand, it is important to note that the distinction that Confucian thinkers emphasize has to do with the distinctive capacities and modes of operation of the heart/mind, rather than with the heart/ mind as a distinctive kind of entity that occupies a "mental" as opposed to a "physical" realm. The character "*xin*", which I have translated as "heart/mind", refers to the organ of the heart, which is a part of the body just like the senses. And just as the heart/mind can operate in the manner described earlier, the senses also have their own modes of operation, such as distinguishing between and being drawn toward certain sensory objects. What distinguishes the heart/mind from other parts of the body is not that it pertains to a mental as opposed to a physical realm, but that its modes of operation are different from and enable it to perform a guiding function in relation to other parts of the body.

Furthermore, there is also a sense in which Confucian thinkers deemphasize the distinction between the heart/mind and other aspects of the person. Earlier, we considered the Confucian emphasis on one's cautiously watching over the minute and subtle activities of the heart/mind, activities that are not yet outwardly manifested. In elaborating on this idea, the relevant texts also emphasize the point that, though initially not discernible from the outside, these activities of the heart/mind will inevitably be manifested outwardly, and so one cannot conceal the way one is from others. Indeed, the different aspects of the person described earlier are all mutually interacting. For example, the life forces (*qi*) that fill the body can be affected by what happens to the body, such as the tastes that the mouth takes in and the sounds that the ear hears; conversely, the life forces can generate speech in the mouth and sight in the eyes. Also, the directions (*zhi*) of the heart/mind can guide and shape the life forces while depending on the life forces for their execution; conversely, the directions of the heart/mind can be swayed if the life forces are not adequately nourished.[8]

It follows from the intimate link between the heart/mind and the life forces, and between the life forces and the body, that the heart/mind is also intimately linked to the body. Various Confucian texts observe how the condition of the heart/mind makes a difference to one's bodily appearance. For example, Mencius observes how one's ethical qualities, while rooted in one's heart/mind, are reflected in one's face, back, and the four limbs, while the *Daxue* observes how ethical qualities adorn the whole person just as riches adorn a house.[9] Thus, while the heart/mind is distinguished from other aspects of the person by its modes of operation and its guiding role, it is at the same time intimately linked to other aspects of the person. It is not a kind of "private" or "inner" entity that eludes observation by others, but its condition is inevitably reflected in other parts of the person. In their emphasis on self-cultivation, the Confucians have in mind a transformation not just of the heart/mind but of the person as a whole.[10] Accordingly, if the self is viewed as the object as well as the subject of self-reflection and self-cultivation, it would be more appropriate to describe the Confucian conception of self as comprising not just the heart/mind but the whole person including various parts of the body.

IV. SELF AND SOCIAL ROLES

Let us turn next to the question in what way the Confucian self is related to the social roles that one occupies. As in the case of the relation between the heart/mind and other aspects of the person, there is a sense in which Confucian thinkers emphasize the independence of the self from the social order, and a sense in which they emphasize their intimate relation.

As we have seen, Confucian thinkers emphasize the capacity of the heart/mind to reflect on one's own life, including the activities of the heart/mind itself, as well as its capacity to reshape one's life and its own activities on the basis of such reflection. By virtue of such a capacity, one also has the capacity to step back from one's place in the social order and reconsider one's relation to it. In the *Analects*, for example, we find passages describing hermit-like individuals who shun the social and political order, at times ridiculing Confucius and his disciples for their persistent and (to these individuals) futile attempts to bring about social and political reform.[11] Other texts such as the *Zhuangzi* and Yangist writings also idealize individuals who shun the social and political order, often because of the danger they see in it. While the Confucians would disapprove of such an attitude, they presumably would still acknowledge the fact that there are individuals who take up such an attitude and hence individuals who are capable of stepping back and reconsidering their place within the social order. Indeed, the Confucian emphasis on the preparedness to deviate from or adapt traditional norms, less explicit in the *Analects* but more conspicuous in the *Mencius* and the *Xunzi*, itself presupposes a capacity of this kind.[12]

In what sense, then, do Confucian thinkers see the self as intimately related to the social roles one occupies, a relation that has led some to present the Confucian view as one that regards the self as constituted by such roles? There are at least four ways in which the Confucians emphasize such a relation. First, in viewing human beings as a species distinct from other animals, they see the distinction as lying in the capacity of human beings to draw social distinctions and to abide by social norms associated with such distinctions. The point is found explicitly in the *Xunzi*, which states that what makes human beings human beings is not their biological or physiological constitution but their capability of social differentiation and distinction.[13] It also accounts for Mencius' observation that someone, like his Mohist opponents, who denies social distinctions or fails to make use of this social capacity is, or has become close to, a lower animal.[14]

Second, given this view of what is distinctive of human beings, Confucian thinkers also advocate an ethical ideal that is informed by the traditional social setup that they advocate. The ideal involves a general observance of traditional norms that govern people's behavior by virtue of the social positions they occupy, such as being a son or an official, or in other kinds of recurring social interactions, such as the host–guest relation or sacrificial ceremonies, as well as the embodiment of certain attitudes appropriate to such behavior. It also involves the cultivation of desirable qualities within various social contexts, such as filial piety within the family or devotion when serving in government. While Confucian thinkers do acknowledge the importance of a preparedness to deviate from or adapt traditional norms, they see such deviation and adaptation as themselves based on a certain rationale underlying the social order that can only be realized in this evolving order. It is through participating in this social order and letting oneself be shaped by it that one becomes fully human.

Third, Confucian thinkers regard human beings as malleable in that they are vulnerable to all kinds of environmental influences, including the social order within which they have been brought up. The audiences they address are concrete individuals who have been brought up within the existing social order, and these are individuals who already share to some extent certain concerns and perspectives that are socially informed. This does not mean that people are not capable of stepping back and reconsidering their place within the social order. As we saw earlier, certain early texts describe, and in some cases even idealize, individuals who shun social and political participation. It does mean, though,

that such reconsideration is itself conducted by individuals whose concerns and perspectives are at least to some extent socially informed. We
see little evidence in Chinese philosophical texts of an attempt to address
someone, like the hypothetical figure of the egoist, who is not already to
some extent moved by certain social considerations. Even the hermit-
like individuals depicted in the *Analects* and those in the *Zhuangzi* and
in Yangist writings are not themselves totally indifferent to such things
as order and harmony in society. Rather, the former advocate withdrawal
from society only because they see no way of restoring order and harmony, while the latter, in advocating the attitude of withdrawal, at the
same time see the sharing of such an attitude as what is needed to restore
order and harmony.[15] This aspect of the Confucian view of the relation
between self and society is highlighted by Joel Kupperman in Chapter 5
in this volume. As Kupperman notes, tradition and community do not
just causally influence the development of the self but are constitutive
of the perspectives that the self develops under such influence. At the
same time, this does not preclude the capacity of the self to reflect on its
relation to the social order, a point that Kupperman puts in terms of the
notion of creativity.

Fourth, there is another sense in which Confucian thinkers regard
the self as intimately related to the social order, and even to the cosmic
order at large, that also provides a sense in which they deemphasize the
distinction between self and others. From the Confucian perspective, not
only do human beings realize their distinctive capacity by upholding the
social order and letting themselves be shaped by it, but their cultivated
character will also have a transformative effect on other human beings.
Furthermore, through proper nourishment of other living things and
appropriate use of resources, they also contribute to enabling everything
in the cosmic order to attain its proper place. This idea is put in early
Confucian texts, such as the *Xunzi* and the *Zhongyong*, in terms of the
transforming and nourishing effect of the sage, an effect compared to
the way the natural process itself operates.[16] In later Confucian thought,
it is expressed by characterizing the ethical ideal in terms of a ceaseless
life-giving force; one who embodies the ideal is one who gives life to and
nourishes the "ten thousand things". It is also expressed by describing the
sage as "forming one body" with the ten thousand things, in that he is
concerned for the well-being and sensitive to the suffering of everything
in the way that he is similarly related to parts of his own body.

This aspect of Confucian thought shows that the Confucians not only
regard the self as shaped by and being fully realized within the evolving
social order but also see it as not sharply distinguished from other human

beings and things. One's own self-cultivation will have a transformative and nourishing effect on other things, and such effect is itself a measure of one's progress in self-cultivation. Earlier, we considered how, while Confucian thinkers emphasize the distinctive role of the heart/mind in guiding other aspects of the person, they also see an intimate link between the heart/mind and the person as a whole. Similarly, while they highlight the capacity of the self to stand back and assess its place in the social order and in the cosmic order at large, they also regard the self as intimately related to everything within that order. Not only do the effects of self-cultivation extend beyond the heart/mind to the person as a whole, but they also extend beyond oneself to other human beings and things.

V. AUTONOMY AND RIGHTS

Let us now consider the implications of the Confucian conception of personhood for the question about the applicability of the notions of autonomy and rights to Confucian thought. These notions are often seen as presupposing a conception of persons as individuals with the capacity to rationally choose their own ends and whose freedom to choose their ends are protected by certain constraints on others' conduct. Thus, Henry Rosemont, Jr., in Chapter 3 in this volume relates the notion of rights to the cluster of notions including autonomy, freedom, reason and choice. The Confucian view of the intimate link between the self and the social roles it occupies raises the question whether the Confucian conception of personhood allows room for the notions of autonomy and rights.

For reasons mentioned earlier, whether these notions are applicable is in part a terminological issue, while the more substantive issue concerns the extent to which the range of phenomena often associated with these notions are instantiated in Confucian thought. In relation to the notion of autonomy, we have seen that Confucian thinkers do ascribe to the heart/mind the capacity to set its own directions in a way that is independent of external control. It has the capacity to reflect on, assess, and shape the person's life as a whole, and it also has the capacity to reflect on and reshape its own activities, however subtle and minute these may be. This capacity of the heart/mind enables it to play a guiding role in one's life; by virtue of this capacity, one is also capable of assessing and redefining one's relation to the social order. So, Confucian thinkers do ascribe to people an "autonomy" in the sense of a capacity to choose and lead their lives in a way that is not determined by external influences.

On the other hand, they do not view this capacity as one of freely choosing one's own ends subject only to certain constraints, whether rational constraints or the constraint that one does not thereby interfere with the exercise of a similar capacity by others. Instead, they regard the exercise of this capacity as related to the social aspects of human life in at least two ways. First, in reflecting on and assessing one's life, one does not do so in a vacuum or in a way that is guided only by self-interest; instead, the considerations that enter into one's reflection are already socially informed. As we have seen, the hypothetical figure of the egoist does not play a role in Chinese ethical thought and Chinese thinkers see their audience as concrete individuals who already share to some extent the concerns and perspectives shaped by the social order within which they have been brought up. Second, for Confucian thinkers, in exercising one's capacity to reflect on and assess one's life as a whole, one should be guided by an understanding of the basic constitution of human beings and their relation to the social order. This involves seeing what is distinctive of human beings in social terms and also seeing that one becomes fully human only in the social context.

Thus, while Confucian thinkers regard human beings as autonomous in having the capacity to reflect on, assess and shape their lives without being determined by external influences, they also regard the exercise of this capacity as intimately linked to the social order. Turning to the notion of rights, Craig Ihara in Chapter 1 in this volume highlights the association of this notion with the idea of claims. That is, the notion of rights has to do in part with the phenomenon of one's having a legitimate claim on others to refrain from infringements of certain kinds against oneself. Should one be a victim of such infringement, one will be in a position to make a legitimate complaint that goes beyond the evaluative judgments that other observers may make about the infringement. Now, Confucian texts do make reference to a phenomenon of this kind. For example, they contain observations about not taking what does not belong to oneself and about the responsibility to fulfill what one has undertaken on others' behalf, with the implication that the property owner or the person to whom one owes an undertaking will have a legitimate complaint against one should one fail to act accordingly. Other examples concern the responsibilities that one has by virtue of a position one occupies, whether it is a position that one has taken up, such as that of an official, or a position that one is born into, such as that of a son. Should one fail in one's responsibilities, the affected parties, such as the people under the care of an official or one's parents, will again have a legitimate complaint.

While Confucian thought does allow room for legitimate claims of this kind, the basis for such claims is not a view of human beings as individuals whose interests require protection either because of competing interests among people or because their freedom to choose their own ends needs to be preserved. The examples just cited are primarily examples in which one's responsibilities, and the legitimate complaints that others may make should one fail in such responsibilities, are generated by some appropriate social contexts, such as the institution of property, a task one has undertaken on others' behalf, or a position one occupies that is associated with specific responsibilities. While some Confucian thinkers, such as Xunzi, do regard the social setup as in part serving the purpose of preempting potential conflict among people in the pursuit of their basic needs, they also emphasize its other functions such as beautifying the emotions. More importantly, even in relation to the function of the social setup in enabling people to satisfy their basic needs, the focus of Confucian thinkers when viewing the legitimate claims that an individual has on others is less on how the claims serve to protect that individual, but more on how they are part of a social setup that is to the communal good. Whether we describe someone with such legitimate claims on others as having "rights" depends on how we construe the notion. If we accept David Wong's proposal in Chapter 2 in this volume to construe the notion of rights broadly in terms of legitimate claims of this kind, however such claims may be grounded, then the notion of rights will be applicable to Confucian thought. On the other hand, if we focus on individual rights of the kind that Ihara discusses, such rights are not part of the Confucian view of the person. The important point, which both Ihara and Wong highlight in their respective chapters in this volume, is that Confucian thinkers regard such claims as based on an understanding of the social dimensions of human life rather than on a conception of human beings as individuals who need protection in the pursuit of their individual ends.

This feature of Confucian thought might lead to the impression that Confucian thought downplays individual interest and subordinates it to the public good, and that when the two are in conflict, the former will be subordinated to the latter. It is important to note, though, that for early Chinese ethical traditions, there is no genuine conflict between individual interest and the public good.[17] The Yangists, with their emphasis on nurturing one's own biological life, regard the public good as promoted by each person's attending to his or her own life. On the other hand, the Mohists, with their emphasis on devotion to the public good, regard the individual's well-being as promoted by each working toward the public good. Daoist and Confucian thought also regard individual interest and public good as converging, though unlike the Yangists and Mohists, they work with a conception of what is in one's real interest that differs from ordinary conceptions. Thus, while Confucian thinkers acknowledge the importance of satisfying basic human needs and promoting material well-being, they also point to various things that human beings regard as more important than these ordinary goods, even more important than life itself. Human beings are primarily social beings and, for the Confucians, their highest accomplishment is to shape and transform themselves to embody certain desirable attributes in a social context. While one may be worse off in material terms in the process, the process is actually to one's real interest.

VI. CONCLUDING REMARKS

As illustrated by some of the other chapters in this volume, different ways of construing certain Western notions can lead to different conclusions about their applicability to Confucian thought. For example, Rosemont construes the notion of autonomy in such a way that it is contrasted with a conception of human beings as relational and argues on such basis that Confucian thinkers do not view human beings as free autonomous individuals. By contrast, Cheng understands the notions of freedom and autonomy in more general terms and uses the notions to describe the Confucian view of human beings as individuals capable of acting under the direction of the heart/mind and independently of determination by external influences. Also, in his discussion of rights, Ihara focuses more on a narrower conception of individual rights that he argues to be absent from Confucian thought. By contrast, Wong construes the notion of rights more broadly and argues that what is distinctive about Confucian thought is not the inapplicability of the notion of rights but the way rights are grounded on certain conceptions of the communal good. While these authors may differ on substantive issues going beyond these terminological differences, it helps to highlight the more substantive issues to shift attention away from the terminological issues. In this chapter, I made the methodological proposal that we do not focus on the question of the applicability of certain Western notions in the study of comparative ethics. Instead, to the extent that we are interested in the substantive issues related to the use of such notions, we should focus on the range of phenomenon associated with these notions and consider the extent to which they are or are not instantiated in Confucian thought. This allows us to focus on the distinctive features of Confucian thought and the way they differ from Western traditions, while sidestepping the terminological issues regarding what content we give to the use of certain Western notions.

In relation to the notion of self and the idea of a mind–body distinction, I argued that Confucian thinkers do regard human beings as capable of self-reflection, having the capacity to reflect both on one's own life and one's place in the social order and to redirect one's life on the basis of such reflection. Such capacity they ascribe to the heart/mind, which is distinguished from other parts of the person in its capacity at reflection and direction, including reflection on and redirection of its own activities. At the same time, the heart/mind is intimately related to other aspects of the person, and transformation of the heart/mind cannot be separated from transformation of the person as a whole, including the body. Furthermore, the whole person is intimately related to the social order and, indeed, to other human beings and other things in the cosmic order; transformation of the person cannot be separated from the transformative and nourishing effect on other human beings and things. In relation to the notion of autonomy and rights, I argued that Confucian thinkers regard a person as being capable of reflecting on, assessing and shaping one's own life in a way that is not determined by external influences, and as having certain legitimate claims on others to refrain from infringements of certain kinds against one's own interest. At the same time, they also regard the exercise of this capacity to reflect on and shape one's own life as inevitably informed by social considerations, and the legitimate claims one has on others as rooted in an understanding of the social dimensions of human life.[18]

Notes

1. Herbert Fingarette argues against using the notion of "self" or "self-cultivation" in discussing Confucius' thinking in "The Problem of the Self in the *Analects*", *Philosophy East and West*, vol. 29 (1979); 129–40. A. C. Graham discusses the applicability of a mind–body or mind–matter dichotomy in *Disputers of the Tao: Philosophical Argument in Early China* (La Salle, IL: Open Court, 1989), pp. 25–7. Commenting on Fingarette's *Confucius: The Secular as Sacred* (New York: Harper and Row, 1972), Graham cites and endorses Fingarette's opposition to employing such a dichotomy in discussing Confucius' thinking.

2. Henry Rosemont, Jr., defends such a position in "Why Take Rights Seriously? A Confucian Critique" in Leroy S. Rouner ed., *Human Rights and the World's Religions* (Notre Dame, IN: University of Notre Dame Press, 1988), pp. 167–82. He argues that the concept of rights is linked to the view of human beings as freely choosing autonomous individuals, and that it has no counterpart in Confucian thought (p. 167). Indeed, for the early Confucians, "there can be no me in isolation", and "I am the totality of the roles I live in relation to specific others" (p. 177).

3. Herbert Fingarette to some extent acknowledges the terminological nature of questions about the applicability of the notion of self in his "Response to Roger T. Ames" in Mary I. Bockover ed., *Rules, Rituals and Responsibilities* (La Salle, IL: Open Court, 1991). According to him, the notion of self that he regards as inapplicable to Confucius' thinking is the notion of some "individualistic, egoistic, particularistic grounds for action" or "a private self, a private willfulness" (p. 197). He claims this to be the normal English meaning of the word "self" but allows for other possible usage (pp. 198–9).

4. The discussion in this chapter will assume the results of the textual studies I conducted in *Mencius and Early Chinese Thought* (Stanford, CA: Stanford University Press, 1997) and *The Development of Confucian-Mencian Thought* (in progress), which contain the appropriate textual references to the primary sources. In this chapter, I will not cite such references except in relation to specific passages.

5. *Analects*, 9.26; *Mencius*, 2A:2. All references to the *Analects* are to book and passage numbers in Yang Bojun, *Lunyu Yichu* (Beijing: Zhonghua shuchu, 1980). All references to the *Mencius* are to book and passage numbers (with book numbers 1A–7B substituted for numbers 1–14) in Yang Bojun, *Mengzi Yichu* (Beijing: Zhonghua shuchu, 1984).

6. *Xunzi*, 17/11–12, 21/44–6. All references to the *Xunzi* are to chapter and line numbers in the *Concordance to the Xunzi*, Harvard-Yenching Institute Sinological Index Series.

7. *Xunzi*, 3/26–34; *Zhongyong*, Chapter 1; *Daxue*, Chapter 6. All references to the *Zhongyong* and the *Daxue* are to chapter numbers (following Zhu Xi's division of the texts) in James Legge trans., *Confucius: Confucian Analects, The Great Learning and The Doctrine of the Mean*, 2nd ed. (Oxford: Clarendon Press, 1893).

8. A point emphasized in *Mencius*, 2A:2.

9. *Mencius*, 7A:21; *Daxue*, Chapter 6.

10. I elaborated on this aspect of Mencius' thinking in *Mencius and Early Chinese Thought*, op. cit., pp. 158–63.

11. *Analects*, 18.5, 18.6.

12. *Mencius*, 4A:17, 4A:26; see also the idea of coping with changes in *Xunzi*, 17/46–8.

13. *Xunzi*, 5/23–8; cf. 9/69–73.

14. *Mencius*, 3B:9, 6A:8.

15. I argue for this interpretation of the Yangist position in *Mencius and Early Chinese Thought*, op. cit., pp. 44–7.

16. See, for example, *Xunzi*, 3/26–34; *Zhongyong*, Chapters 20–3 (cf. *Mencius*, 4A:12).
17. I elaborate on this idea in "Ideas of the Good in Chinese Philosophy" in Eliot Deutsch and Ron Bontekoe eds., *A Companion to World Philosophy* (Cambridge: Blackwell, 1997).
18. Ideas in this eassy were presented at the International Symposium on Bioethics and the Concept of Personhood, Baptist University (Hong Kong; May 11–12, 1998) and the International Conference on Chinese Philosophy and Culture: Contemporary Interpretations, Foundation for the Study of Chinese Philosophy and Culture (Stanford, CA, August 20–22, 1999).

III

COMMENTS

9

Questions for Confucians

*Reflections on the Essays in Comparative Study of Self,
Autonomy, and Community*

Alasdair MacIntyre

These essays are timely. As contributions to academic enquiry into topics central to the Confucian tradition by philosophers at home in both Chinese and American philosophy, they bring us a stage nearer to widespread recognition that American philosophy can only flourish as a conversation of diverse voices from conflicting standpoints, among which a range of Chinese voices have an important place. Earlier scholars as various in their distinction as Wing-Tsit Chan, Angus Graham and David Nivison had already made this recognition possible some time ago. But they did so in a period in which the vast majority of American philosophers took it for granted that the study of Chinese philosophy was eccentric to their own concerns, of interest only to specialists in that field. We are happily moving away from such cultural narrowness, and the present essays are one more sign of progress.

There is however another reason for welcoming these essays at this particular time. We now inhabit a world in which ethical inquiry without a comparative dimension is obviously defective. Chad Hansen raises some of the key issues for comparative ethics with admirable clarity, suggesting that, when we become aware of some rival moral perspective, we may put in question our confidence in what we have hitherto taken for granted, provided that three conditions are satisfied: first, that the rival moral tradition that we encounter differs significantly from our own conceptually or theoretically; second, that it is "an intellectually rich, reflective, hierarchical system of norms"; and third, that it "yields moral insights that impress us from our present moral point of view" (Chapter 4, p. 79). And Hansen goes on to suggest that Westerners who encounter some version of Chinese ethics are more likely to find that it satisfies these three conditions than will be the case in their encounter with various other non-Western modes of moral thought and practice.

It is however much more likely for Westerners to take seriously the claims of Chinese moral thought and practice in some types of situation than in others. And the same is true for those Chinese who encounter some version of Western moral thought and practice. Such situations now occur more frequently and inescapably than during any previous historical period. They are of two main kinds. First, there are those in which a greater number of Chinese individuals and families have made themselves more at home in contemporary Western and especially American society than has ever previously been the case. In so doing they have had to negotiate a new set of cultural and social relationships with those among whom they now live, while Americans and other Westerners have been confronting parallel problems in Chinese settings. Second, there are those Asian situations in which extraordinary political and economic pressure is recurrently exerted by the U.S. government and by American corporations in the name of "globalization," the new mask worn by American imperialism. Those pressures often take the form of demands that the norms governing labor relations and market exchanges should be of a specific kind. In both types of situation, issues that fall under the rubric "comparative ethics" become inescapable, and this in the course of everyday social and political life rather than as a result of philosophical reflection. So one of the questions posed by these essays is: what resources can philosophical enquiry provide for those who confront the questions of comparative ethics at a practical level?

That these essays focus on Confucianism rather than on Chinese ethics more generally is an advantage, in part because Confucianism, more than any other Asian standpoint, challenges some of the key assumptions of modern Western morality effectively, while providing a viable alternative to them, and in part because, in many of the economically advancing societies of the Pacific Rim, Confucianism is the most influential source of non-Western values. In counterposing contemporary Confucian and Western modes of thought and practice, the editors could not have avoided making issues concerning rights central. And the four essays explicitly concerned with rights succeed in identifying and clarifying those issues admirably. Nonetheless I want to quarrel with the editors' decision to begin by raising these issues. Debates concerning rights between Confucians on the one hand and Western protagonists of this or that conception of rights have generally so far been sterile because each of the contending parties has relied upon background assumptions that have determined their attitudes in those debates. It is only perhaps if we begin with some of those background assumptions that we are likely to find less frustrating ways of pursuing answers to questions about rights.

Hansen remarks that "ancient Chinese normative thought does not use any *close* counterpart of human 'reason'" (Chapter 4, p. 75). And correspondingly it does not possess anything like the kind of conception of human beings as by nature rational agents which has informed so much theoretical and practical enquiry in the course of the moral history of the West. This does not mean of course that either ancient or later Chinese normative thought fails to understand human beings as having and giving reasons for what they do and what they believe and as evaluating such reasons as good or bad, better or worse. So one place to begin is by asking, whether for Confucius or for Mencius or for other Confucian thinkers, what counts as a good reason for acting in one way rather than another and how the self that is to weigh these reasons is conceived. And here it is important not to project on to earlier texts too much coherence, ascribing to them a systematic character that may only have emerged later. Kwong-loi Shun's essay on the early Confucian conception of the self is a model in this respect.

Shun's discussion makes it clear that early Confucian uses of expressions about the self are unsystematic in the same way that early Greek linguistic uses are. So Shun remarks that "*shen*" is sometimes used to refer to the body and sometimes to the person as a whole (Chapter 8, p. 187) and that "*xin*" is used both of the heart and of the mind (Chapter 8, p. 187), but without a hint of any dualism of body and mind. Yet through what is said about *shen* and *xin*, the human being is presented as possessing and exercising a variety of embodied powers, among them that of self-reflection, so that *xin* can determine the directions (*zhi*) taken by the human being, just as a commander directs an army, although "while an army can be deprived of its commander, even a common person cannot be deprived" of the direction of *xin* (Chapter 8, p. 188).

Just as there is no systematic body/mind distinction to be found in these texts, so correspondingly there is no systematic distinction between the inner, the realm of thought, and the outer, that of the bodily expression of our thoughts, feelings, and decisions. We are indeed able to reflect upon our thought so as to guide our actions appropriately (Chapter 8, p. 188), but at the same time *xin* is expressed in one's facial expressions and one's bodily comportment (Chapter 8, pp. 189–90). One's bodily movements are the outcome of the direction that has emerged from reflection upon one's thought and decisions. Individuals may therefore develop in different ways and it is up to individuals which line of development they take.

This early Confucian pretheoretical psychology leaves much undetermined. And, while it would be useful to compare it with other such pretheoretical psychologies in other cultures, it would be a mistake to look for analogies between its view of the human being and the well-developed, theoretically informed views of, say, Aristotle or Kant. Like other pretheoretical psychologies it provides a basis for later fuller, richer, and more systematic accounts of the self, and in the later history of Confucianism we can find materials for constructing such accounts. But we still need to distinguish between what we actually find in the texts and what we can construct from the materials provided for us in the texts. Such construction is of course entirely legitimate, and it is one mark of a living tradition that its adherents are apt to present to us as discovered in the texts what has in fact been constructed by them from the texts.

I read Chung-ying Cheng's essay as just such a work of construction. Cheng's claims that "the Mencian or Confucian view of self" includes "the Kantian sense of freedom" and that the self conceived in Confucian or Mencian terms is at once an empiricist and a transcendent self (Chapter 6, pp. 125–6) (incidentally I do not understand how a self conceived in any terms can be both "transcendent" and "a part of nature," as Cheng asserts on in Chapter 6 (pp. 132, 136) and no explanation is offered) could surely not be vindicated by any close reading of the relevant texts. One has only to think of the complexity of Kant's view of freedom, of how it draws upon Kant's account of the a priori, of his understanding of causality, and of his conception of the will, none of which – or anything like them – are to be found in Confucian writings. Cheng allows that we do not find in the texts "the pure will of Kantianism" (Chapter 6, p. 133), but, if that is indeed so, we should not be able to find there either any conception of freedom that is genuinely in a "Kantian sense." So Cheng should perhaps be read, not as reporting what is in the texts, but as constructing out of them a new version of Confucianism that can be more easily compared with Kant's or other Western views.

This is an undeniably interesting project, but one that I take to be, in important respects, premature. For it is that in Confucianism which is most distinctive and least easy to assimilate to familiar Western views that needs to be reckoned with first, if we are to understand adequately the difficulties that confront attempts to generate a conversation in which each of the opposing parties may be able to learn from their opponents. And Shun's characterization of the early Confucian conception of human agency provides just the right starting-point. For of individuals described as able to direct themselves in this way rather than that, we need to ask: what reason do they initially have for directing themselves in one way rather than another, toward conformity to the Confucian ideal rather than away from it? And whence do they derive these reasons? And why do they treat them as good reasons? We know what reasons mature Confucians have for acting as they do and why they treat them as good reasons. Those reasons are of the form "This is the action required by benevolence (*ren*)" or "This is the action required by ritual propriety (*li*)." To identify the Confucian virtues is to identify both the reasons that agents have for acting in one way rather than another and what it is that makes those reasons good reasons. But, if the mature exercise of the virtues is the end toward which rightly directed young individuals move, what reasons do those individuals have for so moving? Their reasons cannot be derived from those virtues, for they do not as yet possess them. But they are already self-directed and so they do need reasons.

The essays by Joel J. Kupperman and Bryan W. Van Norden make a large and significant contribution toward answering this question. Both begin by emphasizing difficulties. Kupperman, by contrasting Aristotle's account of moral education with the relevant passages in the *Analects*, brings out both how much is left unsaid in those particular texts and how what is said, for example about law, is at radical variance with Aristotle's views. Van Norden, emphasizing how different the Mencian catalogue of the virtues is from Western catalogues and how misleading it can be, for example, to translate "*ren*" by "benevolence," joins Kupperman in reminding us that while there are instructive analogies to be found between some Western answers to this question and Confucian answers, they are likely to be genuinely instructive only if full weight has been given to differences as well as to resemblances.

What Kupperman and Van Norden provide are characterizations of important features of the mature Confucian self, of the kind of individual who approximates to the Confucian ideal. So we can understand better the end-state toward which an individual must move, the direction that self-reflection must chart, if an individual is to become someone whose reasons for action are those dictated by the Confucian virtues. If we read Shun's essay as providing us with a characterization of the self that first has to set out on the path that leads toward this end-state, my question becomes that of what reasons individuals have to move from the starting-point characterized by Shun toward the end-state characterized by Kupperman and Van Norden in an appropriately Confucian manner.

This is not so much the question of what Confucian educators must do in order to contribute to the transformation of their students as the question of how those students themselves must contribute to their own transformation, if they are to learn what their instructors are attempting to teach. What reasons do such students have for accepting the guidance of their teachers? To this it may be retorted: students do not have reasons or at least are not guided by reasons in the preliminary stages of their education. Their malleability is that of a prerational, unformed nature, and what the educator has to inculcate is the right set of habits. And it is of course true that much early education does indeed have to concern itself with the nonrational and the prerational. But what this objection ignores is the importance even at relatively early stages of the child's finding its own reasons to develop habits of reasoning. No one was ever conditioned into becoming a reasoner. What then are the students' early reasons, on a Confucian view of the matter?

Consider Van Norden's discussion of "*xiu,*" "*wu,*" "*chi,*" and "*ru.*" What different classical Confucian writers agree in ascribing to individuals is the exercise of a capacity to feel shame in respect of their own actions and a corresponding emotion in respect of the actions of others. Now I take it that to feel shame or some corresponding emotion is inseparable from judging that some particular action is indeed shameful, that the action warrants the response that it evokes. Such emotions give expression to evaluative judgments. So in treating such an action as shameful, students take it that they have good reason for refraining from that type of action. The educator invites them to consider whether such an action does in fact warrant such a response and therefore whether they do indeed have good reason for refraining from such actions. And in so inviting them the educator is asking them to evaluate themselves or others with respect to the virtue of *yi* and to reason accordingly. That is, we are to think of the young as having two capacities, that of responding to her own actions and the actions of others with feelings and with the judgments presupposed by those feelings and that of correcting those responses and those judgments. It is in virtue of possessing these two capacities that individuals are capable of self-direction. So I am suggesting that in their accounts of shame and its relationship to the virtues, and in their discussion of cognate issues, Mencius and Xunzi, albeit in somewhat different ways, are filling out and giving definition to the notion of self-direction.

Kupperman's essay provides a Confucian account of what it is to be a human being in later life. It is to be someone who continues to learn throughout life, someone who overcomes her own one-sidedness and narrowness of view through negotiation of her relationships with others and through harmonizing her responses with those of others through participation in shared rituals (Chapter 5, pp. 113–14). The upbringing that has enabled them to do this has introduced them to various aspects of their familial and social past that have then been transmuted into aspects of their character, so that they are now partly constituted as the individuals that they are by their relationships to the past. Tradition is translated into character (Chapter 5, pp. 111 and 114–15) and into the kind of reasoning that issues from good character. And here again Kupperman contrasts the Confucian view of the self with the Aristotelian and perhaps, more generally, with the Western.

From the discussions by Shun, Kupperman, and Van Norden, an overall view emerges, even if a good deal of the interest of what they say is in the scholarly and philosophical detail. Human nature is taken to be such by Confucian writers that it is developed most adequately when it is guided and self-guided into the practice of the virtues, understood in distinctively Confucian terms, and discharged into social relationships governed by distinctively Confucian norms. All human beings, by reason of their nature, have it in them to become what the teachings of Confucius, Mencius, and Xunzi prescribe that they should become. As Shun notes, there are differences and disagreements between different writers (Chapter 8, p. 187). But there are large agreements, not only in what they advocate but also in what they exclude and reject, either explicitly or by implication. And those rejections include any conception of society as an arena in which competing individuals try to advance their own self-interest and any conception of morality as a set of constraints upon self-interest either in the name of duty or of the greatest happiness of the greatest number or of a social contract. Confucianism therefore seems to be committed, particularly as expounded by Mencius, to holding that characteristically Western moralities, when socially embodied, represent a distortion of or an imposition upon human nature, a suppression of the four sprouts, the four tendencies in human nature that are the precursors of the four virtues, the possession of which makes all human beings potentially virtuous in the Confucian mode (see Chapter 7, p. 149). But Confucianism involves not only a rejection of Western deontology and utilitarianism but also, as Kupperman's comparison of Aristotelian and Confucian views makes clear, a rejection of the basic assumptions of most Western versions of an ethics of virtue. And it is the thoroughgoing nature of this incompatibility between Confucian and Western views that makes it so difficult to find a constructive opening for a conversation between Confucians and Western moral theorists on the subject of rights. But, as I have already suggested, this conversation should not occupy first place on the Confucian agenda. For there is another as important obstacle to the opening up of such a conversation, and one that needs to be engaged with first – the failure of modern Confucians to debate adequately among themselves the crisis within Confucianism that should have been and sometimes has been generated by its encounter with modernity.

That debate became inescapable for Confucians as a result of Western critiques – including those which invoked conceptions of natural or human rights – of the oppressive and exploitative character of those hierarchical Asian societies in which Confucianism had flourished for so long. Confucians did not generally accept and, as Henry Rosemont argues convincingly, had no good reason to accept some of the premises from which those critiques were derived. But they should have recognized and sometimes did that classical Confucianism had to a large degree taken it for granted, and that the statement of its moral doctrines had generally presupposed, that those same hierarchical structures were in fact justified in claiming their allegiance. Just as importantly, they should have recognized, and sometimes did, not only that those hierarchical social, political, and economic structures lacked justification but also that the acceptance of them as legitimate was deeply incompatible with a genuinely Confucian view of human nature. For on the one hand, as Ihara puts it, the orthodox Confucian view is that "All people are by nature good" and potentially members of a harmonious Confucian society (Chapter 1, p. 23). The latter is indeed something about which Mencius and Xunzi are in agreement. Yet the traditional hierarchical structures of Confucian society involved a practical denial of the capacity for reflective self-direction of the vast majority of those whose work sustained them: women, farmers, and fishing crews, more generally those engaged in productive manual labor, most of those to whom the military and civil security of society was entrusted. There was generally and characteristically in traditional Confucian society no recognition of the presence of the Mencian four sprouts in such individuals and no assumption of any responsibility for the frustration of their moral development, let alone for their subjection and exploitation. (Similar charges can of course be brought against Aristotelian polities, and I have argued elsewhere that they are the result of detestable flaws and defects in Aristotle's views.) It is unsurprising that a lasting hatred of Confucianism was generated among many Chinese, something rarely discussed by present-day Confucians and only suggested in these essays by the passage that David Wong quotes from Heiner Roetz's *Confucian Ethics of the Axial Age* and the remarks that he cites by Hall and Ames.

What I am arguing then is that the Confucian way of life, insofar as it presupposes the Confucian view of human nature, as expounded by Shun, Kupperman, and Van Norden, was always to a significant degree in tension with and often in stark contradiction to the presuppositions of the social forms in which it has for most of its long history been embodied. So the question is posed: what social, political, and economic form would a Confucianism take that was not oppressive and exploitative, that gave to women their due place within the family and to workers their due place within political and economic society? This is a question for Confucians to answer; an outsider such as myself can only make tentative suggestions. But the provision of some answer to it is a necessary preliminary to any constructive Confucian enquiry into the sense in which and the way in which concepts of rights might find application within a Confucian framework.

One reason for supposing that this is the right way to proceed is that it will help us avoid conflating two questions that it is important to distinguish. The first is: what conditions must a form of political and social community satisfy, if it is to be accounted genuinely Confucian? The second is: on what terms and through what relationships should Confucians confront the institutional demands of the modern state and the pressures exerted on producers and consumers by present-day national and international market economies? The first of these questions, I will suggest, can and should be answered satisfactorily by Confucians without making any use of any Western conception of individual rights. The second by contrast cannot be answered satisfactorily by Confucians except by finding some way of accommodating themselves to some range of institutionalized practices that make it impossible to avoid in some areas of their lives employing Western conceptions of individual rights.

Craig Ihara argues compellingly against three theses advanced by Joel Feinberg. They are first that without a concept of individual rights, individuals have no grounds for complaining of harms done to them; second and correspondingly that without such a concept individuals cannot treat any benefits as ones to which they have a right, and so all benefits would have to be understood as supererogatory, gratuitous; and third, that without a conception of themselves as possessors of rights individuals would lack a sense of their self-worth and dignity (Chapter 1, p. 17).

Against this Ihara argues that justified grounds for complaint may arise from violations of rules so that an individual may claim that, because harm has been done in violation of an established rule, and because some other rule provides that when such harm has been done restitution to those harmed should be made, restitution should now be made to whomsoever it is that has been harmed – which happens to be that particular individual. She or he may not be able to say, "My rights were infringed," but can certainly say, "That rule was broken." Moreover rules may sometimes provide for the distribution of benefits, so that those benefits are not regarded by those who receive them as gratuitous or supererogatory. And Ihara argues further that an adequate sense of self-worth may arise, not from being regarded as a possessor of rights, but from being regarded as someone by nature fitted to play their part in an harmonious and well-ordered society (Chapter 1, p. 24). So a Confucian society does not need to make use of any conception of individual rights.

To this it might be retorted that Ihara's conclusions appear compelling only because he has covertly introduced a conception of rights. For in the type of society that he pictures, those who point out that some wrong has occurred presumably enjoy the right to say that this is so. Without such a right, they would be unable to appeal to the relevant rules, and so respect for rules in such a society does in fact presuppose the enjoyment of certain rights by those with an interest in the observance of the rules. But this is misleading. In any society in which actions are governed by rules, there will be types of action that are enjoined, types of action that are prohibited, and types of action that fall into neither class, types of action that agents are left free to perform or omit as seems good to them. All that Ihara's imagined society requires is that agents are in this way left free to call attention to violations of rules, if it seems good to them to do so. To call this a right that they enjoy is no more than a *façon de parler*. It is not to ascribe any substantial right, but merely to use the idiom of rights in a way that may disguise their absence.

There is however one aspect of the type of society described by Ihara in characterizing which it seems natural to use the idiom of rights, and where the use of that idiom is illuminating rather than misleading. Ihara in characterizing forms of activity that are Confucian or that resemble those of Confucian societies makes the notion of role as central as or perhaps more central than the notion of rule. But particular roles can never be characterized adequately without reference to certain other roles and to ways in which those individuals who happen to occupy this particular role will only be able to act as the role requires, if those individuals who occupy those other roles provide both the appropriate cues and the appropriate responses. Interdependence in such a role structure is such that each occupier of a role owes it to those whose role performances are integrated with their own to provide the needed cues and responses. And failure to provide them provides grounds for reasonable complaint by those others. It is not just that a rule has been violated, but that those particular agents qua enactors of those roles have been wronged by that violation. That is, we may say nontrivially that those who enact certain roles in a society governed by Confucian norms have a right to expect from others an adequate discharge of their functions as role players.

To this Ihara might well reply that rights so ascribed are not the rights of individuals qua individuals, as understood in Western thought, but rights that attach to individuals only insofar as they occupy certain roles. The right attaches to the role, not to the individual. And this is clearly correct. But it at least suggests that it may be by understanding better how roles and rights are related that we can make progress in our enquiry. A reconsideration of roles must in any case be of central concern to contemporary Confucians, and this in more than one respect. First, we have already noticed how the range and the character of the roles recognized in a Confucian order must give a very different place to, for example, women from that accorded to them by tradition. Wong notes how a duty to speak frankly and freely to rulers and fathers was recognized by Xunzi, but that this was a duty of sons, not of daughters and, we should add, of the sons of the ruling elite, not of the sons and daughters of the common people (Chapter 2, p. 35). But it is not just that the range and types of roles need to be reconceived. It will also be important for a contemporary Confucian to recognize possibilities of movement from one role to another in the course of a lifetime. And this movement will be one that involves the kind of life-long learning to which Kupperman directs our attention when he emphasizes how often Confucius remarked upon how much he himself still had to learn.

So the ruler with the Confucian virtues must govern the ruled in such a way that the ruled in turn learn how to become excellent rulers, just as good parents must educate their children into the virtues, so that those children in time become excellent parents. But sustaining this kind of learning as a social practice requires an assumption of responsibility for the education of the young and the hitherto excluded, throughout the community, so that they are able to realize to the fullest extent the potentialities of their nature as human beings and the four sprouts grow into the four virtues in as many human beings as possible. That is, there is a responsibility to call upon the resources afforded by their human nature, so that they too may become Confucian reasoners, evaluating their reasons in the light of their understanding of the virtues. But in saying this I am doing no more than reiterating a point made compellingly by William de Bary and repeated by Wong (Chapter 2, p. 41).

To assume this large responsibility will involve extensive changes in how communal life is understood among Confucians. The study of the classical texts will remain important to them, but the lessons to be learned from these texts and the ways in which they are transmitted will not be precisely the same as in the past, something already evident in these essays. Xunzi's critique of hereditary titles and his advocacy of merit and desert as standards for promotion, for example, will be supplemented by a recognition of the need to enlarge greatly the opportunities afforded to the hitherto excluded to meet those standards. Mencius' understanding of the connections between participation in rituals and the development of affective capacities will find new applications in the development of new and more inclusive ceremonial forms. And it is through such transformations that traditions will be preserved, so that radical innovation is in the end conservative in its effect. But how then are we to characterize the responsibilities of those who have to undertake and participate in such transformations? And how should we characterize failure to discharge them?

Those responsibilities will have to be understood as among the duties assigned to various roles within an harmonious order. If those who occupy such roles fail to discharge their responsibilities to these latter, then those whose needs have not been met can rightly claim to have been wronged and to have been wronged as individuals. So it can be said of them that, by virtue of their needs and capacities, they must be treated as possessors of a right to be educated for and a right to find a place within the roles of a harmonious social order. And this once again will not be a mere *façon de parler* but will involve the application of a substantial notion of rights. Furthermore these rights attach not to individuals as present occupiers of roles but to individuals as potential occupiers of roles, and they are rights that should be ascribed to every member of a Confucian society.

I may seem at this point to have come very close to arguing after all in favor of the introduction of a Western conception of rights into Confucian social orders. For the rights of which I am now speaking are indeed individual rights. Yet the gap between a modern Western view of rights and a Confucian view has not in fact been closed. Why not? On the type of Western view that I have in mind, rights are ascribed to individuals qua individuals, and those rights are primarily protective of individual liberties. They are rights not to be interfered with, and the liberty that they protect is negative liberty. By contrast, the rights, for whose recognition by Confucian social orders I am now arguing, are rights that individuals possess qua potential contributors to the goods of a harmonious social order, and those individuals who possess those rights have a right to that which they need in order to become such contributors. So the rights ascribed to individuals in a Confucian society will be what Wong calls "communally grounded" rights (Chapter 2). Wong contrasts this type of grounds for ascribing rights to utilitarian justifications, which make the utility by reference to which rights are justified "a function of the welfare of individuals" (Chapter 2, p. 39). He could equally and as sharply have contrasted it with the justifications advanced by those who base their defenses of rights on some conception of individual autonomy.

We need to ask however whether this difference in justification does not require a corresponding difference in content. Wong speaks of a "modern, liberal democratic right to free speech" (Chapter 2, p. 35) and American readers at least are likely to suppose that he is speaking of a right to almost unrestricted freedom of utterance, such as that protected by the First Amendment. But for Confucianism the values of civility, ceremonial decorum, and appropriateness in speech are so important that the question of how a right to freedom of utterance should be defined in a Confucian social order should not be given an American answer, simply by default. And there are of course further issues that should matter to Confucians along with everyone else.[1]

Underlying these differences between a possible Confucian recognition of rights and modern Western traditions is a yet more fundamental contrast. Confucians begin from a well-defined concept of the kind of community within which relationships could be defined by the relevant norms, and the four virtues would provide the standards for practice. If some notion of right is to be introduced, it must be such as to serve the purposes of such communities, and both the justification and the content of those rights are derived from those purposes. But this is not at all how Western conceptions of rights were generated. It is no accident that in the history of the West the development of the nation-state and of large-scale market economies are paralleled by the development of notions of rights as possessed by and even inalienably possessed by individuals. For a central function, perhaps the central function of such rights is to protect individuals from misuses of and abuses of the political power of the state and, in time, the economic power of the competing owners of capital. Rights within Confucian communities are or would be designed to further shared aims and projects. Modern Western rights are designed as obstacles, as barriers, as means for fending off unwanted interventions in one's affairs by government and other bureaucracies.

The need for such obstacles and barriers derives from the nature of the modern nation-state. Modern states have three salient characteristics. First, they allocate to themselves a set of heterogeneous technological and social resources and powers that are vastly greater than those afforded to the governments of earlier periods, resources and powers that are employed to secure both the dependence and the compliance of ordinary citizens. Second, they are governed through a series of compromises between competing economic and social interests. What influence in determining these compromises each interest has is determined by its bargaining power and its ability to ensure that its voice is heard on those occasions when it matters. And what determines both bargaining power and ability is in key part money. So the interrelationships between political and economic elites are always one of the principal determinants of how policy is made. What this excludes is any possibility that the attitudes and policies of government should express the common mind of the members of a community, arrived at by shared enquiry into the nature of their common good, enquiry in which each member of the community is accountable to each of the others both for the quality of her or his argument and for the discharge of her or his responsibilities in effecting that good. Modern political societies cannot be communities, whether Confucian or of some other kind.

Third, in those numerous and varied transactions in which individuals have to deal with this or that agency of the state – paying taxes, securing credentials for achieving employment or going on welfare, buying property, being arrested, getting an education, having the right papers for crossing frontiers – they recurrently and unavoidably encounter administrative rules and regulations whose complexity requires an expertise that is denied to most ordinary citizens. So those citizens are recurrently compelled to put themselves into the hands of experts licensed by the state who advise them and represent them only on terms permitted by the state.

It is these characteristics of modern states that generate among their citizens the demand for legally established and enforceable individual rights and that make appeal to such rights indispensable for any reasonable human being who has to confront the powers of the state. These same characteristics make it impossible for states to give expression to genuinely communal values, except in their official rhetoric. Yet local communities whose members' lives exhibit shared allegiance to some common good and to virtues aimed at achieving that good cannot in the present political and economic world avoid living within the boundaries of some state, so that those members incur whatever obligations and burdens are laid on them as citizens, receiving in return access to certain otherwise unobtainable resources. But their membership in their own community is one thing; their political citizenship is quite another.

It follows that those who are both contemporary Confucians and also inhabitants of a modern state will be forced to lead a double life and that in each of their two lives, as members of a Confucian community and as citizens of some state, they will have to appeal to rights, but to a different conception of rights in each of their two lives. As citizens of modern states, they will discover that many of their relationships to agencies of the state and to other corporate agencies will be intolerably oppressive, unless they enjoy the safeguards afforded by those protective individual rights that are a Western invention. And this will be as much the case in the postcolonial and postimperial states of East Asia as it is in the United States or in other Western countries. Yet at the same time, insofar as their familial and other local relationships are governed by Confucian norms and informed by respect for the four virtues, they will want, so I have suggested, to enlarge their view of what Confucianism requires in a way that commits them to a specifically Confucian conception of rights. But, in understanding how they cannot but lead this kind of double life, Confucians will of course understand themselves and their Confucian allegiance very differently from their predecessors in, say, imperial China or Tokugawa Japan.

Even to suggest this is of course to adopt a perspective not only different from but also incompatible with that of Rosemont's essay. For he treats Mahathir Mohamad's Malaysia and Lee Kuan Yew's Singapore as test cases for the thesis that the life of a modern state can embody the values of Xunzi rather than those of John Locke (Chapter 3, p. 61). It is not of course my view that modern states embody the values of Locke. It is rather that we may need to use a conception of rights that we owe in part to Locke in order to protect ourselves from such states. But my view does involve a denial that any modern state, Asian or Western, could embody the values of a Mencius or Xunzi. The political dimensions of a Confucianism that took either or both of them as its teachers would be those of local community, not of the state.

For an outsider such as myself, someone who is not a Confucian, it is of course appropriate only to make suggestions and to raise questions and both tentatively. It is for Confucians themselves to go beyond this. Yet I shall be surprised if, as discussion proceeds, it does not become increasingly evident both that Confucianism has to develop its own distinctive conception of rights, for which Confucians will find fruitful application in their familial and other communal relationships, and that Confucians nonetheless in their legal and quasi-legal transactions with agencies of the state will find it impossible to avoid appeal to rights conceived in Western individualist fashion, just as do other citizens of modern states.

Note

1. For some of those issues, see Stanley Fish, *There's No Such Thing as Free Speech* (New York: Oxford University Press, 1994) and my "Toleration and the Goods of Conflict" in Susan Mendus ed., *The Politics of Toleration* (Edinburgh: Edinburgh University Press, 1999).

Glossary of Chinese Terms

an	安
budongxin	不動心
bukeyi	不可以
cheng	誠
chengshen	誠身
chengxin	誠心
chengyi	誠意
chi	恥
congxin suoyu, er bu yu ju	從心所欲，而不逾距
da	達
dao	道
daozhi yi de	道之以德
daozhi yi zheng	道之以政
ding	定
dongxin renxing	動心忍性
du	獨
duan	端
en	恩
fanqiu zhuji	反求諸己
haoran zhiqi	浩然之氣
ji	己

ji	及
jing	靜
jinxin	盡心
jinxing	盡性
junzi	君子
keyi	可以
kuoerchong	擴而充
lei	類
li	禮
liming	立命
lu	盧
meng	萌
miao	苗
nian	念
nie	孽
nu	怒
qi	氣
qing	情
qizhi yi li	齊之以禮
qizhi yi xing	齊之以刑
ren	仁
ru	辱
ruojitui er nazhi gouzhong	若己推而納之溝中
shangdi	上帝
shangzhi	尚志
shen	身
shi	實
shi	勢
shouyue	守約
shuai	帥
si	思
ta ziji	他自己
ti	體
tian	天
tianxia	天下
tui	推

wei renmin	為人民
wen	文
wo ziji	我自己
wu	五
wu	惡
wu chizhi	吾恥之
wu ruzhi	吾辱之
wu xiuzhi	吾羞之
xianni	陷溺
xiao	孝
xiaoren	小人
xin	信
xin	心
xinshen	心身
xinxing	心性
xing	性
xing	行
xiu	羞
xiuji	修己
xiushen	修身
xiuwu	羞惡
yi	義
yi	意
yi	宜
yi	以
yong	勇
yu	欲
yuan	怨
zhengji	正己
zhi	志
zhi	智
zhi	知
zhishan	至善
zhitian	知天
zhixing	知性
zhong	忠

zi	自
zibao	自暴
zidao	自道
zide	自德
zifan	自反
zihou	自厚
ziji	自己
ziqi	自棄
ziru	自辱
zisheng	自省
zishi	自使
zisong	自訟
zizheng	自正
zizhi	自制

Index

CPSIA information can be obtained at www.ICGtesting.com
Printed in the USA
LVOW12s1530281114

415994LV00002B/129/P